1/24

ECUMENISM AND INTERRELIGIOUS DIALOGUE

REDISCOVERING VATICAN II

Rediscovering Vatican II is an eight-book series in commemoration of the fortieth anniversary of Vatican II. These books place the council in dialogue with today's church and are not just historical expositions. They answer the question: What do today's Catholics need to know?

This series will appeal to readers who have heard much about Vatican II, but who have never sat down to understand certain aspects of the council. Its main objectives are to educate people as to the origins and developments of Vatican II's key documents as well as to introduce them to the documents' major points; to review how the church (at large and in its many parts) since the council's conclusion has accepted and/or rejected and/or revised the documents' points in practical terms; and to take stock of the council's reforms and paradigm shifts, as well as of the directions that the church appears to be heading.

The completed series will comprise these titles:

Ecumenism and Interreligious Dialogue: Unitatis Redintegratio, Nostra Aetate by Cardinal Edward Cassidy

The Church and the World: Gaudium et Spes, Inter Mirifica by Norman Tanner

The Laity and Christian Education: Apostolicam Actuositatem, Gravissimum Educationis by Dolores Leckey

Liturgy: Sacrosanctum Concilium by Rita Ferrone

Scripture: Dei Verbum by Ronald Witherup

The Nature of the Church: Lumen Gentium, Christus Dominus, Orientalium Ecclesiarum by Richard Gaillardetz

Evangelization and Religious Freedom: Ad Gentes, Dignitatis Humanae by Thomas Stransky

Religious Life and Priesthood: Perfectae Caritatis, Optatam Totius, Presbyterorum Ordinis by Maryanne Confoy

ECUMENISM AND INTERRELIGIOUS DIALOGUE

Unitatis Redintegratio, Nostra Aetate

Edward Idris Cardinal Cassidy

Paulist Press

New York/Mahwah, NJ

Cover design by Amy King

Book design by Celine M. Allen

Library of Congress Cataloging-in-Publication Data

Cassidy, Edward Idris.
   Ecumenism and interreligious dialogue : Unitatis redintegratio, Nostra aetate / Edward Idris Cassidy.
      p.   cm. — (Rediscovering Vatican II)
   Includes bibliographical references and index.
   ISBN 0-8091-4338-0 (alk. paper)
   1. Vatican Council (2nd : 1962–1965). Decretum de oecumenismo. 2. Vatican Council (2nd : 1962–1965). Declaratio de ecclesiae habitudine ad religiones non-Christianas. 3. Catholic Church—Relations. 4. Christian union—Catholic Church. I. Title. II. Series.
   BX1784.C35 2005
   261.2—dc22

                                                        2005006702

Published by Paulist Press
997 Macarthur Boulevard
Mahwah, New Jersey 07430

www.paulistpress.com

Printed and bound in the
United States of America

Dedicated to Pope John Paul II
and
The Pontifical Councils for Promoting Christian Unity
and Interreligious Dialogue
Without Whom All This Could Not Have Been Achieved

Contents

Abbreviations ix

Section I
The Decree on Ecumenism
Unitatis Redintegratio

Part I: The Document 3

Part II: Major Points 13

Part III: Implementation 20

Part IV: The State of the Question 104

Section II
Interreligious Dialogue
Nostra Aetate

Part I: The Document 125

Part II: Major Points 129

Part III: Implementation 132

Part IV: The State of the Question 225

Notes 265

Part V: Further Reading 279

Index 285

ABBREVIATIONS

AAS	*Acta Apostolicae Sedis*
AECAWA	Association of Episcopal Conferences of Anglophone West Africa
AIJAC	Australia/Israel and Jewish Affairs Council
AJC	American Jewish Committee
ARC	National Anglican–Roman Catholic Dialogue Commissions
ARCIC	Anglican–Roman Catholic International Commission
BCCJ	British Council of Christians and Jews
BCEIA	Bishops' Committee for Ecumenical and Interreligious Affairs
BEM	*Baptism, Eucharist and Ministry*
BIRA	Bishops' Institute for Interreligious Affairs
CCEE	Council of Episcopal Conferences of Europe
CCJ	Council of Christians and Jews
CELAM	Consejo Episcopal Latinoamericano
CEC	Conference of European Churches
CEPLA	Comisión Evangelica Pentecostal Latinoamericano y Carabeña
CRRJ	Commission for Religious Relations with the Jews
CWC	Christian World Communions
CWME	Commission on World Mission and Evangelism
DM	*The Attitude of the Church Toward the Followers of Other Religions: Reflections and Orientations on Dialogue and Mission*
DP	*Dialogue and Proclamation: Reflection and Orientations on Interreligious Dialogue and the Proclamation of the Gospel of Jesus Christ*
ED	*Directory for the Application of Principles and Norms on Ecumenism*
EN	*Evangelii Nuntiandi*
F&O	Faith and Order (Commission of the WCC)
FABC	Federation of Asian Bishops Conferences
FUCI	International Federation of Catholic Universities

GS	*Gaudium et Spes*
Guidelines	*Guidelines and Suggestions for Implementing the Conciliar Declaration* Nostra Aetate, *No. 4*
IARCCUM	International Anglican–Roman Catholic Commission for Unity and Mission
ICCI	Interreligious Coordinating Council in Israel
ICCJ	International Council of Christians and Jews
IJCIC	International Jewish Committee for Interreligious Consultations
IJCIR	Israeli Jewish Council for Interreligious Relations
ILC	International Catholic-Jewish Liaison Committee
IS	*Information Service* of the SPCU (PCPCU)
JD	*Joint Declaration on the Doctrine of Justification*
JWG	Joint Working Group (between the Catholic Church and the member churches of the WCC)
LWF	Lutheran World Federation
LG	*Lumen Gentium*
MECC	Middle East Council of Churches
MWC	Mennonite World Conference
NA	*Nostra Aetate:* Declaration on the Relationship of the Church to Non-Christian Religions
Notes	*Notes on the Correct Way to Present Jews and Judaism in Preaching and Catechesis in the Roman Catholic Church*
OR	*L'Osservatore Romano*
PCID	Pontifical Council for Interreligious Dialogue
PCPCU	Pontifical Council for Promoting Christian Unity
RH	*Redemptor Hominis*
SDA	Seventh Day Adventists
SIDIC	Service International de Documentation Judeo-Chrétienne
SPCU	Secretariat for Christian Unity
UR	*Unitatis Redintegratio*
UUS	*Ut Unum Sint*
VIS	*Vatican Information Service*
WARC	World Alliance of Reformed Churches
WCC	World Council of Churches
WEA	World Evangelical Alliance
WMC	World Methodist Council

SECTION I
THE DECREE ON ECUMENISM

Unitatis Redintegratio

PART I

The Document

BACKGROUND

The question of church unity was never removed from the agenda of the Roman Catholic Church. Prayers for Christian unity were offered from time to time, and for many decades before the council a special Week of Prayer for Christian Unity was observed in many churches and religious communities, usually in the month of January, concluding with the feast of the Conversion of St. Paul on January 25. Until 1959 at least, however, the Catholic Church considered the search for Christian unity mainly as a matter of bringing back to the fold those who had wandered away. Pope Pius XI made that very clear in 1928 in his encyclical letter *Mortalium Annos*: "The unity of Christians can be achieved only through a return to the One True Church of Christ of those who are separated from it." It was hoped that with time the Protestants would return to the "one, true church," and the Orthodox schism come to an end.

At the same time, there were within the Catholic Church, especially after the close of the Second World War, bishops and theologians who began to look with interest at developments toward unity within the other Christian communities and to question the traditional Catholic approach. On August 11, 1952, Bishop Charrière of Lausanne, Geneva, and Fribourg chaired a meeting of twenty-four theologians from seven different European countries at his residence. The group decided to establish a *Catholic Conference for Ecumenical Questions*. Their goal was to achieve true collaboration between bishops and theologians in what was virtually an unexplored area of ecumenical rapprochement between the Catholic Church and other Christian communities. Prior to this gathering at Fribourg, exploratory meetings had taken place between bishops, theologians, and some Roman professors, at the initiative of two Dutch priests, Prof. Johannes Willebrands and Franz Thijssen, both members of the board of the Dutch Catholic Association of St. Willibrord, created in 1948 to foster rapprochement between the various Christian denominations in the Netherlands. Jesuit Father Karl Rahner and the Dominican theologian Yves Congar were prominent in the work of the new Catholic Conference for Ecumenical Questions. Yearly meetings were held in different countries, at times focusing on the theme that the World Council of Churches had chosen for its deliberations for that same year. When the Second Vatican Council was announced in 1959, the Catholic Conference began a reflection with the view to passing on the results of its meetings to those who would be taking part in the council. A document was prepared and forwarded to Rome. This document was eventually taken up by the Secretariat for Christian Unity, of which Willebrands was appointed secretary, and incorporated into the documents that the secretariat presented to the council. Several of the suggestions made by the conference can be found in the council decree.

It is interesting to note that Pope John XXIII chose to announce his intention of calling an ecumenical council in the Basilica of St. Paul Outside the Walls precisely on January 25, 1959, at the close of the Week of Prayer for Christian Unity.

In making this announcement, the pope declared that he wanted "an Ecumenical Council for the whole Church." He declared that he would "invite the separated Communities to seek again that unity for which so many souls are longing in these days throughout the world."[1]

There was some speculation as to just what Pope John XXIII had in mind. Some thought that representatives of other Christian communities might be invited to join the Catholic bishops in the council as equal members, an idea that has since been floated more than once as a way to avoid long theological dialogues and achieve Christian unity by a shorter way. But even then it was clear that such a gathering would be impossible to organize, much less come to a fruitful conclusion.

In his first encyclical letter *Ad Petri Cathedram*, issued on June 29, 1959, the pope explained that the Catholic Church had first to reform itself before undertaking similar initiatives with others. The decision was made, however, to ask the Orthodox and Protestant Churches to appoint observers to be present at the council, and Pope John set up a special secretariat to be at their service, with Cardinal Bea at its head. This secretariat had the same status as the other commissions that had been set up to prepare the council documents.

In the document *Humanae Salutis* formally convoking the council, published on December 25, 1961, Pope John XXIII rejoices in the fact that the earlier announcement of his intention to hold a council had been received with "a lively interest, or at least respectful attention, on the part of non-Catholics and even non-Christians." He clearly indicates his desire that the council may contribute to the search for Christian unity:

> At a time of generous and growing efforts which are made in different parts for the purpose of rebuilding that visible unity of all Christians which corresponds to the wishes of the Divine Redeemer, it is very natural that the forthcoming council should provide premises of doctrinal clarity and of mutual charity that will make still more alive in our separated brothers the wish for the hoped-for return to unity and will smooth the way.

One sees already in these words a reflection of the preconciliar thinking of a "hoped-for return," with an indication of the "rebuilding of visible unity of all Christians" that is certainly more in harmony with the thinking of the council itself. Toward the end of this document, Pope John XXIII requests the prayers of "all Christians of Churches separated from Rome, that the council may also be to their advantage." He continues:

> We know that many of these sons are anxious for a return of unity and of peace, according to the teachings and the prayer of Christ to the Father. And we know that the announcement of the council has been accepted by them not only with joy but also that not a few have already promised to offer their prayers for its success, and that they hope to send representatives of their communities to follow its work at close quarters. All this has been for us a reason of great comfort

and hope, and precisely for the purpose of facilitating these contacts we instituted some time ago the secretariat for this specific purpose.

AT THE COUNCIL

Again, in his opening address to the council on October 11, 1962, the pope includes a reflection that was to be of special importance in the theological dialogue that would follow the council. I believe it is well to quote the whole of this passage, given its special significance for future dialogue:

> The substance of the ancient doctrine of the deposit of faith is one thing, and the way in which it is presented is another. And it is the latter that must be taken into great consideration with patience if necessary, everything being measured in the forms and proportions of a magisterium which is predominantly pastoral in character.
>
> The Catholic Church, raising the torch of religious truth by means of this Ecumenical Council, desires to show herself the loving mother of all, benign, patient, full of mercy and goodness toward the brethren who are separated from her.

For Pope John XXIII, there is a vital link between knowledge of the truth as revealed by God and a complete and firm unity of minds, with which are associated true peace and eternal salvation. He continues:

> Unfortunately, the entire Christian family has not yet attained this visible unity in truth. The Catholic Church, therefore, considers it her duty to work actively so that there may be fulfilled the great mystery of that unity, which Jesus Christ invoked with fervor and prayer from his Heavenly Father on the eve of his sacrifice.

Finally, Pope John was anxious to present this unity as part of God's plan for all mankind, and for an earthly city resembling "the heavenly city where truth reigns, charity is the law, and whose extent is eternity."

From all this, it was evident that Christian unity would have a special place in the agenda of the Second Vatican Council. Indeed, right from the first session when documents on liturgy and sources of revelation were discussed, the desire for Christian unity often found a positive echo. The hope was expressed that liturgical renewal would play a role in advancing this cause. The document on the sources of revelation was recalled for revision as a result of the criticism expressed in the council, and among that criticism was the fact that the text before the assembly would not encourage dialogue.

Moreover, Christian unity was dealt with in two other documents submitted to the council fathers during the first session of the council. The Theological Commission included a chapter on Christian unity in the first draft of a document on the church, while the question also formed part of the schema prepared by the Commission for the Eastern Churches. In the meantime, the secretariat set up by Pope John XXIII for Christian unity was busy preparing its own draft. Before the close of the first session, the council voted 2068 to 36 to have all this material included in a special document on ecumenism, to be composed by the secretariat.

The first version of the decree on ecumenism was shown to Pope John XXIII before he died. On his authority it was sent around the world to the bishops for study and recommendations. The Secretariat for Christian Unity brought the new document to the second session of the council, where it was introduced by the archbishop of Rouen, Most Rev. Dr. J. M. Martin. In doing so, he explained that it was considered necessary to give Catholics a better understanding of the nature, attitude, and providential significance of the ecumenical movement—words which already indicated the direction in which the document was heading.

The document was discussed from November 18 to December 2, 1963. It contained five chapters: the first three dealt with the principles and practice of ecumenism, and relations with other Christian communities; chapter four was dedicated to Catholic-Jewish relations; and chapter five to religious freedom.

On November 21, the council was asked to vote on the first three chapters as providing a basis for further discussion. Of the council fathers present, 1970 voted in the affirmative with 86 against. Two questions—relations with the Jews and religious freedom—were taken out of the document to be treated in other documents. The first, as we shall see, became a part of the Declaration on the Relation of the Church to non-Christian Religions (*Nostra Aetate*), while a special council document was prepared on religious freedom.

During the third session, in 1964, the council fathers were presented with the Decree on Ecumenism (*Unitatis Redintegratio*). About one thousand changes and recommendations to the former document had in the meantime been examined. This new version was voted on by the council fathers on November 20, 1964, and approved by 2054 affirmative votes to 64 negative. On the day before the final ceremonial vote, Pope Paul VI introduced nineteen minor changes in the text. Though nothing essential was altered, and in some cases greater clarity achieved, there was a certain resentment among some council fathers and observers that these changes had been made when no further discussion on the text was possible. In the ceremonial vote of November 21, 1964, only eleven negative votes were presented, and the document was promulgated that day. On that same day, the council approved the Dogmatic Constitution on the Church. Any study of *Unitatis Redintegratio* needs to be accompanied by a reading of both the Dogmatic Constitution on the Church (*Lumen Gentium*), and of the Declaration on Religious Freedom (*Dignitatis Humanae*).

As the council came to a close in early December, 1965, a first important fruit was received by the Roman Catholic and Orthodox Churches in the form of a declaration removing "from memory and the midst of the Church the sentences of excommunication that had been leveled against each other in 1054." The sentence of excommunication leveled against Patriarch Michael Cerularius and two other persons by the legates from Rome under the leadership of Cardinal Humbertus in that year had been followed by similar sentences pronounced by the patriarch and the synod of Constantinople against the Roman legates. While the rupture of ecclesial communion came later, there is no doubt that the events of 1054 played a decisive role in this sad development.

On December 7, 1965, Pope Paul VI in Rome and Patriarch Athenagoras in Istanbul issued a solemn declaration in which they recognized the excesses that accompanied the events of 1054 and led to consequences "which, in so far as we can judge, went much further than their authors had intended and foreseen." The document explains that those responsible for the excommunications had directed their censures against the persons concerned and not against the churches. They were not intended to break ecclesial communion between the See of Rome and Constantinople. In common agreement, the pope and the patriarch with his synod therefore made the following declaration:

> Regret is expressed for the offensive words, the reproaches without foundation, and the reprehensible gestures that, on both sides, marked or accompanied the sad events of this period.
>
> Similarly, the two Church leaders express regret and remove both from the memory and the midst of the Church the sentences of excommunication which followed these events, the memory of which has influenced actions up to our day and has hindered closer relations in charity; and they commit these excommunications to oblivion.
>
> Finally, they deplore the preceding and later vexing events which, under the influence of various factors—among which, lack of understanding and mutual trust—eventually led to the effective rupture of ecclesial communion.[2]

OBSERVERS AT THE SECOND VATICAN COUNCIL

As already indicated above, Pope John XXIII, in *Humanae Salutis*, rejoices in the fact that his intention to call the Second Vatican Council had been received with "a lively interest, or at least respectful attention, on the part of non-Catholics and even non-Christians." In fact, an extraordinary and vital part of the council's proceedings over the period of the four sessions was the presence in the assembly of delegated observers officially invited and hosted by the Secretariat for Christian Unity (SPCU).

Their presence was the result of complicated and delicate negotiations by the secretariat with the Eastern and Oriental Orthodox Churches, with the Anglican and Old Catholic communities, with seven world confessional bodies, and with the World Council of

Churches. These were represented by delegated observers, while others were invited *ad personam* or as representatives of an institution or a Christian church or community not included in the above categories. As Rev. Thomas Stransky, who was an original member of the SPCU, points out:

> The observers' church traditions had widely, different dealings with the Catholic Church. They carried in mental bags varied lists of wishes and desires (*vota et desideria*), as they arrived in Rome, with differing expectations, not all positive. In fact, most initial expectations of Vatican II in the Orthodox and Protestant worlds were anything but positive.[3]

There were 38 observers and SPCU guests at the opening session of the council, and three others—including the two Russian Orthodox observers—arrived in the following days. The observers had a privileged place within the *aula* (St. Peter's Basilica) and mixed freely with the council fathers in the coffee bars. Outside the assembly, they had the opportunity to meet among themselves, with the members of the SPCU and with invited members of the council.

Father Stransky states that the observers not only observed but also, by the end of the first session, had learned various ways to make their opinions and observations known. He gives various examples of how some of these observations were taken up by council fathers and had an important influence on the council documents. An important example of this for our purpose here is what he calls the "*iter* of the expression *hierarchy of truths*, N. 11 in the Decree on Ecumenism":

> At the Pensione Castel Sant'Angelo, Oscar Cullman, a few other observers, SPCU Consulters Canadian Gregory Baum and Swiss Johannes Feiner, had been conversing about "the hierarchy of truths" in different Church traditions as a subject for dialogue. Feiner then approached his friend Archbishop Andrea Pangrazio of Gorizia with an orderly text. Pater Pangrazio used it almost verbatim in a speech in *aula* (November 25, 1963)—in toto published in English, German and French collections of notable interventions. SPCU introduced the paragraph "hierarchy of truths" in its new draft in

the third session. When that new schema was discussed...
Cullman announced (and later published) that he regarded
the passage as "the most revolutionary to be found, not only
in the ecumenism schema but in any of the schema."[4]

Time has gone by and history will never know just to what extent
the presence of the observers influenced the council decisions. Individual conversations between Paul VI and the observers and, of
course, between the council fathers and the observers certainly had an
influence. In fact, at the close of the second session, some council
fathers from Latin America, Italy, and Spain asked the Holy Father the
rhetorical question: "Were not the observers becoming too influential
on the Council in a negative way?" Pope Paul VI wrote to Cardinal
Bea on April 24, 1964, asking him to consider if the presence and
"mentalia" of "the separated brethren" were "excessively dominating
the Council, and diminishing its psychological freedom." It seems that
the possibility was considered of "dis-inviting" the observers. Fortunately nothing of this followed, and we have much for which to thank
the observers for their contribution to the work of the council.

In fact, a notable change took place during the council in the attitude of other churches to the work of the council. It is not my intention to refer here to the response of other churches to this new
approach on the part of the Catholic Church. Very briefly, I think it
true to state that in general the Anglican and Protestant Churches
reacted favorably, as witnessed to by Dr. Oscar Cullman, who observed:
"This is more than the opening of a door; new ground has been broken. No Catholic document has ever spoken of non-Catholic Christians in this way.[5]

The response of the Orthodox theologian Alexander Schmemann
was less encouraging.[6] There is in his remarks an acknowledgment of
positive elements in the document. The recognition of the Eastern
tradition as being "equal in dignity" with that of the West is, he
states, a decisive step forward. At the same time he points out what he
sees as a fundamental error in the council's approach, namely, that
differences are reduced to the sole area of rites, discipline, and "way
of life." It is precisely this that the Orthodox reject. The liturgical and
canonical tradition of the East cannot be isolated from doctrinal principles that it implies. For Schmemann, this is the real issue, and it has

been neglected in a document that he describes as "a Latin text about Eastern tradition." While acknowledging equality of tradition, he considers that the decree formulates and regulates it in terms of Western and even juridical ecclesiology, hardly adequate to spiritual orientations. He also expresses criticism of the importance that the document gives to patriarchates, since in the Eastern tradition the patriarch does not have jurisdiction over other bishops. He is simply *primus inter pares*.

Finally, Schmemann reminds Catholics that so-called Uniatism (the presence in Orthodox territories of churches in full communion with Rome that follow identical traditions with the local Orthodox Church, but are not in communion with that church) is always considered by the Orthodox as one of the major obstacles to any sincere theological confrontation with the Roman Catholic Church. For the Orthodox, there remains in this whole question of Uniatism a deep ambiguity to which they are extremely sensitive.

This response has seemed worthy of particular mention in view of the place that these very ideas would come to play in the future official Roman Catholic–Orthodox theological dialogue.

A further sign of the change that had taken place in both the Catholic Church and other churches during the Second Vatican Council came on December 4, 1965, when Pope Paul VI took part in an ecumenical prayer service for unity in St. Paul's Basilica Outside the Walls, in Rome. His Holiness did not preside at this service, but participated together with Orthodox, Protestants, and Catholics in a reading of the Sacred Scriptures. The intention of Rome was clear. Now, it is for us to see how this intention has been realized in the period 1965–2005.

PART II

Major Points

CATHOLIC PRINCIPLES OF ECUMENISM

It does not take long to discover the fundamental change that the Decree on Ecumenism seeks to bring to the Catholic understanding of the relationship with the other Christian communities. *Unitatis Redintegratio* states at once that "the restoration of unity among all Christians is one of the principal concerns of the Second Vatican Council" (*UR*, 1). Reading the signs of the times, the Council Fathers have come to see that "division among Christians openly contradicts the will of Christ, scandalizes the world, and damages the holy cause of preaching of the Gospel to every creature" (*UR*, 1).

In a clear and radical departure from precouncil teaching, the council presents the ecumenical movement as being "fostered by the grace of the Holy Spirit," and desires in this document "to set before all Catholics the ways and means by which they too can respond to this grace and to this divine call" (*UR*, 1).

While the council clearly teaches that there is only one church of God, the Decree on Ecumenism acknowledges that "often enough men of both sides were to blame" (*UR*, 3) for the rifts that occurred in the course of centuries, impeding full communion between the Catholic Church and other large communities of Christians. Children born into those communities today are not to be accused of the sin involved in separation, but to be embraced as brothers with respect and affection. Later on, in the 1995 encyclical letter *Ut Unum Sint* (On Commitment to Ecumenism), Pope John Paul II presents "brotherhood rediscovered" as one of the principal fruits of the ecumenical dialogue that had taken place. He states that the "universal brotherhood of Christians" has become a firm ecumenical conviction. It was the Second Vatican

Council that opened the way to this understanding by referring to other Christians as "brothers" and pointing out that this was not just a polite expression, "for men who believe in Christ and have been truly baptized are in communion with the Catholic Church even though this communion is imperfect." Despite the differences that exist between them and the Catholic Church, "it remains true that all who have been justified by faith in Baptism are members of Christ's body and have a right to be called Christian, and so are correctly accepted as brothers by the children of the Catholic Church" (*UR*, 3).

To make sure that this teaching would not be interpreted falsely as referring only to individual Christians, considered apart from their membership of a community, the Decree on Ecumenism refers to the churches and communities not in full communion with the Catholic Church as possessing "many of the elements and endowments which together go to build up and give life to the Church itself." Liturgical actions in those communities "most certainly can engender a life of grace, giving access to the community of salvation." The Holy Spirit has not refrained from using them as means of salvation (*UR*, 3).

The document points out the importance of the differences in doctrine and discipline that still persist, creating obstacles to full communion. Other churches or communities are seen to be lacking "that unity which Jesus Christ wishes to bestow on those who through Him were born again into one body" (*UR*, 3). This unity "subsists in the Catholic Church as something she can never lose" (*UR*, 4). The use of the word "subsists" was the result of heated discussion within the council. The draft document identified the Catholic Church as the "one and only church." The use of the word "subsists" means that the one, true church can be found in the Catholic Church, but does not automatically close the discussion about the relationship between other churches and the one, true church. This expression would have an important positive influence on subsequent ecumenical dialogue.

In the concluding section of the first part of the decree *Unitatis Redintegratio*, the council "exhorts all the Catholic faithful to recognize the signs of the times and to take an active and intelligent part in the work of ecumenism," and "commends this work to the bishops everywhere in the world to be vigorously stimulated by them and guided with prudence" (*UR*, 4).

THE PRACTICE OF ECUMENISM

After calling on the whole church, faithful and shepherds alike, to be concerned for the attainment of Christian unity, the council sees this concern being expressed in the first place by renewal in the Catholic Church in fidelity to its own calling. Deficiencies in church discipline, in the moral conduct of its members, "or even in the way the Church teaching has been formulated" (*UR*, 6) are seen as having in the past contributed to division, and church renewal has therefore notable ecumenical significance.

Such spiritual renewal should pervade every action within the church, be it at the leadership level or within the community. "There can be no ecumenism worthy of the name without a change in heart." All the faithful are called upon to live holier lives and to pray to the Holy Spirit for the grace "to be genuinely self-denying, humble, gentle in the service of others, and to have a brotherly generosity toward them" (*UR*, 7).

Prayer, both public and private, should accompany this renewal. Together with a change of heart and a holier life, prayer is an essential element in promoting Christian Unity. Such *spiritual ecumenism* "should be regarded as the soul of the whole ecumenical movement" (*UR*, 8). Pope John Paul II will later refer to "the primacy of prayer" in the search for Christian Unity (*Ut Unum Sint*, 21). It was not usual until then for Catholics to join with other Christians in prayer, but the council proposes prayer in common as desirable for Catholics and "an effective means of obtaining the grace of unity" (*UR*, 8).

This chapter of the document concludes with significant suggestions regarding the *dialogue of truth*. It encourages all those involved in ecumenical dialogue to seek to understand the outlook of their partners in dialogue, their respective doctrines, their history, their spiritual and liturgical life, their religious psychology, and their general background (*UR*, 9). Each side is to meet on an equal footing and "the way and method in which the Catholic faith is expressed should never become an obstacle to dialogue with our brethren" (*UR*, 11).

Catholic doctrine must of course be presented in its entirety, for "nothing is so foreign to the spirit of ecumenism as a false irenicism, in which the purity of Catholic doctrine suffers loss and its genuine

and certain meaning is clouded" (*UR*, 11). The council then made
two statements that were to prove invaluable in ecumenical dialogue.
First, "Catholic theologians standing fast by the teaching of the
Church and investigating the divine mysteries with the separated
brethren must proceed with a love for the truth, with charity and with
humility." Second, "when comparing doctrines with one another, they
should remember that in Catholic doctrine there exists a *hierarchy* of
truths, since they vary in their relation to the fundamental Christian
faith" (*UR*, 11).

"Sacred theology and other branches of knowledge, especially of
a historical nature, must be taught with regard to the ecumenical
point of view, so that they may correspond more exactly with the
facts" (*UR*, 10). Polemics are to be avoided and theology taught in
this way during the formation of future priests. Certainly, even after
forty years much still has to be achieved in this connection within the
Catholic Church.

Finally, the council fathers point out the value of ecumenical
cooperation, by which Christians together bear witness to their common hope and vividly express the relationship that in fact already
unites them, while setting in clearer relief the features of Christ the
Servant (*UR*, 12).

CHURCHES AND ECCLESIAL COMMUNITIES
SEPARATED FROM THE ROMAN APOSTOLIC SEE

In this chapter of the document, the council considers the relationship between the Roman Apostolic See and other churches and ecclesial communities, under a broad division of "Eastern Churches" and
"Churches and ecclesial communities in the West."

Special consideration is given to relations with the Eastern
Churches, and the council urges especially those who will devote
themselves to the restoration of full communion between the Catholic Church and the Churches of the East to give due consideration
to the origin of these ancient churches and to the historic links that
for so many centuries characterized their relations with the Roman
See.

The council acknowledges that, even after separation, these churches "possess true sacraments and above all, by apostolic succession, the priesthood and the Eucharist," whereby they are linked with the Church of Rome in closest intimacy. Through the celebration of the Eucharist, "the Church of God is built up and grows in stature." Similarly, it is acknowledged that in these churches, high tribute is paid to Mary ever Virgin. "Many also are the saints whose praise they sing, among them the Fathers of the universal Church" (*UR*, 15).

Having all this in mind, the council considers that, given suitable circumstances and the approval of church authority, "some worship in common (*communicatio in sacris*) is not only possible but to be encouraged" (*UR*, 15).

The decree makes particular reference to the riches of spiritual traditions to be found in the East, especially in monastic life. It was from the East that monastic spirituality flowed over into the Western world, providing the source from which Latin monastic life took its rise.

Unitatis Redintegratio then sets out important considerations that would need to be taken into serious account in seeking to restore full communion between the Eastern Churches and the Church of Rome:

- The very rich liturgical and spiritual heritage of the Eastern Churches should be known, venerated, and preserved by all.
- A certain diversity of customs and observances, far from being an obstacle to the church's unity, adds rather to its splendor.
- The council solemnly declares that the Churches of the East, while remembering the necessary unity of the whole church, have the power to govern themselves according to the disciplines proper to them.
- What has just been said about the lawful variety that can exist in the church must also be taken to apply to the differences in theological expression of doctrine. Often these various theological expressions are to be considered as mutually complementary rather than conflicting.

The document concludes this section by an important declaration that will later become a fundamental principle of ecumenical dialogue: "After taking all these factors into consideration, this Sacred Council solemnly repeats the declaration of previous Councils and Roman Pontiffs, that for the restoration or the maintenance of unity and communion it is necessary 'to impose no burden beyond what is essential'" (*UR*, 18).

CONCLUSION

Before moving on to consider how the Catholic Church has acted in order to implement the principles and recommendations approved in this document by the Second Vatican Council, I would point out just a few of the remarkable changes that took place during the council sessions with regard to the understanding of the Catholic Church in relation to other Christian Communities.

In the first place, there is the fundamental move away from a church awaiting the return of the separated brethren to a new understanding of a pilgrim church moving together with other Christians toward Christ. At times in the years following the Second Vatican Council, one may still find echoes of this former attitude within the Church of Rome, but the official voice of the church would remain constant on this. The former Catholic understanding of the search for Christian unity has, however, remained a basic approach of the Orthodox Churches toward other Christians. This was clearly shown in an address given by the Russian Bishop Hilarion Alfeyev of Vienna and Austria in a paper delivered at an International Symposium on Orthodox Theology and Ecumenical Dialogue in Thessaloniki, Greece, on June 2, 2003. Referring to the work of the Special Commission on Orthodox Participation in the World Council of Churches, he explained:

> We, the Orthodox, do not aim at imposing our culture, ethos, rite and other peculiarities of "Byzantine" Orthodoxy on to other Christians. At the same time we firmly believe that all major features of the original Christian Tradition have been preserved intact by the Orthodox Church. We believe therefore that the restoration of full communion among the various denominations is possible only within this Tradition, *which has to be rediscovered by those Christians who for various*

reasons have lost or modified it in their doctrine and practice (emphasis added).[7]

Among other affirmations made by the council in *Unitatis Redintegratio* that would prove to be of special importance for future dialogue, these are worthy of note:

- That Jesus is at work, in the Spirit, in the other Christian churches and communities
- That baptized persons are truly reborn and so are brothers and sisters with each other and with Roman Catholics
- That the worship of other Christians in their communities is accepted by God, who uses it to sanctify and save them
- That Catholics have also admitted their own guilt for the divisions that have occurred down through the centuries

With this decree, the Catholic Church entered fully into the ecumenical movement. Catholics were challenged to undergo a change of heart and to become involved in this new experience.

PART III

Implementation

It was obvious that a great deal of effort would be needed within the Catholic Church before the decisions of the Second Vatican Council on ecumenism would became a normal part of the attitude and activity of the bishops, priests, and faithful throughout the world. During the council discussions on the Decree on Ecumenism, several bishops asked for detailed directives and guidelines for the pastoral application of the decisions taken. The SPCU, which had been set up to oversee the *iter* of the decree *Unitatis Redintegratio* through the council, now became a *dicastery*, a permanent administrative body of the Roman curia, and was entrusted with providing such directives. With Cardinal Bea as the president and Bishop Johannes Willebrands as the secretary, the new dicastery set out to present the universal Catholic Church with guidelines for offering an effective response to their new calling; namely, as the council had requested, "to recognize the signs of the times and take an active and intelligent part in the work of ecumenism" (*UR*, 4).

The First Ecumenical Directory and Other Early Publications

The first ecumenical directory, entitled *Directory for the Application of the Decisions of the Second Ecumenical Council of the Vatican concerning Ecumenical Matters*, was published in 1967. In Part 1 of this document, directives were given to help Catholics throughout the world understand the significance of the recognition of the validity of baptism conferred by other Christian communities. They were encouraged to develop "spiritual communion" and participate in spiritual activities, including liturgical worship. Special attention was given to the importance of setting up diocesan and national ecumenical commissions.[8]

Part II of this directory, which followed in 1970, directed its attention particularly to *ecumenism in higher education.* It had become obvious to those involved in ecumenism that there was a particular problem regarding education and theological formation. The directory stated, *"Ecumenism should bear on all theological disciplines as one of its necessary determining factors, making for the richer manifestation of the fullness of Christ"* (71). For the first time, mention was made of a special course in ecumenism being provided. Should that not be possible, ecumenism could at least be the theme of some lectures given in the main dogma courses.

This section of the first ecumenical directory then set out in some detail what should be taught in a course on ecumenism (72), and provided directions concerning the ecumenical aspect to be proposed in the teaching of the separate branches of theology (73). Of particular interest in looking back at this document is a paragraph with the heading *"Conditions of a genuine ecumenical mind in theology."*[9]

Also in 1970, the secretariat issued the declarations *The Position of the Catholic Church Concerning a Common Eucharist between Christians of Different Confessions,*[10] and *Reflections and Suggestions Concerning Ecumenical Dialogue.*[11] On the delicate question of eucharistic sharing, the secretariat made public on June 1, 1972, *Instruction Concerning Cases When Other Christians May Be Admitted to Eucharistic Communion in the Catholic Church.*[12] This was followed in October of the following year by "Note About Certain Interpretations of the Instruction."[13] The document *Ecumenical Collaboration at the Regional, National, and Local Levels* in 1975 brought to a close this series of publications aimed at providing guidance and encouragement to the universal church in bringing to life in the local churches the decisions on ecumenism of the Second Vatican Council. From time to time norms, directives, suggestions, and warnings on various topics with an ecumenical dimension—such as mixed marriages, evangelizations, and catechesis—were also issued.

With the promulgation of the revised *Code of Canon Law* in 1983 and of the *Code of Canons of the Eastern Churches* in 1990, a new and determining factor appeared that naturally affected ecumenical activity within the Catholic Church. In response to all these factors, the Pontifical Council for Promoting Christian Unity (as the SPCU was now called) decided on a complete update of the ecumenical directory that would have two basic characteristics:

- To gather and bring together the essential principles and norms that had been issued by the Catholic Church in the ecumenical forum
- To present such legislation in a coherent, logical, and consistent way, so that the new directory not only would be one for consultation, but also would provide a valuable instrument for ecumenical formation

The Second Ecumenical Directory

On March 27, 1993, the cardinal secretary of state, Angelo Sodano, announced the Holy Father's authorization for the publication of the *Directory for the Application of Principles and Norms on Ecumenism* (*ED*),[14] with the following formula: "On March 25, His Holiness Pope John Paul II approved this directory, confirmed it with his authority and ordered it to be published—anything to the contrary notwithstanding."

From the council onwards, fraternal relations with churches and ecclesial communities not in full communion with the Catholic Church had intensified and theological dialogues had notably expanded. This document was conceived as a response to these developments (*ED*, 3–5). It was also intended as a companion and in-depth directory for those involved in ecumenical activity within the Catholic Church.

Chapter I of the Directory

Perhaps the most striking feature of this new directory is the first chapter itself, "The Search for Christian Unity." Here we find for the first time in an ecumenical directory a reflection on the doctrinal basis of the involvement of the Catholic Church in the ecumenical movement. Theological in character, it establishes the doctrinal principles on which the Catholic Church's commitment to ecumenism is established, referring in particular to the decree *Unitatis Redintegratio*, chapter 1, and to the Dogmatic Constitution on the Church, *Lumen Gentium*, nos. 8 and 15. Of special note is the approach to ecumenical research based on an *ecclesiology of communion*, which is today at the heart of ecumenical understanding:

> Thus united in the threefold bond of faith, sacramental life and hierarchical ministry, the whole people of God comes to be what the tradition of faith from the Old Testament onwards has always called *koinonia*/communion. This is a key concept that inspired the ecclesiology of the Second Vatican Council and to which recent teaching of the magisterium has given great importance. (12)

Awareness of the real yet imperfect communion existing between the Catholic Church and other churches and ecclesial communions is essential for an understanding of the nature of ecumenism and for progress toward Christian unity. The directory presents four basic points with respect to the application of this principle:

- *The Church of Christ subsists in the Catholic Church.* "Catholics hold the firm conviction that the one Church of Christ subsists in the Catholic Church, 'which is governed by the successor of Peter and by the Bishops in communion with him'" (17, quoting *LG*, 8). The directory then recalls the following words from the Second Vatican Council decree *Unitatis Redintegratio:* "This unity, we believe, subsists in the Catholic Church as something she can never lose, and we hope that it will continue to increase until the end of time" (18, quoting *UR*, 4).

- *Communion among Christians has never been destroyed.* Despite the divisions that have intervened because of "human folly and human sinfulness," and for which often enough men of both sides were to blame, communion among Christians has never been destroyed.

In fact, "other Churches and ecclesial Communities, though not in full communion with the Catholic Church, retain in reality a certain communion with it" (*ED*, 18).

- *This communion is differentiated.* For all churches and ecclesial communities, the ecumenical directory makes the general affirmation that "the Spirit of Christ has not refrained from using them as the means of salvation" (*ED*, 18, quoting *UR*, 3). In this context, *Unitatis Redintegratio* indicated that "some, even very many, of the most significant elements and endowments which go together to build up and give life to the church itself can exist outside the visible boundaries of the Catholic Church" (3). But, as already mentioned above, the directory says, "Between the Catholic Church and the Eastern Churches not in full communion with it, there is still a very close communion in matters of faith. Moreover, through the celebration of the Eucharist of the Lord in each of these Churches, the Church of God is built up and grows in stature ... these Churches still possess true sacraments, above all—by apostolic succession—the priesthood and the Eucharist" (122).

- *No Christian should be satisfied with these forms of communion.* They do not respond to the will of Christ, and weaken his church in the exercise of its mission (19).

Chapter II of the Directory

A second chapter deals with *the organization of the Catholic Church* at the service of Christian unity. It takes up much of what was already prescribed for diocesan ecumenical commissions and ecumenical commissions of episcopal conferences in chapter 1 of the 1967 directory. While reinforcing those norms, however, the new directory indicates other areas and structures that should promote ecumenism: supranational bodies that exist in various forms for assuring cooperation and assistance among episcopal conferences, institutes of consecrated life, and societies of apostolic life—organizations of Catholic faithful in a particular territory or nation, as well as at the international level, dealing with questions such as spiritual renewal, action for peace and social justice, education, and economic aid and development. In short, the directory wishes to involve in the ecumenical task persons and structures at all levels of the church's life. It refers especially to those persons and structures particularly engaged in promoting Christian unity and sets out norms that govern their activities. The chapter closes with a brief description of the competence and task of the Pontifical Council for Promoting Christian Unity, regarding which it points out the importance of this council being informed of important initiatives taken at various levels of the life of the church, especially when such initiatives have international implications.

Chapter III of the Directory

The third chapter takes up the question of *ecumenical formation* for all involved in promoting ecumenism within the Catholic Church and enters more deeply into this question, referring to the various categories of persons involved in formation, to the scope and methods of formation, as well as to their various doctrinal and practical aspects. The new directory draws on the second part of the former directory, especially the section on *ecumenism in higher education*. The treatment here is broader and embraces all the components of the church: the faithful in general, those directly engaged in pastoral work, ecclesiastical faculties, Catholic universities, and specialized ecumenical institutes. A final word is devoted to permanent formation since "doctrinal formation and learning experience are not limited to the period of formation, but ask for a continuous '*aggiornamento*' of the ordained ministers and pastoral workers, in view of the continual evolution within the ecumenical movement" (91). The directory mentions also the possibility of interconfessional meetings aimed at improving reciprocal relationships and at trying to resolve pastoral problems together. To give concrete form to these initiatives, it might be useful to create local and regional clergy councils or associations.

Having set the scene, as it were, in the first three chapters, the ecumenical directory goes on to consider ecumenical activity: in chapter IV looking at *spiritual activity*, and in chapter V *cooperation*, *dialogue*, and *common witness*.

Chapter IV of the Directory

Chapter IV is of particular interest since it refers to *"spiritual ecumenism,"* which, as we shall see, is receiving renewed attention in the new Christian millennium. The chapter begins with a section on the existing communion with other Christians that is based on the sacramental bond of baptism. The sacrament of baptism is treated at some length, since it is through this sacrament that Christians share a real communion, one with the other, even when that communion is not yet perfect. Hence, it is important to ascertain the validity of baptism conferred by ministers of other churches and ecclesial communities. Useful guidelines are given in this connection (99), and rules are also included concerning godparents from a church or community not in full communion with the Catholic Church (98).

The directory encourages Christians to share spiritual activities and resources through prayer in common, participation in liturgical worship in the strict sense, and common use of places of worship and all necessary objects for worship. Two very important principles are enunciated:

- In spite of the serious difficulties that prevent full ecclesial communion, it is clear that all those who by baptism are incorporated into Christ share many elements of the Christian life. Thus, there exists a real, even if imperfect, communion among Christians that can be expressed in many ways, including sharing in prayer and liturgical worship.

- Since this communion is incomplete because of differences of faith and understanding, unrestricted sharing of spiritual endowments is not possible.

This is a complex reality and requires norms that take into account the diverse ecclesial situations of the churches and communities involved. On the one hand, Christians are able to esteem and rejoice in the spiritual riches they have in common; on the other hand, they are also made aware of the necessity of overcoming the separations that still exist. "Since eucharistic concelebration is a visible manifestation of full communion of faith, worship and community life of the Catholic Church, expressed by ministers of that church, it is not permitted to celebrate the Eucharist with ministers of other churches or ecclesial Communities" (104).

The directory reminds us that "the Churches and ecclesial Communities not in full communion with the Catholic Church have by no means been deprived of significance and value in the mystery of salvation, for the Spirit of Christ has not refrained from using them as means of salvation." Hence, it is recommended that consultations on spiritual sharing, which should include a certain reciprocity, take place between appropriate Catholic authorities and those of other communions.

Prayer in common is in itself a way to spiritual reconciliation and is strongly encouraged in the directory. Shared prayer should be particularly concerned with the restoration of Christian unity, but may be appropriate whenever Catholics and other Christians wish to place before the Lord common concerns. "Under the direction of those who have proper formation and experience, it may be helpful in certain cases to arrange for spiritual sharing in the form of days of recollection, spiritual exercises, groups for study and sharing of traditions of spirituality, and more stable associations for a deeper exploration of a common spiritual life" (114). While representatives of the churches, ecclesial communities, and other groups are encouraged to arrange common prayer services, the directory states that it is not advisable to have these take place on Sundays, since Catholics are bound to attend Mass on that day and on days of precept.

Of particular interest is the section on *sharing in nonsacramental liturgical worship*. Liturgical worship is defined as "worship carried out according to books, prescriptions and customs of a Church or ecclesial Community, presided over by a minister or delegate of that Church or ecclesial Community," and may be the celebration of one or more sacraments, or simply nonsacramental worship (116). Catholics are encouraged to take part on appropriate occasions in the nonsacramental liturgical worship of other churches and ecclesial communities.

With regard to *sharing in the sacramental life of other churches and communities, especially the Eucharist*, certain fundamental distinctions must be kept in mind:

- Between the Catholic Church and the Eastern Churches not in full communion with it, there is still a very close communion in matters of faith. Through the celebration of the Eucharist of the Lord in each of these churches, the church of God is built up and grows in stature. They possess true sacraments, above all—by apostolic succession—the priesthood and the Eucharist (Cf. *UR*, 14). "This offers ecclesiological and sacramental grounds, according to the understanding of the Catholic Church, for allowing and even encouraging some sharing in liturgical worship, even of the Eucharist, with these Churches" (122). At the same time, the directory respects the fact that these Eastern Churches, on the basis of their own ecclesiological understanding, may have more restrictive disciplines in this matter.

- The situation is not the same with regard to other churches and ecclesial communities. The Catholic Church cannot make the same affirmations about the priesthood and the Eucharist; there is not a unity in faith sufficient to allow sacramental sharing, except in very special circumstances. Hence, in general, says the directory, the Catholic Church "permits access to its Eucharistic communion and to the sacraments of penance and anointing of the sick, only to those who share its oneness in faith, worship and ecclesial life" (129). The directory gives guidelines that should be of help to those who have difficult decisions to make in this connection. The sharing of churches and church buildings—including, in certain circumstances, common ownership—is strongly recommended by the directory, which also speaks of cooperation at the spiritual level in Catholic schools, hospitals, and homes for the aged.

- Finally, there are guidelines on specific issues related to *mixed marriages*, which are constantly on the increase and create a special challenge for the ecumenical movement. The directory insists on the need to prepare adequately those about to enter a mixed marriage and suggests that, where possible, contact be made with the minister of the other church or community involved. This support should be available also after the marriage takes place. In this connection, there are directives on eucharistic sharing in mixed marriages, at the time of the celebration and later on. It makes clear that "although the spouses in a mixed marriage share the sacraments of baptism and marriage, Eucharistic sharing can only be exceptional and in each case the norms stated above [in the directory] concerning the admission of a non-Catholic Christian to Eucharistic communion, as well as those concerning the participation of a Catholic in Eucharistic communion in another Church, must be observed" (160).

Chapter V of the Directory

A fifth and final chapter encourages ecumenical cooperation, dialogue, and common witness. As is the case with the first chapter, this chapter is new. It does, however, draw largely on the document published by the SPCU in 1975: *Ecumenical Collaboration on Regional, National, and Local Levels*. It also takes in, from the second part (1970) of the former directory, the section on collaboration in institutes of higher education. At the same time, the 1993 directory considers some entirely new areas of cooperation, such as ecumenical collaboration in missionary activity, based on the conciliar decree *Ad Gentes*, the apostolic exhortation *Evangelii Nuntiandi* (December 8, 1975), and the encyclical *Redemptoris Missio* (December 7, 1990). The directory also considers ecumenical collaboration in the field of catechesis, based on the directives of the apostolic exhortation *Catechesi Tradendae* (October 16, 1979).

The final chapter of the directory begins with a powerful declaration about the value of common witness in our present age:

> When Christians live and pray together in the way described in Chapter IV, they are giving witness to the faith which they share and to their baptism, in the name of God, the Father of all, in his Son, Jesus, the Redeemer of all, and in the Holy Spirit who transforms and unites all things through the power of love. Based on this communion of life and spiritual gifts, there are many other forms of ecumenical cooperation that express and promote unity and enhance the witness to the saving power of the Gospel that Christians give to the world. (161)

The council's Decree on Ecumenism, *Unitatis Redintegratio*, pointed out the value for ecumenism of practical cooperation among Christians (12). Such cooperation, it states, not only "profoundly expresses that unity which already exists between them and illuminates more fully the face of Christ the servant," but also enables them to learn "how to smooth the way toward unity." Taking up this challenge, the new directory examines the possibility of cooperation in social and cultural life, of the common study of social and ethical questions, and of collaboration in the development of important areas of human need, including the stewardship of creation, the medical field, and the means of social communication.

There are important guidelines concerning the structuring of ecumenical cooperation, such as in councils of churches and Christian councils, in the common work of translating and distributing the Bible, and in dialogue with other religions. Finally, it is here in chapter V that we find directives on ecumenical dialogue and its needs.

For those who express frustration at the slow pace of ecumenical progress, this fifth chapter offers a great variety of possible initiatives that, if taken up widely, could help advance the cause of Christian unity and hasten the day of a restoration of full, visible communion among all Christians.

THE ENCYCLICAL *UT UNUM SINT*

A final document that cannot be ignored if one is to understand the extent of the ongoing commitment of the Catholic Church to the search for Christian unity is the encyclical letter of Pope John Paul II entitled *Ut Unum Sint* (On Commitment to Ecumenism) published May 25, 1995. This was not only the first such document ever to be issued by a bishop of Rome on ecumenism, but it is unique up to now in the ecumenical movement. Unless I am mistaken, no other church or ecclesial communion has offered to the one ecumenical movement a similar official declaration of its understanding of and commitment to the restoration of full, visible unity of the Christian family.

If, however, one looks back at this pope's activity during his long pontificate, his decision to write an encyclical letter on this subject does not appear strange. A constant feature of his pontificate has been his own personal commitment to the search for Christian unity. As a young member of the Polish hierarchy, and after 1964 the archbishop of Krakow, Karol Wojtyla participated in the Second Vatican Council and signed the Decree on Ecumenism, *Unitatis Redintegratio.* Thirty years later, in this encyclical letter On Commitment to Ecumenism, *Ut Unum Sint,* John Paul II reflected in the light of his experience, especially that gained during his pontificate from 1978 to 1995, on the hopes and expectations of the council fathers. The encyclical letter can be seen as a personal response to his own appeal in the apostolic letter *Tertio Millennio Adveniente,* published just some six months earlier, for the "promotion of fitting ecumenical initiatives, so that we can celebrate the Great Jubilee, if not completely united, at least much closer to overcoming the divisions of the second millennium."[15]

Chapter 1: On Commitment to Ecumenism

In this encyclical, Pope John Paul II took up the question of the commitment to ecumenism of the Second Vatican Council and removed all doubt about its meaning and gravity. He stated, "At the Second Vatican Council, the Catholic Church committed herself *irrevocably* to following the path of the ecumenical venture, thus heeding the Spirit of the Lord, who teaches people to interpret carefully the 'signs of the times'" (3). And then, after declaring that "the way of ecumenism is the way of the Church" (7), the pope wrote: "The Catholic Church embraces with hope the commitment to ecumenism as a duty of the Christian conscience enlightened by faith and guided by love" (9).

His Holiness saw the unity we seek as having its divine source in the trinitarian unity of the Father, the Son, and the Holy Spirit. He reminded the reader that Christ himself, at the hour of his passion, prayed "that they may all be one":

This unity, which the Lord has bestowed on his Church, and in which he wishes to embrace all people, is not something added on, but stands at the very heart of Christ's mission. Nor is it some secondary attribute of the community of his disciples. Rather, it belongs to the very essence of this community.

God wills the Church, because he wills unity, and unity is an expression of the whole depth of his *agape*. (9)

The Second Vatican Council had stated that concern for restoring unity was to be considered a task for all the members of the church, according to the ability of each (*UR*, 5), and Pope John Paul II came to the following conclusion, which is of great importance for the future activity of the Catholic Church:

> Thus it is absolutely clear that ecumenism . . . *is not just some sort of "appendix"* which is added to the Church's traditional activity. Rather, ecumenism is an organic part of her life and work, and consequently must pervade all that she is and does; it must be like the fruit borne by a healthy and flourishing tree which grows to its full stature. (20)

No occasion has been allowed to pass without a valuable contribution from Pope John Paul II to the ecumenical cause. He has taught by word and deed that the church that he has been called to lead is fully and irrevocably committed to the promotion of Christian unity. This clear commitment to unity on behalf of the Catholic Church is perhaps best summed up in the pope's own very beautiful and striking words with which he declared that "to believe in Christ means to desire unity; to desire unity means to desire the Church; to desire the Church means to desire the communion of grace which corresponds to the Father's plan from all eternity. Such is the meaning of Christ's prayer: *'Ut Unum Sint'*" (9).

The above statements of Pope John Paul II should cause every member of the Catholic Church to reflect and examine his or her conscience in this connection. If, as the Holy Father stated, "ecumenism is an organic part of the Church's life and work," then it must be part of the life and work of each bishop and responsible person in the church—and indeed of every member of the church, since as the Second Vatican Council has declared, "the concern for restoring unity involves the whole Church, faithful and clergy alike" (*UR*, 5). If "to believe in Christ is to desire unity," then we must ask whether one can be considered fully a citizen of the Church of Christ and not desire this unity.

Chapter 2: The Fruits of Dialogue

Right at the beginning of the encyclical, Pope John Paul II seeks to encourage those who may be victims of a certain frustration or who are disillusioned by the slow progress being made and the difficulties being encountered in the ecumenical movement. In his introductory remarks, the Holy Father thanks the Lord "that he has led us to make progress along the path of unity and communion between Christians, a path so difficult but full of joy" (2).

To illustrate this important point, the encyclical's second chapter is titled "The Fruits of Dialogue." A first fruit is the fact that Christians of one confession no longer consider other Christians as enemies or strangers. Already the Second Vatican Council had solemnly declared: "All those justified by faith through baptism are incorporated into Christ. They therefore have a right to be honored by the title of Christian, and are properly regarded as brothers in the Lord by the sons and daughters of the Catholic Church" (*UR*, 3).

The pope points out that new expressions are now used to indicate new attitudes based on a common awareness "that we all belong to Christist.... The 'universal brotherhood' of Christians has become a firm ecumenical conviction" (42). His Holiness speaks of *brotherhood rediscovered*, a brotherhood that "is not the consequence of a large-hearted philanthropy or a vague family spirit [but] is rooted in recognition of the oneness of baptism and the subsequent duty to glorify God in his work" (42). These attitudes, moreover, are not just expressed in words, but are given practical application in various forms of cooperation and solidarity in the service of humanity.

Renewed and frequent contacts between the churches have strengthened the bonds that unite them and have made possible substantial progress in the various theological dialogues. "The process has been slow and arduous, yet a source of great joy" (51). The real, though imperfect, communion that the Second Vatican Council found to be existing between the baptized has continued to grow and be strengthened, especially through prayer and dialogue. Those involved in the ecumenical ministry have experienced in their own lives important fruits resulting just from being so involved, and it would certainly seem to be the case also with Pope John Paul II.

His Holiness concludes his reflection on the progress made in the theological dialogue with the following evaluation:

> This dialogue has been and continues to be fruitful and full of promise. The topics suggested by the Council decree have already been addressed, or will be in the future. The reflections of the various bilateral dialogues, conducted with a dedication which deserves the praise of all those committed to ecumenism, have concentrated on many disputed questions such as Baptism, the Eucharist, the ordained ministry, the sacramentality and authority of the Church and apostolic succession. As a result, unexpected possibilities for resolving these questions have come to light, while at the same time there has been a realization that certain questions need to be studied more deeply. (69)

Chapter 3: Future Dialogue

In the third chapter of the encyclical, His Holiness asks, "How much further must we still travel until that blessed day when full unity in faith will be attained and we can celebrate together in peace the Holy Eucharist of the Lord" (77).

At the beginning of this chapter of the encyclical, the Holy Father speaks of the ecumenical journey as requiring patient and courageous efforts, and then makes what I believe to be an important statement that has still to be widely received in the various dialogues. He speaks of the journey toward necessary and sufficient visible unity, in the communion of the one church willed by Christ. In this journey, therefore, "one must not impose any burden beyond that which is necessary" (cf. Acts 15:28)" (78). The churches are not involved in a search for uniformity of doctrinal expression, but in a quest for unity in faith. The late Rev. Max Thurian, a founder-member of the Taizé community in France and later a convert to Catholicism, who was well-known and highly esteemed in ecumenical circles, made the following comment while speaking on Vatican Radio (Radiogiornale del Radio Vaticano) on this particular point:

Today it is necessary for us to deepen together ever more fully the faith that we have in common. One delightful aspect of the encyclical is when the Pope stresses that we must seek only what is necessary and sufficient to bring about unity.... There is no question of some coming out winners and others as losers. (June 1, 1995)

Pope John Paul II reminds his readers—and perhaps theologians in particular—of the distinction recommended by Pope John XXIII in his opening address to the Catholic bishops gathered in the Second Vatican Council, between the deposit of faith and the formulation in which it is expressed. This distinction, writes Pope John Paul II, "will be of great help methodologically" in examining the results of the theological dialogues and in carrying forward, with the assistance of the Holy Spirit, the process of reconciliation (81).

At the same time, the pope calls upon the members of his church "to avoid false irenicism and indifference to the Church's ordinances" (79). Ecumenism, in fact, does not relativize or diminish the unique claims of the Catholic Church. On the contrary, it is the unique status of the Catholic Church that makes ecumenism mandatory. Ecumenism is not a program of the Catholic Church; ecumenism is in the nature of being the Catholic Church. The Catholic Church cannot be true to itself unless it is ecumenical.[16] This is a truth too little appreciated by many Catholics, and the encyclical points out that the same "transparency and prudence of faith" that require us to avoid compromise on questions of faith urge us "to reject a half-hearted commitment to unity and, even more, a prejudicial opposition or a defeatism which tends to see everything in negative terms" (79).

Pope John Paul II identifies the areas in need of fuller study before a true consensus of faith can be achieved, namely:

- The relationship between Sacred Scripture, as the highest authority in matters of faith, and Sacred Tradition, as indispensable to the interpretation of the Word of God
- The Eucharist, as the sacrament of the Body and Blood of Christ, an offering of praise to the Father, the sacrificial memorial and

real presence of Christ, and the sanctifying outpouring of the
Holy Spirit
- Ordination, as a sacrament, to the threefold ministry of the episcopate, presbyterate, and diaconate
- The magisterium of the church, entrusted to the pope and the
bishops in communion with him, understood as a responsibility
and an authority exercised in the name of Christ for teaching and
safeguarding the faith
- The Virgin Mary, as Mother of God and icon of the church, the
spiritual Mother who intercedes for Christ's disciples and for all
humanity (79)

In this connection, an interesting aspect of the encyclical is the
section entitled "Contribution of the Catholic Church to the Quest
for Christian Unity" (nos. 86 and 87), which is immediately followed
by a reflection of the Holy Father, "Ministry of Unity of the Bishop
of Rome" (nos. 88–96).

It seems that, in writing this reflection, Pope John Paul II was
faced with a dramatic paradox. While expressing his strong commitment to ecumenism, both as an individual and as head of the Catholic
Church, he realized that, in the view of many of precisely those people
he wished to challenge with this encyclical, the primacy of the pope as
the successor of Peter is the principal obstacle to unity.

We observe this in his presentation of the ministry of the bishop
of Rome as being primarily a ministry of unity, yet one that can be a
source of "painful recollections" and a difficulty for most other Christians. His Holiness joined his predecessor Pope Paul VI in asking forgiveness "to the extent that we are responsible for these" (88). At the
same time, the pope expressed encouragement that other churches
and ecclesial communities, after centuries of bitter controversies, are
more and more taking a fresh look at the question of the primacy of
the bishop of Rome. At the conclusion of this profound reflection on
the role of the papacy in the search for unity, Pope John Paul II
states:

I am convinced that I have a particular responsibility in this
regard, above all in acknowledging the ecumenical aspirations
of the majority of the Christian Communities and in heeding

the request made of me to find a way of exercising the primacy which, while in no way renouncing what is essential to its mission, is nonetheless open to a new situation. (95)

In his homily during the Mass celebrated in St. Peter's Basilica on December 6, 1987, in the presence of His Holiness Patriarch Dimitrios I of Constantinople, Pope John Paul II had already expressed his hope that "the Holy Spirit may shine his light upon us, enlightening all the Pastors and theologians of our Churches, that we may seek—together, of course—the forms in which this ministry may accomplish a service of love recognized by all concerned" (95).[17]

While acknowledging now that this is "an immense task, which we cannot refuse and which I cannot carry out on by myself," Pope John Paul II renews his appeal to church leaders and their theologians to engage with him in a patient and fraternal dialogue on this subject, "a dialogue in which, leaving useless controversies behind, we could listen to one another, keeping before us only the will of Christ for his Church, and allowing ourselves to be deeply moved by his plea 'that they may all be one ... so that the world may believe that you have sent me' (John 17:21)" (96).

These reflections have elicited great interest and not a little comment. Rev. Richard John Neuhaus has written, "I am confident that we would not go wrong in understanding the Holy Father to be saying that unity is more important than jurisdiction. Christians in the East have been waiting a thousand years to hear a Bishop of Rome say that, and now it is being said."[18]

Comments on and Responses to the Encyclical

I doubt if any other papal document has received such attention outside the Catholic Church as the encyclical *Ut Unum Sint*. In general, the comments have been very encouraging. Certainly, not all those who have referred particularly to the question of the papacy have reacted positively to the pope's request. As was to be expected, the most negative comments in this connection have come from the Reformed Communions. It is indeed difficult to find a place for the primacy of the bishop of Rome in an ecclesiology that does not have a significant role for the ministry of the ordained bishop. And yet there have been several thoughtful and hopeful statements even from members of these communities.

Official replies were received from several churches and ecumenical organizations. Among these I would mention those of the *Faith and Order Commission of the World Council of Churches*[19] (WCC) and those of the *house of bishops of the Church of England.*

Pope John Paul II was praised in many of the replies for the encyclical's and the Catholic Church's strong commitment to ecumenism. The replies expressed appreciation for his spiritual insights and for his emphasis on spiritual ecumenism. The replies also referred to his strong presentation of the theology of baptism, to his clear endorsement of legitimate diversity within the unity of the churches, to his understanding of the intrinsic link between mission and the unity of the church, and to his insight on the ecumenism of the martyrs. At the same time, various responses noted his sense of realism and spirit of humility.

On the negative side, the document from the *Faith and Order Commission of the WCC*, while "appreciating the combination of personal courtesy and theological candor with which the encyclical speaks of other churches and Ecclesial Communions," considered unsatisfactory some of the references to these churches in the encyclical.

Several of the responses made particular reference to the primacy and to the pope's request for "Church leaders and their theologians to engage with me in a patient and fraternal dialogue on this subject" (96). Special attention was given to this subject in the response of the house of bishops of the Church of England, who see the role of the bishop of Rome in the church as central to dialogue between Roman Catholics and other Christians. In the Occasional Paper "May They All Be One,"[20] the bishops state that "Anglicans and Catholics are at one in their understanding of the episcopate as a ministry involving not only oversight of each local church but also a care for the universal communion of which each church is a member." Recalling the earlier statement of the Anglican–Roman Catholic International Commission (ARCIC) on the office of universal primacy, the bishops affirm:

Anglicans are thus by no means opposed to the principle and practice of a personal ministry at the world level in the service of unity. Indeed, increasingly their experience of the Anglican Communion is leading them to appreciate the proper need, alongside communal and collegial ministries, for a personal service of unity in the faith. (44)

The house of bishops would not rule out "the universal primacy of the bishop of Rome as the person who particularly signifies the unity and the universality of the Church," and they would be ready "to acknowledge his special responsibilities for maintaining unity in the truth and ordering things in love . . .''; but despite this, they would have reservations in so doing and noted the serious obstacles that still exist "because of the present Roman Catholic understanding of the jurisdiction attributed to the primacy of the Bishop of Rome" over the whole church. They make it clear, however, that they do not consider this "an argument for a primacy of honor only, or for the exclusion from a universal primacy of the authority necessary for a worldwide ministry in the service of unity" (46 and 47).

Ecumenical Patriarch Bartholomew I of Constantinople, in a brief, general comment, stated that the encyclical *Ut Unum Sint* would "undoubtedly have been accepted with gratitude" by all denominations if the Catholic Church had been ready to consider the papal office in line with the "pentarchy." The pentarchy is an Orthodox concept in which the five ancient patriarchates—Rome, Constantinople, Antioch, Alexandria, and Jerusalem—have a special place of honor among all the churches, with Rome as first, but among equals. "This means," Bartholomew I said, that the encyclical would have been accepted "if the Church and its theologians had been prepared to see the pope as coordinator and senior leader without extremes and theologically mistaken demands for a world primacy in the jurisdictional sense—or even worse, for personal infallibility over the whole church and independently of it."[21]

I would just mention two other important responses from the Orthodox Church that merit special attention. Immediately after the publication of the encyclical, on June 1, 1995, Metropolitan Damaskinos of Switzerland contributed a long and very positive article to the French newspaper *La Croix*, and issued a shorter version of the same to all the mass media. He did not hesitate to state that this encyclical letter was a remarkable and constructive contribution by His Holiness

Pope John Paul II "to the search which the Catholic Church is carrying out with other Churches and Ecclesial Communities for the reestablishment of the unity of all the baptized."

Responding to *Ut Unum Sint* on the same date, in the paper *Le Monde*, Olivier Clément, a professor at the Orthodox *Institut Sainte-Serge*, Paris, found that the encyclical gives the ecumenical movement a properly spiritual foundation, "a method based on common prayer in the sincere discovery of the other, and on repentance." It should signify, he hoped, "the end of accusation of the other." In a subsequent interview with the Italian daily *Avvenire*, Clément made the following interesting observation. He referred to the pope's invitation for a dialogue on the exercise of the primacy as "an unprecedented and prophetic initiative," and then went on to state: "I find it inadmissible that the proposal has gone almost unheard. I would hope that the Oriental Patriarchs would get to work and be in a position to present their reflections to Pope John Paul II . . . in 1999."[22]

In an interview reported by *Catholic News Service* in July 1996, the secretary-general of the WCC, the Rev. Konrad Raiser, expressed the opinion that, while the encyclical had raised the question of "how to find a way of exercising primacy, which is open to the new ecumenical situation, without rejecting anything essential from its mission," he could see "no sign yet that the pope is ready to consider the necessary self-relativization of his primacy." For Rev. Konrad Raiser, the papal office remains the "foremost obstacle" to reunification.[23]

As already mentioned, one notes in general a certain reserve among representatives of the Reformed Churches, especially as regards the Petrine primacy. Milan Opocensky, general secretary of the World Alliance of Reformed Churches (WARC), in an early comment on the encyclical, gave a broad welcome to the initiative to strengthen and deepen ecumenical cooperation but found it "unthinkable to accept the Papacy as a symbol of unity among Christians."[24] Lukas Vischer, a Swiss Reformed theologian and former Director of Faith and Order at the World Council of Churches, said that the encyclical presented a "dilemma" for churches of the Reformation. Let me quote his words as published in the French newspaper *Le Monde*, also on June 1, 1995:

On the one hand we can only welcome the fundamental convictions contained in the text. To a large extent they correspond with the convictions declared by the World Council over the years. On the other hand, the text comes from the supreme authority of the Roman Catholic Church where, according to Catholic doctrine, the ministry of the pope is crucial to the reestablishment of unity, and thus the encyclical necessarily becomes a plea for the ministry of unity of the Pope."

Lukas Vischer doubted that this vision of the pope's ministry of unity could be put at the service of the church and expressed his conviction that the Reformation churches cannot in good conscience associate themselves with such a vision. A recent symposium of the evangelical faculty of Vienna found no place in reformed thinking for a personal primacy or for dogmas in the church.

Not all Reformed comment has been so negative. Rev. Paul Crow, the ecumenical officer of the Christian Church–Disciples of Christ, stated:

I'm one of those who believes the office of the papacy is not only essential for the Roman Catholic Church, but is an important office for all Christians. We can debate him (Pope John Paul II)...but it's not an office Protestants can ignore. His invitation to rethink how he exercises that role is thus an invitation to shared ministry.[25]

There have been many other responses that deserve attention, but those cited seem to be the most important and hopefully give an indication of the manner in which the pope's encyclical was received.

Ut Unum Sint—Contribution and Inspiration

In conclusion, it seems obvious that the encyclical *Ut Unum Sint* has made a valuable contribution to the ecumenical movement. In declaring so strongly the commitment of the Roman Catholic Church to the search for the full, visible unity of all the disciples of the Lord, it has challenged other churches and ecclesial communions to examine and declare their commitment to "this most noble task" (3). At the same time, the papal document has been an inspiration to the bishops, clergy, religious, and faithful of the Catholic Church in their efforts to promote greater Christian unity.

The encyclical, however, is also proof of the fact that much work remains to be done within the Church of Rome before Pope John Paul's vision of the ecumenical commitment is fully shared by all the members of the church. He has shown the way; he has clearly indicated the direction and illustrated the means to be adopted. In this document, he has made it clear that, as disciples of Christ, Catholics are called to unity, and this not for their own satisfaction, but "so that the world may believe" (John 17:21). The pope asks,

> How indeed can we proclaim the Gospel of reconciliation without at the same time being committed to working for reconciliation between Christians? . . . When non-believers meet missionaries who do not agree among themselves, even though they all appeal to Christ, will they be in a position to receive the true message? Will they not think that the Gospel is a cause of division, despite the fact that it is presented as the fundamental law of love? (98)

Ut Unum Sint continues to attract attention, study, and serious debate. During a visit to His All-Holiness the Patriarch of Constantinople Bartholomew I, at the Phanar on May 8, 1998, the then Archbishop of Milan, Cardinal Carlo Maria Martini, stated:

> The need of purifying the memory and healing still-open wounds of the past should not be separated from the need to discern, in a side-by-side comparison of our two traditions, which of our differences are the result of the work of the one who divides or of the sin of man, and which, on the other hand, come from the Spirit who diversifies forms so as to bring them together in a unity that is no longer carnal but spiritual.[26]

This reflection seems to echo the closing exhortation to Pope John Paul's encyclical, in which he asks the members of his church to seek the gift of unity from the Holy Spirit, for it is the Spirit who is able to banish from their midst the painful memories of their separation and grant them clear-sightedness, strength, and courage to take whatever steps are necessary, so that their commitment may be ever more authentic (102). The encyclical closes on a note full of faith and hope:

> There is no doubt that the Holy Spirit is active in this endeavor and is leading the Church to the full realization of the Father's plan, in conformity with the will of Christ. This will was expressed with heartfelt urgency in the prayer which, according to the Fourth Gospel, he uttered at the moment when he entered upon the saving mystery of the Passover. Just as he did then, today too Christ calls everyone to renew their commitment to work for full and visible communion. (100)

It is on the response of Christians, especially their leaders, to this call that the future of the ecumenical movement will depend in the long run. Nothing is lacking on the part of the Lord. He has given us his Spirit to guide and inspire us. The big question remains: To what degree are the churches ready to listen to what the Spirit is saying to them?

FORTY YEARS OF DIALOGUE

The Second Vatican Council indicated the path that the church was to follow in order to restore its relations with other Christian Communities. The ecumenical movement, as seen by the council fathers in *Unitatis Redintegratio*, would be built upon three basic pillars. First, there would be an effort "to avoid expressions, judgments, and actions which do not represent the condition of our separated brethren with truth and fairness and so make mutual relations with them more difficult." Second, dialogue between competent experts from different churches and communities would follow. "Through such dialogue everyone gains a truer knowledge and more just appreciation of the teaching and religious life of both communions." This would be accompanied by intensive cooperation in carrying out any duties for the common good of humanity that are demanded by every Christian conscience. And, third, there should be "common prayer, where this is permitted" (*UR*, 4).

In the encyclical *Ut Unum Sint*, Pope John Paul II takes up these indications and develops them, as has already been mentioned. For the Holy Father, the most important indication is prayer, especially common prayer, which he sees as the "soul" of ecumenical renewal and of the yearning for unity. He sees dialogue as "an indispensable step along the path toward human self-realization, the self-realization both of each individual and of every human community" (28). Dialogue, he states, is not simply an exchange of ideas. In some way it is always an "exchange of gifts" (21ff.).

Already during the Second Vatican Council, the seeds of future theological dialogue between the Catholic Church and other churches and communities had been sown. This dialogue, we can say, began informally, thanks to the presence of the observers from other Christian communities at the council, and then developed quickly into formal bilateral dialogues with most of the other churches. In the forty years that have followed, bilateral dialogue between the Catholic Church and other Christian communions has developed extensively and has produced extraordinary results.

Within a few years of the solemn closing of the council, the Church of Rome was in dialogue with the Anglican Communion (ARCIC), the Lutheran World Federation, the World Methodist Council, the World Alliance of Reformed Churches, and the Disciples of Christ.

Dialogue with the Oriental Orthodox Eastern Churches—the Coptic Orthodox Church, the Armenian Apostolic Church, the Malankara Orthodox Churches, and the Assyrian Church of the East—has been conducted separately with each of these churches and in different forms, according to the particular history of the partner involved, but this has produced some of the most important results. An official dialogue with the Orthodox Churches had to wait until 1980 to begin its work. And then in more recent years, there has been a bilateral dialogue between the Catholic Church and some Pentecostals within the International Catholic-Pentecostal Dialogue, and also with the Mennonite World Conference, the Baptist World Alliance, and the World Evangelical Alliance.

The Importance of Bilateral Dialogue

In the understanding of the Catholic Church, bilateral dialogue is seen as an essential element in the search for Christian unity. Multilateral dialogue has, undoubtedly, an important role to play in this search, and the Catholic Church has given its support to, and taken part in, the work of the Commission on Faith and Order of the World Council of Churches. Given, however, the nature of the questions that continue to prevent full communion among the churches and the varying approaches to these questions on the part of different churches, Rome has been convinced from the beginning of the need for bilateral dialogue if the goal of Christian unity is to be reached.

For example, in dialogue with the Oriental Orthodox or the Orthodox, questions relating to the Eucharist or ministry in the church could be fruitfully discussed with the hope of reaching agreement. These, however, are among the questions that create the greatest obstacles to unity with churches coming out of the Reform. For each bilateral dialogue, a common ground has to be found on which a fruitful dialogue can be built. From that established base, the dialogue can then hope to move ahead into areas where the partners hold contrary, or seemingly contrary, beliefs. Experience has shown that to begin with the most difficult questions does not lead to any fruitful conclusion.

Some Dialogue Experiences

Oriental Orthodox Churches

The experience in respect of these churches varies. Until very recently, it had not been possible to have a dialogue with all of them together, and there had not been any ongoing formal dialogue with either the Armenians or Syrians. A Joint International Commission for Theological Dialogue between the Catholic Church and the Coptic Church did some good work until suspended by the Coptic partner in the early nineties. In Southern India the Catholic Church has been engaged in official dialogues with both the Orthodox Syrian Churches of Malabar, through the Joint International Commission for Theological Dialogue between the Catholic Church and the Malankara Orthodox Syrian Church and the Joint Commission for Theological Dialogue between the Catholic Church and the Malankara Syrian Orthodox Church. Regular meetings have taken place since the 1980s, with both dialogues following a more or less parallel program, dealing mainly with the history of the church, the local and universal church, the Petrine ministry, and possible common witness. At the same time efforts are being made to reconcile and reunite these two churches. As indicated below, in recent years the Catholic Church and the *Assyrian Church of the East* have also carried on a fruitful dialogue.

Despite the obvious delicate relations with these churches, the Catholic Church succeeded in coming to an understanding with each of them at various times on one of the great questions that had divided the church already in the fourth century, namely, the christological understanding concerning the two natures in Jesus Christ. It was the definition of the Council of Chalcedon (AD 451) in particular that led to the parting of the ways between the Oriental Orthodox Churches and the rest of the then Christian world. In contrast to the Chalcedonian formula of one person and two natures in Christ, these churches affirmed the formula of Cyril of Alexandria, who spoke of "the one incarnate nature of the Word of God." For the Oriental Orthodox, those who accepted the Chalcedonian formula were seen as holding an essentially Nestorian Christology that compromised the unity of Christ's person. For those who accepted Chalcedon, the "one incarnate nature" formula of the Oriental Orthodox seemed indistinguishable from the monophysite position of Eutyches, who taught that Jesus' humanity was totally subsumed into his divinity.

Since the Second Vatican Council, it has been possible for the Catholic Church and the patriarchs of several of these churches to declare their common faith in Jesus Christ, true God and true man, putting aside fifteen hundred years of controversy by stressing the common faith behind different expressions of that faith. Agreement was reached with the Syrian Church in 1971, with the Coptic in 1973, with the Ethiopian in 1993, and with the Assyrian Church of the East in 1994 (see *Ut Unum Sint*, 62). The 1996 common declaration of Pope John Paul II and the Armenian Catholicos Karekin I spoke of their "fundamental common faith in God and in Jesus

Christ." This is a particularly important distinction for ecumenical dialogue in general, as has became clear over and over again in subsequent agreements with other churches.

Five unofficial theological consultations have also been held between Catholic and Oriental Orthodox theologians—under the auspices of the *Pro Oriente* foundation in Vienna—in 1971, 1973, 1976, 1978, and 1988.

In 1998, Pope Shenouda III, the Syrian Patriarch Mar Zakka I Iwas, and Armenian Patriarch Aram I of Cilicia agreed not to undertake dialogues with other churches and ecclesial communions unless this could be done jointly. Subsequent discussions with the Pontifical Council for Promoting Christian Unity resulted in the setting up of a Catholic Church–Oriental Orthodox Churches International Joint Commission for Dialogue. The Oriental Orthodox Churches represented in this joint commission are the Coptic Orthodox Church, Syrian Orthodox Church, Armenian Apostolic Church (Catholicosate of All Armenians), Armenian Apostolic Church (Catholicosate of Cilicia), Ethiopian Orthodox Church, Malankara Orthodox Syrian Church, and Eritrean Orthodox Church. Although these belong to different traditions, they see themselves as belonging to the same ecclesial family. They recognize the validity of each other's sacraments and allow eucharistic concelebration.

This joint commission was formally set up in Rome in January 2003, with the strong encouragement of Pope John Paul II, who welcomed the representatives to Rome and addressed them as follows:

> Substantial ecumenical progress has already been made between the Catholic Church and the different Oriental Orthodox Churches. Essential clarifications have been reached with regard to traditional controversies about Christology, and this has enabled us to profess together the faith we hold in common. This progress is most encouraging since "it shows us that the path followed is the right one and that we can reasonably hope to discover together the solution to other disputed questions" (*Ut Unum Sint*, 63). May your efforts to establish a Joint Commission for Theological Dialogue prove a major step forward toward full communion in truth and charity.[27]

The commission had its first meeting in Cairo in January 2004. Following a review of the many conversations, declarations, and dialogue meetings that had already taken place between the Oriental Orthodox Churches and the Catholic Church over the past thirty years, it was decided to begin the future program with a study of the "church as communion." Three principal aspects of this theme are indicated:

- The notion of communion and its constitutive elements
- Communion at the regional and universal levels, as well as the meaning of the notions "Sister Churches" and "Family of Churches"
- Full communion and levels of communion in light of common ecumenical goal

The Cairo meeting was held in a cordial and constructive atmosphere. The discussions indicated the progress already made in building unity at three levels: the level of faith through the various christological declarations; the level of sacraments, as witnessed by the agreements reached between the Catholic Church and some of the member churches; and the level of ecclesiology, through advances in discussion.[28]

The churches represented in this commission are also in dialogue together with the Orthodox Church and the Anglican Communion. Although it forms part of the commission, the Malankara Syrian Orthodox Church intends to continue its own particular dialogue with the Catholic Church along the lines already established. The rapprochement between the various churches originating from the original St. Thomas tradition requires individual study and dialogue.[29] The Joint Commission for Dialogue between the Catholic Church and the Malankara Syrian Orthodox Church is concentrating on issues concerning the nature of the church, ecclesial communion, and common witness with reference to their 1993 agreement on mixed marriages. The Joint Commission for Dialogue between the Catholic Church and the Malankara Orthodox Syrian Church has been discussing the concept of primacy in the church, and in October 2003 signed an "Agreed Statement on Proselytism." In this dialogue, however, the pastoral question of mixed marriages remains without agreement.[30]

The *Assyrian Church of the East* is still considered by some other Oriental Orthodox as "Nestorian" in faith. Consequently, it has not been possible for it to be admitted as a member of the Middle East Council of Churches (MECC) or to have it take part in the Catholic Church–Oriental Orthodox Churches International Joint Commission for Dialogue.

The Assyrian Church of the East developed in Mesopotamia, or Persia, in the early years of the Christian era, and spread over a large area to the east outside the borders of the Roman Empire. Later on it suffered greatly from the Muslim expansion in the Middle East and Asia. At that time it was simply called the "Church of the East." In 1552 part of this church entered into full communion with Rome and has since usually been known as the Chaldean Church, while the remaining section took the name of the Assyrian Church of the East. Both particular churches, however, still share the same theological, liturgical, and spiritual tradition; they both celebrate the sacraments or sacred mysteries according to the East-Syrian tradition.

On November 11, 1994, Pope John Paul II and Mar Dinka IV, Patriarch of the Assyrian Church of the East, signed the *Common Christological Declaration*. This declaration removed the main doctrinal obstacle dividing the Catholic Church and the Assyrian Church of the East. In this declaration, both leaders not only expressed a common christological faith, but pledged themselves "to do everything possible to dispel the obstacles of the past which still prevent the attainment of full communion between our Churches, so that we can better respond to the Lord's call for the unity of his own, a unity which has of course to be expressed visibly."[31]

For this purpose a Joint Committee for Theological Discussion between the Catholic Church and the Assyrian Church of the East was established and began its work in 1995. During its annual meetings the committee studied mainly questions of sacramental theology and in 2000 issued an agreed-upon document, *A Common Statement on Sacramental Life*, which was then submitted to the competent authorities of both churches for approval. Amendments from the Holy Synod of the Assyrian Church and the Roman Congregation for the Doctrine of Faith were received and introduced into the text, which was then submitted for official ratification. This was then

granted on behalf of the Catholic Church by the Congregation for
the Doctrine of the Faith.

The agreed statement on sacramental life is seen as important,
not only for its doctrinal affirmations, but also for its promise to serve
both the Chaldean Church and the Assyrian Church of the East in
future common pastoral and catechetical work.

Meanwhile there has been significant progress in the theological
dialogue, as well as a fruitful ongoing process of ecumenical rapprochement that has taken place between the Assyrian Church of the
East and the Chaldean Church. In November 1996, Patriarch Mar
Raphael Bidawid and Patriarch Mar Dinka IV signed a list of common proposals with a view to the reestablishment of ecclesial unity
between these historical heirs of the ancient Church of the East, and
in 1997 this program was approved by the respective synods and confirmed by a joint synodal decree.

This opened the way for a study of a pressing practical problem
regarding admission to the Eucharist that was being widely experienced. Assyrian and Chaldean faithful are to be found in many different parts of the world, though often in small numbers: in Scandinavia,
Western Europe, Australia, and North America. Since there cannot
always be a priest of both churches available to a local community in
such a widespread diaspora, Chaldean and Assyrian faithful are often
confronted with a situation of pastoral necessity with regard to the
administration of sacraments.

The Joint Committee for Theological Discussion between the Catholic Church and the Assyrian Church of the East studied the question
and proposed the document *Guidelines for Admission to the Eucharist between the Chaldean Church and the Assyrian Church of the East.*
The Pontifical Council for Promoting Christian Unity elaborated the
guidelines, in agreement with the Congregation for the Doctrine of
the Faith and the Congregation for Oriental Churches.[32]

The main doctrinal problem encountered by the Catholic Church in
approving the guidelines arose from the use by the Assyrian Church of
the East of an ancient canon or anaphora for the eucharistic celebration,
the *Anaphora of Addai and Mari*, which does not contain the words of the
eucharistic institution, which the Catholic Church considers a constitutive and therefore indispensable part of the prayer. This was solved
when the Congregation for the Doctrine of Faith, on January 17, 2001,

was able to conclude that, despite the absence of the words of institution, the Anaphora of Addai and Mari can be considered valid. This decision was based on the fact that "the Anaphora of Addai and Mari is one of the most ancient Anaphoras, dating back to the time of the very early Church; it was composed and used with the clear intention of celebrating the Eucharist in full continuity with the Last Supper according to the intention of the Church; its validity was never officially contested, neither in the Christian East or the Christian West."[33]

The guidelines allow the Assyrian faithful, when necessity requires, to participate and to receive Holy Communion in a Chaldean celebration of the Holy Eucharist. In the same way, Chaldean faithful for whom it is physically or morally impossible to approach a Catholic minister are permitted to participate and to receive holy communion in an Assyrian celebration of the Eucharist (1). "When Chaldean faithful are participating an Assyrian celebration of the Eucharist, the Assyrian minister is warmly invited to insert the words of the Institution in the Anaphora of Addai and Mari, as allowed by the Holy Synod of the Assyrian Church of the East" (3).

The present phase of dialogue within the Joint Theological Committee deals with questions related to the constitution of the church. Particular attention is being given to the Petrine ministry in the New Testament and in the first millennium. Both the Catholic Church and the Assyrian Church of the East acknowledge the particular role given to Peter by Jesus Christ, a role that can be defined as a "ministry of unity." Their liturgical traditions, moreover, give witness to that particular position and mission of Peter. Discussion has centered also on the relation of mutuality or of intrinsic reciprocity between the local church and the universal church. The commission is also continuing its study of the christological tradition of the Church of the East, and this was a major theme in the meeting held in 2004.

The Orthodox Churches

When the Joint International Commission for the Theological Dialogue between the Catholic Church and the Orthodox Church was established in 1979, great hopes were expressed in the possibility of this dialogue rapidly bringing these ancient churches together again in the full communion of the first Christian millennium. During the following ten years, the commission did excellent work and produced three documents mainly regarding the sacramental life of the Catholic and Orthodox Churches.[34]

As a result, it was possible for Pope John Paul II and the Ecumenical Patriarch Dimitrios I to state in 1987 that "the Catholic Church and the Orthodox Church can already profess together that common faith in the mystery of the Church and the bond between faith and sacraments." They also affirmed that "in these Churches apostolic succession is fundamental for the sanctification and the unity of the people of God" (*Ut Unum Sint*, 59).

When the commission met in Munich, in 1990, it had before it a new document that dealt with authority in the church. It was expected that this document, which earlier in the year had received the approval of the coordinating committee of the dialogue, would have brought the two partners close to discussing the fundamental reason for their divisions, namely, the position of the Roman pontiff in the exercise of authority in the universal church. Unfortunately, this paper was never discussed. The fall of Communism in Central and Eastern Europe had reopened in those areas an old and bitter source of division, namely, "Uniatism": the existence in traditional Orthodox territories of a church that follows Orthodox traditions, but is in full communion with Rome rather than the Orthodox patriarch of that territory. The Communist regimes in the Soviet Union and Romania had declared these churches illegal and confiscated their properties. Now they were able to return to life legally and to reclaim their former churches and other confiscated property; however, by this time, much of this property was in Orthodox hands. By June 1990, the situation in certain areas had become tense and relations were severely strained.

The question of Uniatism had been present in ecumenical dialogues, in one form or another, since the first plenary session of the commission (Patmos-Rhodes 1980) and was scheduled to be discussed at a later stage. The theological commission was not really the place to discuss certain aspects of the problems that were being faced in Eastern Europe, but was given no option by the Orthodox partner. A statement was prepared by the dialogue commission and published at the close of the meeting.

For the Orthodox Churches, the time had come for the whole question of Uniatism to be discussed and hopefully condemned. The Catholic members of the commission, on the other hand, could not see how any discussion on this subject could be successful unless there had first been dialogue on the role of the Roman pontiff in the universal church. In 1991 the coordinating committee of the dialogue prepared a draft document for consideration at the next plenary, entitled "Uniatism, Method of Union of the Past, and the Present Search for Full Communion."[35]

The plenary met at Balamand, in Lebanon, in 1993, and approved an agreed statement. This was not an attempt to solve the problem, but rather to bring back a climate of peace in the troubled areas of Central and Eastern Europe, so that the formal theological dialogue could be resumed. Known as the Balamand Document from the place of meeting, the text is based on three fundamental principles:

1. *"The inviolable freedom of persons and their obligation to follow the requirements of their conscience"* (15). This principle is the basis of the whole document, and justifies both the personal choice to adhere to the Catholic Church or to the Orthodox Church, and offers the possibility of "returning to the Catholic Church for those communities which in 1945–49 had been forced by Communist regimes to become part of the Orthodox Church, as happened in the Ukraine, Romania, and Slovakia."

2. *"The right of the Oriental Catholic Churches to exist and to act in answer to the spiritual needs of their faithful"* (3).

3. The recognition that *"Uniatism is not the present method in the search for full unity"* (4). The document states: "On each side it is recognized that what Christ has entrusted to his Church—profession of the apostolic faith, participation in the same sacraments, above all the one priesthood celebrating the one sacrifice of Christ, the apostolic succession of bishops—cannot be considered the exclusive property of one of our Churches" (13).

From this, the document draws the two following conclusions:

1. The local Catholic and Orthodox Churches recognize each other as "Sister Churches" that have the responsibility to work for the restoration of unity between them (cf. 14).

2. "In this context it is clear that any rebaptism must be avoided" (13).

The document then seeks to give some practical rules, based on the above ecclesiological principles with a view to overcoming the tense relationships between Orthodox and Eastern Catholics in certain places, and in the hope of encouraging a genuine growth in "mutual respect between the Churches which find themselves in difficult situations" (19).

Some Orthodox Churches unfortunately rejected the Balamand document. In fact, the Church of Greece and five other Orthodox Churches (Jerusalem, Serbia, Bulgaria, Georgia, and the Czech Republic and Slovakia) had refused to participate in the Balamand meeting and were not at all happy with the agreed statement. Some objections came also from the Romanian Greek-Catholic Church, but the Ukrainian major archbishop, Cardinal Lubachivsky, immediately accepted the document. The Balamand Document receives a positive presentation in the encyclical *Ut Unum Sint* (60) and in the common declaration signed by Pope John Paul II and Patriarch Bartholomew I at the conclusion of the patriarch's visit to Rome in June 1995.[36]

The next plenary was due to be held in Rome in 1996, but no agreement could be reached on the theme for such a meeting. For the Catholic partner, it was time to return to the theological dialogue and discuss the document prepared and approved by the coordinating committee in 1990. The Orthodox partner refused, however, to discuss any question other than Uniatism until further progress could be made toward the final solution to this problem. The coordinating committee met at Ariccia, just outside of Rome in June 1999, and a full meeting of the commission followed in Baltimore, Maryland, in July 2000. It proved impossible, however, to move beyond Balamand, and for the present the international dialogue remains suspended. Consultations between the Ecumenical Patriarchate and the other Orthodox Churches are in process, with a view to finding ways to continue the dialogue. Internal difficulties between these churches do not make the solution any easier. In a 2004 interview given at the close of the Week of Prayer for Christian Unity, Bishop Brian Farrell, secretary of the PCPCU, indicated that progress was being made in an attempt to restart the international dialogue. He indicated that the coordinating committee of the dialogue would be convened in the near future to suggest a path forward.[37]

This experience shows how difficult theological dialogue can be when the partners bring along with them sad memories of former centuries and old suspicions that destroy mutual trust. Without mutual trust there can be no genuine dialogue. Similarly, there can be little hope of a positive outcome when there is no agreement on the agenda to be followed. On the most fundamental level of doctrine and sacraments, Catholics and Orthodox see themselves as closer to each other than to any other church or Christian community. As Cardinal Kasper told the plenary meeting of the members of the Pontifical Council for Promoting Christian Unity in November 2003: "We are very close to these churches in terms of faith, sacraments and Episcopal ministry, and we are bound to them in a 'community of faith and charity,' in 'family ties which ought to thrive between local churches, as between sisters.'" Experience with regard to Orthodox-Catholic relations shows, however, that there is nothing so delicate and potentially painful as a family feud. The stakes, moreover, are particularly high, since the possibility of full and visible communion is real.

Since Baltimore in 2000, the Pontifical Council for Promoting Christian Unity has concentrated its efforts on fostering better relations and promoting cooperation with individual Orthodox Churches in order to build trust and dispel concerns. This has resulted in more frequent visits of delegations, some of them without precedent in recent years. Of special importance were the visit of Pope John Paul II to Greece in 2002 and the return visit of a delegation of the Church of Greece to Rome in February 2003. Cardinal Kasper has been in Serbia and also met with a delegation of the Orthodox Church of Serbia in Rome in February 2003. Cardinal Kasper was able to state in November 2003: "The change in climate in relations with the Orthodox Church in Greece and Bulgaria, as with the Serbian Orthodox Church, can only be defined as simply astonishing."[38]

Such regular contact offers the possibility of exchanging ideas and fostering better understanding. The future of Europe and the acknowledgment of its Christian roots has also provided a common challenge for joint action to Catholic and Orthodox Churches.

In May 2003, the PCPCU organized an academic symposium on the Petrine ministry. Relations were presented by both a Catholic and an Orthodox scholar for each of the four themes chosen for consideration during this meeting. It is expected that the acts of this symposium will be published and should be a valuable contribution to a question that is of fundamental importance for all theological dialogue in which the Catholic Church is engaged.

The Anglican Communion

A very different atmosphere has accompanied the *Anglican–Roman Catholic International Commission* (ARCIC) and its work over the years. The first ARCIC produced a final report on three basic questions of faith, namely Eucharist, ministry, and authority. The 1988 Lambeth Conference found the statements on Eucharist and ministry "consonant with Anglican tradition," while the section on authority was seen as a good foundation for further discussion. A first Vatican response was not so positive, and it was possible only after much discussion within the Vatican for the Pontifical Council for Promoting Christian Unity to respond with a more encouraging reply. The discussions led to "clarifications," which in turn were accepted by ARCIC, and eventually, as president of the Pontifical Council, I was able to confirm officially that no further work needed to be done on the presentation of Anglican and Catholic faith in the Eucharist. It was possible to state also that there was agreement on the nature of ministry in the church, although the question of the person of the minister able to celebrate the Eucharist remained unsolved. Like the Anglican partner, the Catholic Church also saw the section of the final report dealing with authority in the church as most promising, but needing further study.

A second ARCIC has carried on the dialogue and has produced several excellent documents that have not as yet been submitted for official approval. I would like to mention especially the following:

- *The Church as Communion*, 1990. This document made a significant contribution to the present understanding of the church as communion, a theme that has been taken up in a number of other dialogues and contexts.

- *Life in Christ: Morals, Communion and the Church*, 1993. Among the many international dialogues (bilateral and multilateral) among divided Christians, the Anglican–Roman Catholic International Commission was the first to have directly attempted a study on the subject of morals. The commission had received many requests to take up this question since there was a growing belief that Roman Catholics and Anglicans are as much, if not more, divided on questions of morals as on doctrinal matters. As the then presidents of ARCIC explained in an introduction to their report on *Life in Christ: Morals, Communion and the Church*: "This belief in turn reflects the profound and true conviction that authentic Christian unity is as much a matter of life as of faith. Those who share one faith in Christ will share one life in Christ. Hence the title of this statement: *Life in Christ: Morals, Communion and the Church*."[39]

- *The Gift of Authority*, 1999. As already mentioned, the question of authority in the church was one of the three topics dealt with by ARCIC I in their final report. The statements there were seen to provide a good foundation for further study, and ARCIC II undertook such a study. The result, in the form of an agreed statement entitled *The Gift of Authority*, was published in 1999 and is a valuable contribution to a question that is of importance in all dialogues. In this document, authority is seen as a gift that God gives to his church and that calls for a response of "yes" from the members of that body. There is qualified acknowledgment of papal primacy, together with the need for greater collegiality. The document *The Gift of Authority* challenges the Anglican Communion and the Catholic Church to move beyond their traditional differences of expression, so as to converge around their common basic understanding of authority. This means that the Anglican Communion would grow from opposition to the papal primacy to acceptance of a universal primacy, while the Catholic Church, in the spirit of the Second Vatican Council, would develop greater collegiality. In February 2004, the General Synod of the Church of England dedicated time to an examination of this document.

ARCIC II has since turned its attention to the role of Mary in the life and doctrine of the church, with special attention given to the dogmatic definitions of the immaculate conception and the assumption of Mary. According to reports by the Anglican Communion News and other ecumenical agencies, the commission has agreed on a methodology based on scripture and theological reflection in an attempt to go behind what it describes as "entrenched positions" on the Virgin Mary. During its meeting in Seattle in early 2004, the commission completed work on the text of a statement: *Mary, Grace and Hope in Christ.* It expressed the hope that the document, when published, will make an ecumenical contribution of value, even beyond the partners of Anglican-Catholic dialogue. The place of the Blessed Virgin Mary in the life of the church had been addressed briefly by ARCIC I in *Authority in the Church II* (1981), paragraph 30, and a considerable level of agreement had been registered there. The Marian dogmas of the assumption and the immaculate conception, together with the practice of invoking Mary in intercessory prayer, remained as areas of divergence. It was principally with the aim of addressing these particular areas of Marian doctrine and devotion that ARCIC II took up a special study of the role of Mary in the faith and practice of the church.

With reference to the dogma of the assumption of Mary, the agreed statement notes that "we can together affirm that God took the Blessed Virgin Mary, in the fullness of her personal being, into his glory." The text proceeds to affirm: "what this definition teaches about Mary is not contrary to the teaching of Scripture, but received support from it, and can only be understood in the light of Scripture."

With regard to the content of the dogma of the immaculate conception, the agreed statement affirms that in Mary's acceptance of the divine will one can see "her prior preparation from the very beginning of her existence." Hence the commission "can together affirm that God was at work in Mary from her mother's womb, preparing her for the unique vocation of bearing in her own flesh the new Adam 'in whom all things in heaven and earth hold together' (Colossians 1:17)." Again here, the dogma is declared not to be contrary to scripture, but to receive support from it.

The commission has looked at the doctrines themselves, and has not finalized its treatment of the authoritative claims of dogmatic definitions. Experience within the Ecumenical Society of the Blessed Virgin Mary, an English-based society, indicates that there is indeed reason to hope that in due course Mary will be seen by the Christian churches not as an obstacle to unity, but as a "Mother of God and Icon of the Church, the spiritual Mother who intercedes for Christ's disciples and all humanity" (*Ut Unum Sint*, 79).[40]

Mention should be made here of the Mississauga Consultation that took place in May 2000, in Mississauga, Ontario, since on this occasion Anglicans and Roman Catholics took an initiative that could interest other churches in their bilateral relations. When the then archbishop of Canterbury, Dr. George Carey, and I met in Malines in August 1996, on the occasion of the commemoration of the seventy-fifth anniversary of the informal Malines conversations between representatives of the Catholic Church and the Church of England, the question was asked: Is ARCIC the responsible body for taking the Anglican–Roman Catholic search for unity forward, or is it not rather a theological commission at the service of the churches as they seek unity? Since both churches are hierarchical in structure, it seemed to us that responsibility for promoting unity should first and foremost be that of the bishops of the two communions. It was therefore decided to call together a number of bishops of both communities from countries having a significant Anglican-Catholic presence to consider how the relationship between the Anglican Communion and the Catholic Church might progress.

In May of 2000, pairs of senior bishops, one Anglican and the other Catholic, from thirteen countries gathered at a retreat house in Mississauga, Ontario, under the chairmanship of Archbishop Carey and myself. We all lived together and worshipped together, and after most fruitful discussions, were able to produce a draft plan of action and an agreed statement from the participants. It was recommended that a new International Anglican–Roman Catholic Working group be set up of eight members (of whom four would be bishops) from

each side. The International Anglican–Roman Catholic Commission
for Unity and Mission (IARCCUM) was officially launched at the
end of 2001 in Lambeth Palace, London, and in Rome, and received
strong encouragement for its work from both Archbishop Carey of
Canterbury and Pope John Paul II. Work would be directed toward
three areas in which it seemed further progress toward visible unity
between the Anglican Communion and the Roman Catholic Church
would strengthen the mission of the Church of Christ. In particular,
work began in 2002 on preparing a first draft of a "common declaration which would formally express the degree of agreement in faith
that already exists between Anglicans and Catholics, consolidate the
results of more than thirty years of dialogue and commit the dialogue
partners to a deeper sharing in common life and witness."[41]

Other areas of study would focus on practical recommendations for
facilitating the ongoing process of ecumenical reception, with special
attention to the reception of ARCIC documents, while attention would
be given to pastoral and practical strategies to help the two communions, especially in local contexts, to do together even now whatever is
possible in the actual stage of real but imperfect communion.

A second meeting of the commission was held in Malta from
November 19–23, 2002. The work already done was discussed thoroughly, and practical proposals were made, especially for the reception of ARCIC texts through mutual study and understanding, rather
than by formal response.[42]

After a third meeting in 2003, IARCCUM suffered a severe set-
back, as a result of difficulties that the Anglican Communion was
experiencing as a consequence of deep divisions among the provinces
with regard to the priestly ordination of practicing homosexual ministers, and of Gene Robinson, an openly gay priest, even as bishop of
New Hampshire. The primates of the Anglican Communion met at
Lambeth in October 2003 and decided to set up a commission to
examine how to create order in the church. The Anglican Communion being in such disarray, and indeed in danger of breaking up, the
members of IARCCUM decided in November 2003 to suspend tem-
porarily their commission's activity before proceeding further, so as to
leave the Anglican Communion room to find a solution to its own
internal problems.

The experience of Mississauga was judged by all who took part as being of great value, since it allowed the participants to actually live during those days the real, though not yet complete, communion that Anglicans and Catholics already share. The statement issued by the meeting speaks of "a profound atmosphere of friendship and spiritual communion," and this was certainly my own experience.

The Lutheran World Federation

The Lutheran–Roman Catholic dialogue is held between the Lutheran World Federation (LWF) and the Pontifical Council for Promoting Christian Unity (PCPCU). It began its work soon after the conclusion of the Second Vatican Council and has completed three phases. The first (1967–71) focused on the gospel and the church; the second (1973–84) on the Eucharist and ecclesial ministry; and the third (1986–93) on church and justification.

One of the most significant and personally satisfying experiences of my years as president of the Pontifical Council for Promoting Christian Unity was undoubtedly the signing in Augsburg, on October 31, 1999, of the statement *Joint Declaration on the Doctrine of Justification* (JD), which was an outcome of the earlier work of the dialogue commission, and in particular of its third phase. After thirty years of serious bilateral theological and ecumenical dialogue, the International Lutheran/Roman Catholic Commission for Unity had come to the conviction that the two seemingly opposing understandings by Lutherans and Catholics of the doctrine of justification could be reconciled. A joint declaration was drawn up and officially submitted by the commission to the two churches for approval.

The process of approval was itself interesting from the ecumenical point of view, since this was probably the first such attempt by a Reformed Church. But of course it is the document itself and the method followed that offers encouragement and throws light on the whole movement toward the unity of Christians. Neither side was asked to abandon traditional teaching or change their fundamental approach to such a basic Christian belief as justification.

The aim was to see if traditional expressions of faith were in fact contradictory—as was claimed and seemed true for several centuries—

or could they be considered complementary and even as enriching one another. Both Lutherans and Catholics are usually particularly bound to their own expressions of faith, and hence this was no easy task. Yet in the end both the Catholic Church and the Lutheran World Federation were able officially to sign the joint declaration, and so open the way for further progress in dialogue.

The Anglican Communion gave an early positive response to the joint declaration, while the World Methodist Council (WMC), after first issuing a statement of congratulations and appreciation, took the initiative to propose a meeting with the LWF and the Catholic Church in order to discuss how the JD might have favorable consequences for those other than the two partners to the declaration. The idea developed into a consultation, hosted by the PCPCU and the LWF, and attended by representatives of the World Methodist Council and the World Alliance of Reformed Churches (WARC). This was held in Columbus, Ohio, from November 27–30, 2001, and focused on theological and procedural issues involved in a possible formal adherence of the Methodist and Reformed ecclesial families to the agreements reached in the JD.

Following on this meeting, the World Methodist Council prepared a statement on the Methodist understanding of justification and its relationship to the agreements reached in the joint declaration. This text was submitted to the PCPCU and the LWF, and suggested changes incorporated into the document that will now be submitted to the member churches of the WMC, hopefully culminating in an endorsement by the WMC Conference. The draft indicates an acceptance by the Methodists of the basic consensus stated in the common confessions of the JD. Similarly, it declares that the explanations that Lutherans and Catholics give in the JD concerning their respective positions on key aspects of the doctrine of justification are not considered sufficient cause for division between Methodists and either of these two churches. The text concludes with a formal statement of fundamental doctrinal agreement with the teaching expressed in the JD by the WMC and its member churches, on terms that the text makes clear.

This process has significant implications not only for Methodist-Catholic relations, but also on possible future attempts by a third partner to become part of an agreement established by two others. It signals a new genre of ecumenical text and a new means of advancing the search for unity.

On the fifth anniversary of the signing of the JD, Rev. Dr. Ismael Noko, secretary general of the LWF, and Cardinal Walter Kasper, president of the PCPCU, wrote a joint letter calling for celebrations by Lutheran and Catholic communities on October 31, 2004. They referred to work being done to follow up on the joint declaration, mentioning in particular a study program on the contemporary meaning of justification, "Justification in the World's Context," as well as a biblical symposium being organized to broaden the biblical section of the declaration.[43]

The International Lutheran/Roman Catholic Commission for Unity has now turned its attention to the subjects in the document, *Apostolicity of the Church, Ministry and Church Teaching*. The discussions cover such subjects as these: New Testament foundations; the apostolic Gospel and the apostolicity of the Church; the ordained ministry from the Lutheran perspective; scripture and church teaching in a Reformation perspective, and concept and understanding of the magisterium in Catholic theology from the Council of Trent to the Second Vatican Council; and the ministry of apostolic teaching.

After the official signing of the JD and the experience of the great ecumenical celebrations of the Jubilee Year 2000, relationships between Catholics and Lutherans have continued to develop. Leaders of the LWF and the PCPCU meet at least twice a year for discussions, alternatively in Geneva and Rome. Discussions deal with present-day issues, plans for the international Lutheran-Catholic dialogue, and ecumenical relations in general. Cardinal Kasper personally led the Catholic delegation to the plenary assembly of the LWF of 2003 that was held in Winnipeg, Canada, which had as its theme "For the Healing of the World."

The World Methodist Council

An International Methodist-Catholic Dialogue Commission began its work in 1967, soon after the close of the Second Vatican Council. During this time there have been seven five-year phases that have produced four reports. The most recent reports show a constant concern with teaching authority in the two churches: *The Apostolic Tradition*

(1991); *The Word of Life—A Statement on Revelation and Faith* (1996); and *Speaking the Truth in Love* (2001), which deals specifically with authority in the church and is very similar to the Anglican statement *The Gift of Authority*.

From the beginning, this dialogue has preferred to present its agreed conclusions as "reports," rather than "agreed statements." The results of the dialogue have been indeed most promising, as stated in the following presentation to the 2001 plenary of the Pontifical Council for Promoting Christian Unity:

> Increasingly, they have been able to find common language in the topics discussed, but frequently follow statements of common faith with divergent Catholic and Methodist interpretations, and with questions that each side would wish to put to the other. The texts are thus characterized by a careful theological plodding which has been productive beyond expectations. While the initial aim of the dialogue was greater mutual understanding and the fostering of better local relationships, since the Report of 1986 on the church, the goal, while remaining a long way off, is now explicitly full communion in faith, mission and sacramental life. The Reports have not been presented for any formal evaluation by either side.[44]

This constructive working relationship between the members of the commission will be of great assistance as they now undertake a topic that has never been addressed so directly in a bilateral dialogue: a study of how the dialogue partners interpret each other ecclesiologically. What place do Methodists claim for themselves in the church, and what place do they see Catholics as having? How might Catholics locate Methodism ecclesiologically? The study will surely take up the Second Vatican Council's teaching that the one Church of Christ "subsists" in the Catholic Church, while many elements of that one church are also found outside the visible boundaries of the Catholic Church. Of importance will also be the 2000 document *Dominus Jesus* of the Congregation of the Doctrine of the Faith and the WMC's response to it.

During a public discussion on Catholic-Methodist relations in Rome on March 11, 2004, the two cochairs of the International Methodist-

Catholic Dialogue Commission expressed confident hope in the future of this dialogue. The Catholic cochair, Bishop Michael Putney of Townsville in Australia, said he believes firmly that the Christian churches will eventually be one. "It is unfolding before my eyes," he said. "Where it is going and when it will end I do not know and, in many ways, I do not care. I'm just enjoying the ride." In a joint statement with the Methodist cochair, Rev. Geoffrey Wainwright, he said he is "waiting to be surprised" at how it finally happens.[45]

Other Theological Dialogues

Not all the bilateral dialogues have produced such outstanding results, but all are making a worthwhile contribution to the search for Christian unity. The Pontifical Council for Promoting Christian Unity pursues with interest and deep commitment each of the dialogues in which it is engaged. As mentioned earlier, besides those already referred to, such dialogues are regularly carried on with the following:

- The World Alliance of Reformed Churches
- The Disciples of Christ (Christian Church)
- The Baptist World Alliance
- The Mennonite World Conference
- Classical Pentecostal Churches and Leaders
- The World Evangelical Alliance
- Seventh Day Adventists
- The Old Catholic Churches of the Union of Utrecht

I shall seek to give at least a brief overview of each of these as they are at the time of writing.

The World Alliance of Reformed Churches

The World Alliance of Reformed Churches (WARC) includes more than 220 member churches, comprising altogether about 75 million Christians of Presbyterian, Reformed, or Congregational traditions. There is a great diversity among the Alliance's member churches, although the Calvinist tradition is central to its heritage.

The Roman Catholic–World Alliance of Reformed Churches Dialogue thought it necessary to begin with a fundamental topic, *Presence of Christ in the Church and in the World* (1970–77), and then move toward the theme *Toward a Common Understanding of the Church* (1984–90). The present phase of dialogue, which began in 1998, has before it reflections on the topic *Church as Community of Common Witness to the Kingdom of God.*

A major aspect of this third phase of dialogue has been a concentrated study of the notion of the "kingdom of God," hoping to see if this concept can both throw light on the search for common ecclesiological ground, and also give impetus to exploration of the possibilities of common witness. Much emphasis has been given in this particular dialogue to the experience of Reformed/Roman Catholic relations in various parts of the world: Canada, South Africa, and Northern Ireland in particular. Certain fundamental approaches of the two partners make this a difficult dialogue. There is a tension between doctrine and people's experience, as between the contextual and the universal. Unresolved issues coming from the time of the Reformation and subsequent developments also influence the dialogue.

There has been a marked development in the focus of this third consultation when compared to the first two. Whereas the earlier discussions concentrated on "confrontation or dialogue," the third phase emphasizes "dialogue not confrontation." The subtitle for the dialogue—"Exploring Ways for Minority Churches and Majority Churches to Work Together and to Relate to the State"—acknowledges that churches that are majority churches in some countries may also be minority churches in others. Given the history of struggles between majority and minority churches in Europe over the centuries, and to some extent even today, the evolution of this third consultation to a more positive intention must be considered an important development.

The Disciples of Christ (Christian Church)

The first phase of the Disciples of Christ–Roman Catholic Dialogue (1977–81) took up the theme *Apostolicity and Catholicity in the Visible Unity of the Church.* Discussion focused attention on common rootedness in baptism, the importance of spiritual ecumenism, the nature of unity, and the relation between faith and tradition. Continuing the same theme of unity of the church, the second phase (1983–92) concentrated on the theme *The Church as Communion in Christ.* In 1995, a third phase of dialogue focused on a topic identified in the second phase as needing further study, namely, "the rule of faith *(regula fidei)* expressed in the teaching of the Church down the ages." In May 2002, an official report on this phase was issued with the title *Receiving and Handing on the Faith: The Mission and Responsibility of the Church.* In releasing this document, the cochairs of the commission, Most Rev. Daniel Buechlein, archbishop of Indianapolis, and Rev. Dr. Paul Crow, Jr., retired president of the Council on Christian Unity of the Christian Church (Disciples of Christ), noted several important agreements that may lead to continuing work. The following is the brief text issued by the cochairs on completion of the third phase:

> The Agreed Statement *(Receiving and Handing on the Faith: The Mission and Responsibility of the Church)* begins with the common affirmation that "the Church is essentially a missionary community, a community of those sent into the world to proclaim the offer of God's gifts to all persons." It addresses the topics of the Word of God, proclaimed and received; holding to the faith, in the formation of the Canon, the Councils, the discerning of the Gospel in every age; receiving the faith; conscience and teaching authority; and handing on the faith as the mission of the whole Church.

The conclusion of the agreed text—while focusing upon technical understandings of teaching authority in the Church and the role of scripture, confessions, and individual conscience—identified that both communions understand the task of teaching and handing on the faith as essential to the evangelization of the world. Dr. Crow states, "In this dialogue, Disciples [of Christ] have been able to articulate in a new way our catholicity as we have been challenged to expand our historical memory as a church."[46]

In a comment on this document Cardinal Avery Dulles stresses the "many points of agreement that have never before been so explicitly stated." He considers the agreements on the sacraments of baptism and the Eucharist as being quite remarkable, while noting similarities in the approach Catholics and Disciples take to the primacy of evangelization among the tasks of the church and to the effectiveness of the lives and examples of committed Christians as a means of bearing witness to the gospel.

This international dialogue between the Disciples of Christ and the Catholic Church has produced most encouraging results. It may be well to recall that, as is the case with the Methodists, there was never a historical breaking of communion between Disciples and Catholics. From the beginning, in the early nineteenth century, the Disciples moreover had a twofold aim: to overcome the denominationalism that was splintering the Protestant world and to work for Christian unity on the basis of the New Testament. The Disciples regarded Christian unity as essential for the mission of the church and the conversion of the world. While seeking to be completely faithful to the apostolic church of the New Testament, they were distrustful of the multitude of creeds, confessions, and dogmas that had accumulated in the course of centuries.

In May 2003, a planning subcommission of the international dialogue commission met to prepare and shape the theme and content for the fourth phase of the dialogue, which will have as its general theme *The Presence of Christ in the Church, with Special Reference to the Eucharist.*

The Baptist World Alliance

Ecumenical contacts with the Baptist World Alliance have developed from the participation of representatives of the Pontifical Council for Promoting Christian Unity and the Baptist World Alliance during the annual meetings of the Conference of Secretaries of Christian World Communions. Since at least 1985, the Baptist World Alliance has invited the PCPCU to send a fraternal delegate to its World Congress every five years, while Baptists have been among the fraternal delegates at several of the synods of bishops held in Rome.

A first phase of international dialogue between the Catholic Church and the Baptist World Alliance took place in 1984–88; this produced a report published in 1990 entitled *Summons to Witness to Christ in Today's World.* Due to opposition from within the Baptist World Alliance, it has not been possible to begin a second phase of dialogue. Contacts continue, however, between the Pontifical Council and the World Baptist Alliance. Brief consultations of an informal nature took place in Rome in 2000, in Buenos Aires in 2001, and again in Rome in 2003.

The meeting in Buenos Aires looked at "the theological issues between Baptists and Catholics in Latin America." A number of important doctrines on which Baptists and Catholics are divided were mentioned, including the hierarchical organization of the church, the Petrine office, Marian dogma, and the sacraments. Cardinal Kasper, who led the Catholic delegation, suggested that the group consider the concept of *communio* as a framework within which such issues could be more fruitfully discussed.

At the suggestion of the Baptists, the third encounter, in Rome in 2003, dedicated the first day to consideration of the *Joint Declaration on the Doctrine of Justification* signed by the Catholic Church and the LWF in 1999. The "Petrine ministry" formed the agenda for the second day. A Baptist presentation stated that the formulation of the doctrine of justification in the JD (nos. 14–18) "can be endorsed by all Baptists without hesitation. Those paragraphs showing the Lutheran-Catholic consensus deserve full Baptist support" (referring to nos. 19, 22, 31, and 37 of the JD, each beginning with "We confess"). Numbers 25 and 28 of the JD could be accepted with the exception of what they state about baptism. In fact, the Baptist scholars present had a serious problem with the way baptism is dealt with in the declaration. Baptists also would have liked to see two questions emphasized more in the JD: the notion of "*sola fides*," and justification as "imputed," that is, bestowed by God on persons who are without God and without any merit.

All agreed that these encounters are most useful in clarifying for each other the Baptist and Catholic understanding on the topics discussed. Another two-day consultation was planned to take place in a year's time. Hope has also been expressed that an official phase of dialogue can eventually be taken up again.[47]

The Mennonite World Conference

One of the more recent dialogues into which the Catholic Church has entered is that with the Mennonite World Conference (MWC). This is the first Catholic international dialogue with one of the so-called "historic peace churches," and aims to create better understanding between the two communities.

Mennonites come from the more radical side of the Reformation, from the Anabaptist tradition. They differ from the mainstream Reformist churches in that they sought an even more radical break with the Christianity of the sixteenth century: complete separation of church and state, the denial of the validity of infant baptism, and a more biblically based Christianity. They were given the title of "anabaptist," meaning to rebaptize, and suffered greatly at the hands of the Reformed and Lutherans as well as of the Catholics.

The Mennonite World Conference has its headquarters in Strasbourg, France, and comprises some ninety conferences in fifty-two countries, numbering about 1.3 million people. It is described as a lightly structured network that invites all Anabaptist Churches around the world to send representatives to its General Council. Their International General Council is composed of a hundred representatives from the more than 170 conferences and meets every three years.

The international dialogue that began in 1998 has thus far moved on two tracks. One seeks a better understanding of the current life and theology of each communion. Papers on this track have included, in 1998, a profile by each describing for the other "who we are"; in 1999, a contemporary view of the church from each side; and in 2000, the respective understandings of each party of what is "a peace church."[48]

The second track is historical and aims to clarify issues of the past in order to move toward a healing of memories. Papers on this track included, in 1998, "Anabaptist Images of Roman Catholics during the Sixteenth Century" and "The Catholic Response to the Anabaptist Movement in the Sixteenth Century"; in 1999, "The Anabaptist Idea of the Restitution of the Early Church," complemented by a Catholic paper on "The Anabaptist/Mennonite Tradition of Faith and Spirituality and Its Medieval Roots"; and in 2000, an interpretation from each side of the theme, "The Impact of the Constantinian Shift on the Church."

At the conclusion of this first five-year phase of dialogue, a report was published under the title *Called Together to Be Peacemakers*. A first chapter gathers together the results of the historical discussions; a second chapter is dedicated to considering theology together; and then a third chapter looks to a healing of memories.

The historical section considers the Constantinian Era, the Middle Ages, and the rupture between Catholics and Anabaptists in the sixteenth century. The theological chapter examines the nature of the Church, baptism, the Eucharist or Lord's Supper, and the meaning of a "peace church." A considerable amount of basic convergence was achieved on a number of these questions, while on other aspects differences of understanding remain. For instance, Catholics and Mennonites agree on significant aspects of the meaning of the Eucharist or Lord's Supper, namely, that the celebration of the Eucharist is rooted in God's grace made available to all by virtue of the suffering, death, and resurrection of Christ, and recalls those saving events. Both Catholics and Mennonites agree that the risen Christ is present at the celebration of the Eucharist: Christ invites to the meal; he is present in the faithful gathered in his name; he is present in the proclaimed word. But for Mennonites, the Lord's Supper is primarily a sign or symbol that points to Jesus' suffering, death, and resurrection, while it keeps his memory alive until his return. For Catholics, on the other hand, the Eucharist is the source and summit of the whole life of the church, in which Christ's sacrifice, offered once and for all on the cross, is made really present under the species of the consecrated bread and wine.[49]

It has not been easy for the Mennonite World Conference to enter into such a dialogue with the Catholic Church. There are bitter memories that made the dialogue difficult, especially for the Mennonite representatives. This first phase of dialogue is intended to contribute to "a healing of memories," through rigorous historical-theological judgment, a readiness to ask pardon of God and of one another for past conflicts, and a conscious move away from the stereotypes and prejudices of the past.

The PCPCU expressed the belief that this first phase of dialogue with the Mennonite World Conference has created a good atmosphere in helping to foster reconciliation between Mennonites and Catholics.[50] A sign of this progress was the invitation to the PCPCU to send a delegate to the 14th Mennonite World Assembly, August 11–17, 2003, in Bulawayo, Zimbabwe, which was attended by about seven thousand people. A smaller decision-making council meeting at the same time discussed the report of the International Mennonite-Catholic Dialogue referred to above. The need for healing of memories was reflected during the discussion and some delegates, especially from Latin America, expressed concern about the dialogue. They spoke of tensions experienced with the Catholic Church in their countries and were anxious to defend their particular interpretation of God's word. In the end, however, the council agreed to a recommendation to promote Catholic-Mennonite consultations in different regions, and to accept an invitation from the PCPCU for a delegation to visit the PCPCU in Rome.[51]

Classical Pentecostal Churches and Leaders

The dialogue between the Roman Catholic Church and a group of leaders and communities of Classical Pentecostals began in 1972 with the aim of promoting mutual respect and understanding between Catholics and Pentecostals. This dialogue seeks to encourage a better knowledge of the different confessional expressions, pointing to convergences and divergences, while highlighting the fields requiring further discussion. Four documents have been published: *Final Report* (1972–76); *Final Report* (1977–82); *Perspectives on Koinonia* (1984–89); and *Evangelization, Proselytism and Common Witness* (1990–97).

In the present fifth phase, the dialogue has studied the following topics from a patristic and biblical perspective: *Baptism in the Spirit and Christian Initiation* (1998); *Faith and Christian Initiation* (1999); *Conversion and Christian Initiation* (2000); *Christian Experience in the Community* (2001); and *Christian Discipleship and Formation* (2002). The real novelty of this phase is the attempt to become more familiar with the patristic perspectives on these topics that are fundamental for both communities.

The 2003 meeting focused entirely on the preparation of the first draft of the *Final Report* of this phase of dialogue, on the basis of papers prepared by a drafting committee. Another plenary session is needed in order to finalize this report.

Reports on the dialogue over the years indicate that the members of the joint commission have succeeded in attaining greater mutual understanding in terms of confessional reality and experience of faith. This does not, however, always mean that there has been convergence. Agreement has been even less frequent among the members. In this last phase difficulties came from a lack of familiarity with the patristic writings. Moreover, there were deep discrepancies concerning the intrinsic value and the authority that patristic writings have in the life of the church. Pentecostals could admit that "the Holy Spirit spoke through the fathers," but would never affirm that there is a difference between the value of the interventions of the fathers of the church and "the interventions realized by the Spirit in recent years, through the Pentecostal fathers and mothers." The intrinsic authority of patristic writings depends on the context in which such writings were presented.

A particular limitation with respect to this dialogue is the fact that on the Pentecostal side most participants come from the United States. There is scant geographical representation. There is a particular need to promote dialogue between Catholics and Pentecostals in Latin America. Some moves have been made recently in this regard, and there is hope that a working group may be established in South America sponsored by the Consejo Episcopal Latinoamericano (CELAM) and the Comisión Evangelica Pentecostal Latinoamericano y Carabeña (CEPLA).[52]

The World Evangelical Alliance

In recent years there has been a notable change in the relations between Evangelicals and Catholics. Though these two Christian communities remain far apart in respect of doctrinal understandings, they often find themselves today in the public forum sharing a common approach to situations in which Christian moral values are endangered.

A first series of conversations between the PCPCU and individual members of Evangelical communities took place between 1977[53] and 1984.[54] A report was published entitled *The Evangelical–Roman Catholic Dialogue on Mission.*[55]

A more formal group of conversations between the PCPCU and the World Evangelical Fellowship began in 1993 as a result of contacts within the Conference of Secretaries of Christian World Communions in 1988 and 1990. The World Evangelical Alliance (WEA) is a global network of 120 national and regional evangelical church alliances, 104 organizational ministries, and six specialized ministries serving the worldwide church through WEA.

The dialogue between the WEA and the Catholic Church is not a formal dialogue, but rather a type of international theological consultation, coordinated by the PCPCU and a task force on ecumenism of the World Evangelical Alliance. From the beginning the general aim of the consultations has been to foster greater mutual understanding and promote better relations between Catholics and Evangelicals.

The series of consultations between 1993 and 2001 allowed the participants to identify and discuss the issues that tend to divide Evangelicals and Catholics. Early in the consultations, it became evident that two issues in particular kept Evangelicals and Catholics apart, namely, the nature of the church as communion, and the nature and practice of mission and evangelization. At the same time, as the consultations proceeded, participants came to realize that Catholics and Evangelicals have the possibility of sharing a real fellowship in Christ as a consequence of their common faith in him as their Lord and Savior. A new methodology was adopted: after the initial reflection on the specific questions requiring clarification, the group focused on the topic *Revelation: Scriptures and Tradition,* and then studied ecclesiological issues. Two collaboratively written papers were produced that were then used as the basis for an initial draft of the *Final Report,* which was finalized in 2001–2.

Entitled *Church, Evangelization and the Bonds of Koinonia,* this report is intended to assist Evangelicals and Catholics to better understand each other's convictions on the nature of the church and its mission. It seeks to clarify misunderstandings and, while pointing out differences, indicates possible areas of convergence. But it is not an authoritative statement of either the Catholic Church or the WEA.

Part I of this report presents the respective Catholic and Evangelical understanding on issues concerning the nature of the church; the criteria to determine degrees of communion between Christians; the *elementa ecclesiae*/the living faith in Jesus Christ; the visible/invisible church and the church as *unam realitatem complexam* (*LG*, 8); the relation between the local and universal church. In part II of the text, the consultation adopts a different methodological approach in presenting its contribution to the discussion on evangelization, proselytism, and common witness in the light of koinonia, drawing on both Catholic and Evangelical official documents and other ecumenical sources. This is a particularly valuable statement in view of the difficulties encountered in the relations between Evangelicals and Catholics in this field in various parts of the world.[56]

This final report has been presented to the WEA International Council and was well received. The council decided to circulate the document, facilitating its release with the WEA community.

Seventh Day Adventists

Since 2001 there have been consultations between the Catholic Church and the Seventh Day Adventists (SDA). For many years the Seventh Day Adventists have taken part in the annual meeting of the Secretaries of Christian World Communions. The Adventists are not members of the WCC, but have had bilateral discussions with the LWF, the WARC, and representatives of the WEA. Discussions between the Catholic Church and the SDA are delicate for both sides. There are frequent complaints from local Catholic Churches of Adventist proselytism directed at their members, while Adventists in many places continue to consider the Church of Rome as a "spiritual Babylon," with reference to the Book of Revelation 17:5.

Three rather low-key meetings have been held in Geneva in the period 2001–3. The consultations have taken the following course:

1. The meeting of April 8–9, 2001, focused on the "27 basic beliefs" of the Seventh Day Adventists.

2. The meeting of May 20–22, 2002, considered a basic difference in the practice of Sabbath/Sunday.[57]

3. A third consultation in Geneva, May 19–21, 2003, considered the topic *Principles of Biblical Interpretation.* Catholics interpret the scriptures within the living tradition of the whole church, while Adventists do this only by reference to other scripture passages, following the principle of biblical intertextuality. This difference in interpretation leads to divergent understandings regarding matters such as purgatory, the veneration and efficacious intercession of the saints, indulgences and Mariology. The conversations

also manifested differences in fundamental theological issues between the two traditions, paramount among them being the relationship between faith and reason, based on the Catholic principle that grace perfects nature. Adventists distrust the use of unaided reason, whereas Catholics see a complementarity between the two.[58]

Old Catholic Churches of the Union of Utrecht

Although there have been official dialogues at the national level in several countries between the Catholic Church and the Old Catholic Churches of the Union of Utrecht, it was only in 2003 that a joint working group drafted a proposal for the establishment of an international dialogue commission of the International Old Catholics Episcopal Conference of the Union of Utrecht and the PCPCU. This commission is expected to meet twice yearly and take up questions concerning authority in the church, with particular reference to the Petrine ministry, theological development in both churches, and problems connected with the passage of priests and laypeople from the Catholic Church to the Old Catholic Church, with special reference to canons 1364 and 844 of the Code of Canon Law.

Concluding Thoughts on Forty Years of Bilateral Dialogue

As can be seen from this brief overview of the theological dialogues between the Catholic Church and other churches and ecclesial communions, the discussions tend very rightly to begin by seeking to define more clearly common ground and to clarify misunderstandings. Only then can the participants move on to more divisive, or seemingly divisive, issues. Two important general trends in the dialogues of recent years have been a realization of the need for a common understanding of authority in the church as a prerequisite of agreement on many other questions, and a desire on the part of the dialogue members to orientate their discussions more to unity, rather than simply to seek a better appreciation of the traditions of the other partner.

More and more, it becomes obvious to all involved in dialogue that one of the basic questions to be confronted in theological dialogue is ecclesiology. All speak of the one church of Jesus Christ and of themselves as being "churches." Yet they have great difficulty in coming to a common understanding of what is meant by these terms. A basic common understanding of the church and then of the exercise of authority within that church would seem to be necessary before agreement can be reached on other essential doctrines, such as those concerning ministry and Eucharist.

The dialogue at the international level, if it is to be effective in bringing about a new relationship between the communions involved, must be closely related to national dialogues. Otherwise its good work may be like passing clouds that promise much, yet produce little rain, with the result that not a great deal is really achieved. The results of the international dialogue must become the property of the local churches and form part of their heritage. On the other hand, the international dialogue can be greatly assisted by the work done at the national level, as has already been the case, for example, with the *Joint Declaration on the Doctrine of Justification* between the Catholic Church and the Lutheran World Federation. In this case, the international dialogue was able to profit greatly from the work done on this same topic in Germany and in the United States of America by the dialogue commissions there.

A final consideration concerns what has been called "the dialogue of love." Experience over the past forty years has shown clearly that there is a close link between the two dialogues: the dialogue of truth and the dialogue of love. St. Paul urges the early Christians "to speak the truth in love" (Eph 4:15). The more the various Christian communions come to know each other, to respect one another, to appreciate and learn from one another, and to enter into the life and liturgy of the other, the greater the possibility of reaching a common understanding of doctrines that continue to keep them apart at the altar. Pope Paul VI and Pope John Paul II have both described dialogue as "an exchange of gifts." Members of one community can be greatly enriched in their own spiritual life by receiving from dialogue partners the gifts that they bring to the discussion, for the dialogue then becomes not just an intellectual exercise but a profound spiritual experience. Head and heart are both challenged.

In an address to the Catholic Committee for Cultural Cooperation with the Orthodox Churches and the Oriental Orthodox Churches,

Pope John Paul II had some words to say that would seem to challenge all those who are involved in ecumenical dialogue:

> At the beginning of a new millennium, in this period of transition between *what has been achieved and what we are called upon to achieve* in order to promote ecumenism right up to point of full communion, we have an inescapable duty... namely to promote the reception of the results that have been achieved in the various ecumenical initiatives. The time of ignoring one another has passed; now is the time for coming together and sharing each other's gifts, on the basis of an objective and deep knowledge of one another.[59]

THE WORLD COUNCIL OF CHURCHES
AND THE ROMAN CATHOLIC CHURCH

One of the questions often discussed in ecumenical circles is the special relationship of the Roman Catholic Church with the World Council of Churches. From the time when, in 1948, the World Council of Churches came officially into being, until the Second Vatican Council, the attitude of the Church of Rome to this new organization was in general rather negative, or at least coldly indifferent. Yet, as mentioned in the earlier section of this study, not all Catholic theologians or members of the hierarchy were so indifferent. Some even began to attend the general assemblies of the WCC as unofficial observers, while the Catholic Conference for Ecumenical Questions at its annual gatherings at times focused its attention on the same theme that the WCC had chosen for its deliberations.

After the Second Vatican Council, a new relationship gradually developed. The Vatican Secretariat for Christian Unity sought successfully to build a working relationship with the WCC. The question of WCC membership of the Catholic Church, however, has never been considered feasible by Catholic authorities. A Roman Catholic Church membership in the WCC would face a number of problems. There is the very size of the membership of the Catholic Church and subsequent proportional representation, which could cause grave concern among many smaller WCC members. To give such a community just one vote would be ridiculous, but then how would this community be represented: by dioceses (some four thousand) or provinces or national conferences? The question of decision-making within the WCC is already a matter of concern for the Orthodox Churches and would certainly not be acceptable in its present form by the Roman Catholic Church.

There is, however, a very positive aspect to all this, for in fact the Roman Catholic Church and the WCC have established over the years a close working relationship, which in many ways is far more effective than that of some of the member churches themselves of the WCC.

The primary form of collaboration between the Catholic Church and the World Council of Churches takes place within the framework of the Joint Working Group (JWG). Established in 1965 for the general purpose of exploring possibilities of dialogue and cooperation, the JWG is given a mandate by its parent bodies to study themes of mutual interest that help to deepen *koinonia* between the Catholic Church and the member churches of the WCC. It seeks to encourage and evaluate bilateral relations between their respective organs and programs. The JWG consists of seventeen members on each side, appointed by the WCC and PCPCU for a period of seven years, and chosen from different parts of the world. In addition, the PCPCU has two full-time Catholics attached to the staff of the WCC and three representatives on the WCC Commission on World Mission and Evangelism (CWME). Some nine Catholic experts are invited regularly by the WCC to different programs.

The relationship of the Catholic Church to one of the important organs of the WCC, the Faith and Order Commission, is more official. In fact, twelve Catholic theologians are members of this commission, as shall be seen later.

The present mandate of the JWG is for the period 1999–2005. It has been asked in particular:

- To work toward a common, integrated vision of the one ecumenical movement, on the basis of official documents of the Catholic Church (*Ut Unum Sint*, 28–38; *Unitatis Redintegratio*, 161–65; and a 1970 document of the PCPCU entitled *Reflections and Sugges-tions Concerning Ecumenical Dialogue*), and of the JWG study doc-ument of 1967 *Ecumenical Dialogue*

- To be concerned about any tension that may threaten the coher-ence of the ecumenical movement, especially in the social field
- To examine the contribution of the national and regional councils to the search for Christian unity, keeping in mind the growing presence of the Catholic Church in these councils and practical questions that this development has raised in some cases
- To consider the ecclesiological consequences of baptism, with the purpose of identifying the fundamental theological issues under-lying the topic, while focusing attention on the meaning of mutual recognition of baptism, the relation between baptism and faith, as well as the nature of incorporation into the church through baptism.

Other issues receiving attention from the JWG during its present mandate are interchurch marriages in terms of their ecumenical role, theological anthropology, and social thought and action.

On a less formal basis, regular contact occurs between the WCC and the Catholic Church at various levels. The principal opportunity for establishing valuable friendships in a wide context is offered by the Assemblies of the World Council of Churches, which take place every seven years. This was evident at Canberra in 1991 and again in Harare in 1998. At this last assembly there were an estimated four thousand participants, excluding day visitors. The official observer delegation from the Catholic Church consisted of twenty-three mem-bers from a wide range of countries, under the leadership of the then-bishop of Aberdeen, Monsignor Mario Conti. Another hundred Catholics were at the assembly under various categories of participa-tion. During his more than twenty-five years as bishop of Rome, Pope John Paul II has sent a message to each WCC Assembly, and this action has been generally much appreciated.[60] In Harare, the moderator of the Central Committee of the WCC, His Holiness Aram I (Catholicos of the Armenian Catholicosate of Cilicia) made special reference to the encyclical of Pope John Paul II *Ut Unum Sint* and other Catholic documents on ecumenism. He stated, "Although these documents addressed the internal ecumenical life of the Roman Catholic Church, their potential transcends the Roman Catholic Church."

Ample opportunities for promoting deeper ecumenical relations between participants and the Catholic delegation are available also outside the assembly sessions. In Harare, for example, Bishop Mario Conti offered several informative sessions on the Catholic Church in the ecumenical movement, which were well attended.

Other valuable forms of regular contact between the Roman Catholic Church and the WCC include the following:

- The PCPCU is now routinely invited to send observers to the 158-member WCC Central Committee meetings each eighteen months. Two officials of the Pontifical Council were at the meeting of August 26–September 3, 2002, during which the commission received the final report of the Special Commission on Orthodox Participation in the WCC. This report is of particular interest to the Catholic Church since it examines matters such as ecclesiology, social and ethical questions, common prayer, and the consensus model of decision-making.

- The WCC was invited to send a representative as a fraternal delegate to the Vatican Central Committee preparing the Jubilee Year 2000.

- WCC delegates took part in the ecumenical gatherings connected with the celebration in Rome of the Jubilee, at St. Paul's Outside the Walls on January 18, 2000, and January 25, 2001, as well as the Commemoration of Witnesses to the Faith in the Twentieth Century, at the Colosseum on May 7, 2000.

- There are also frequent visits and contacts between Rome and Geneva on a more informal basis by members of the staff on both sides. These help greatly in establishing personal trust and understanding between those seeking to promote the official relationship, while providing the occasion for an exchange of information and views on how best to proceed to this end.

The PCPCU cooperates with the WCC in various programs. Since 1985, the council has appointed Catholic experts on mission and evangelization to work with the corresponding offices of the WCC in this field. A religious sister from a Catholic missionary institute is attached full-time to the WCC headquarters in Geneva as a consultant on mission questions. Part of her work is to help the WCC staff team to make use of the available resources in terms of information, expertise, and documentation from Catholic sources.

For some years now, the PCPCU has made it possible for a full-time, highly competent Catholic priest-professor to teach at the WCC Ecumenical Institute of Bossey, near Geneva, which offers young Orthodox and Protestants a four-month course in ecumenical formation. As the course draws to a close each year, the staff and students are invited by the PCPCU to visit Rome for several days so that they may experience Catholic life firsthand. They meet with curial officials and with representatives of educational and missionary institutes, and before returning to Geneva have a private audience with the pope.

One of the most successful aspects of the relationship between the Catholic Church and the World Council of Churches is collaboration in the area of interreligious contact. The Pontifical Council for Interreligious Dialogue (PCID) works in this field with the WCC Office for Interreligious Relations. Information is exchanged and joint studies on issues of mutual interest are promoted. Staff from the two offices have reflected together on interreligious marriages and interreligious prayer, and each year there is a visit by the Roman Pontifical Council to Geneva, or by the WCC Office to Rome.

It is obvious from what has been stated above that the relationship between the WCC and the Catholic Church is quite positive. The contribution of the Catholic Church to the work of the World Council is greatly appreciated by the authorities in Geneva, since it certainly provides valuable assistance to the WCC in certain fields of its activities.

FAITH AND ORDER

Within the context of the multilateral theological dialogue, the Commission on Faith and Order (F&O) of the World Council of

Churches has a special role in promoting the search for greater doctrinal unity among the churches. It is good to remember that the World Council of Churches traces its origin to two earlier ecumenical movements, the International Missionary Council and the Faith and Order movement.

Faith and Order came into being in 1920, after some years of discussion, and held its first world conference in Lausanne in 1927. A second world conference in Edinburgh in 1937 agreed to unite Faith and Order with the Movement for Life and Work "to form a council of Churches." This led to the formation of the WCC in 1948.[61]

The Faith and Order movement serves the churches by leading them into theological dialogue as a means of overcoming obstacles to and opening up ways toward the manifestation of their unity given in Jesus Christ. The commission consists of 120 theologians who come from the various member churches of the WCC and also from some nonmembers. Since the Uppsala Assembly of the WCC in 1968, twelve of the 120 members of the commission have been Catholic theologians, appointed by F&O in collaboration with the PCPCU. They serve as full voting participants. The commission meets every three or four years and aims, according to its bylaws, "to proclaim the oneness of the Church of Jesus Christ and to call the churches to the goal of visible unity in one faith and one Eucharistic fellowship, expressed in worship and in common life in Christ, in order that the world may believe."[62] A standing commission of thirty members, of whom three are Catholic, meets annually. From time to time, F&O calls a world conference. These large assemblies have been held at Lausanne (1927), Edinburgh (1937), Lund, Sweden (1952), Montreal (1963), and Compostella (1993). The seventy-fifth anniversary of the First World Conference on Faith and Order was celebrated in August 2002 in Lausanne. The value and importance of the world conference is that it reaches out to involve more people in F&O issues than those who would normally work with them. In this way, it can enable F&O efforts to achieve visible unity to have a greater impact on the various churches and ecclesial communities.

Three major studies of the F&O Commission deserve special mention: *Baptism, Eucharist and Ministry* (BEM), the *Apostolic Faith Study*, and the study *The Unity of the Church and the Renewal of Humankind*.

The best known of these is the BEM document, which was sent to the churches in 1982 with the request that a response to it would be forthcoming "at the highest appropriate level of authority." More than 180 official responses were sent over the next several years, and these have been published in six volumes, edited by the late Max Thurian with the title *Churches Respond to BEM: Official Responses to the Baptism, Eucharist and Ministry Text*, published by the World Council of Churches, Geneva (1986–88).

Since the twelve Catholic theologian members of the F&O Commission contributed to the development of BEM, the Catholic Church also sent an official response to the document. This was the first such official response to an ecumenical document by the Catholic Church and took some five years to prepare. After obtaining the comments of a number of episcopal conferences, the PCPCU developed a draft response that was then brought to a final form in collaboration with the Congregation for the Doctrine of the Faith. A study of the responses indicated major issues demanding further study, especially scripture and tradition, sacrament and sacramentality, and perspectives on ecclesiology in the churches.[63] The conclusion states that "BEM is a significant result and contribution to the ecumenical movement. It demonstrates clearly that serious progress is being made in the quest for visible Christian unity." For the Catholic Church, the truths of faith are not divided from one another, but constitute a unique organic whole. "Therefore full agreement on the sacraments is related to agreement on the nature of the Church." Nevertheless, "the study of BEM has been for many Catholics an enriching experience. Catholics can find in BEM much that they can agree with.... We rejoice in the convergence that has taken place and look to further growth toward unity."[64]

A second important study undertaken by the F&O Commission has as its aim to bring the Christian Churches to a common confession of the apostolic faith. The study entitled *Toward a Common Expression of the Apostolic Faith Today* concentrates on the Nicene-Constantinopolitan Creed of 381, which has been more universally received than any other symbol of the faith as a normative expression of the apostolic faith. A first step in this process has been the preparation of the document *Confessing One Faith* that presents the churches with an explication of this creed. This study has been sent to the

churches for "consideration and study." Eventually, it would be followed by two other steps: a common *recognition* and then a common
confession of the apostolic faith in our time.

The importance of this study, following on BEM, is obvious if
one recalls the three conditions identified by the ecumenical movement as necessary for full, visible unity: (1) the common confession of
the apostolic faith; (2) the common recognition of baptism, Eucharist,
and ministry; and (3) common structures for decision-making and
teaching authoritatively.

A third document that has been the object of study by F&O is
entitled *The Church and the World: The Unity of the Church and the
Renewal of the Human Community.* This document seeks to capture the
fundamental common concerns of the relationship of the unity of the
Christians to the spreading of the gospel in the world. In 1993, this
document study was followed up by two studies, *Ecclesiology and Ethics
and Ecumenical Hermeneutics.*

In 1998, F&O published a document (paper 181) titled *The Nature
and Purpose of the Church.* In this document F&O seeks for the first
time to make a substantial statement on the nature of the church.
Many of the responses to the BEM document had called for a deeper
exploration of ecclesiology as a way of providing the correct context
for an understanding of the sacraments and ministry in the church.
This paper was presented as "a stage on the way to a common statement," and comments and suggestions were invited. Some forty
responses have been forthcoming, among them a lengthy though not
official Catholic analysis of the paper by a group of Catholic theologians under the auspices of the PCPCU.[65]

A revised text was published in 2003, which is notable for the
greater emphasis now placed on the church as *communio* or koinonia.
Much more attention is also given to *primacy* in this new version of
the document. The 1998 text had little to say on primacy, and a ministry of unity at the universal level was not specifically mentioned. It
was just referred to in a box indicating that much work has to be done
to reconcile differences in this regard. The 2003 text instead dedi-
cates seven sections to the question of primacy, including historical
and classical perspectives, and more recent developments. While the
complexity of the issue is indicated, the text now roots the discussion
in the 1993 statement on "a universal ministry of Christian unity" by

the Fifth World Conference on Faith and Order. After referring briefly to some aspects of the state of the question today, the document states: "Many disagreements remain, but also several avenues of agreement seem to have opened up." One is that "there seems to be a wide agreement that a personal 'universal ministry of Christian unity' needs to be exercised in a communal and collegial way, resembling Faith and Order's viewpoint about ministry in *Baptism, Eucharist and Ministry* 1982." It also notes that "the very historically conditioned exercise of such a ministry is often being distinguished from what is essential to it, leaving room for possible changes from ways in which this ministry has been exercised in the past."[66] While this text is not as yet finalized, the evolution it has undergone in just a few years is very significant.

The president of the PCPCU, Cardinal Walter Kasper, was invited to the celebration in 2002 of the seventy-fifth anniversary of the First World Conference on Faith and Order, which took place in Lausanne, Switzerland, from August 3–21, 1927. Cardinal Kasper, who had been at one time a Catholic member of F&O, spoke on two aspects of the commission's activity that he considers important for the ecumenical movement today: the spiritual and theological basis of ecumenism, and the contribution of F&O to reconciliation among churches by overcoming historical divisions.[67]

The F&O Commission is responsible, together with the PCPCU, for the preparation and distribution of material for use each year during the Week of Prayer for Christian Unity by Christian communities throughout the world. (More about this joint contribution in fellowship in worship and spirituality will be found later in this study).

Rev. Günter Gassman, Lutheran theologian and longtime member of F&O, in the conclusion to the section "Faith and Order" in the *Dictionary of the Ecumenical Movement* (2002), gives the following description of the place of F&O in the ecumenical movement:

> Within the wider ecumenical movement, and as part of the structure of the WCC, the communion on F&O sees its task in a concentrated theological effort to assist the churches in overcoming their dividing doctrinal differences, in sharing their diverse theological insights and forms of life as a source

of mutual renewal, and in reappropriating and expressing their common apostolic Tradition. All these efforts have as their goal the manifestation of the visible unity of the Church of Jesus Christ. On the way to this goal the churches are called to become a credible sign and instrument of God's plan for the salvation and transformation of humanity and all creation. With such a commitment F&O has rendered a significant contribution to the radically changed relationships between the churches and the many steps that have been taken to express their full (or at least their growing) unity.[68]

CHRISTIAN WORLD COMMUNIONS

Though not an organ of the WCC, the Conference of the Secretaries of Christian World Communions (CWC) provides a global forum to promote dialogues and their reception, deepen and expand relationships, and contribute to the thinking of interchurch relations today. The secretaries of several churches or ecclesial communions that are not members of the WCC are regular participants in these meetings, which then provide them with an entry into the one ecumenical movement. In October 2003, the conference carried out a process of evaluation with regard to its nature and purpose, and during the meeting the secretaries decided to establish six working groups with particular focus on how to contribute actively to a better understanding of the ecumenical role of the CWC. Since 1957, the conference of the CWC has been meeting annually, mainly for informal exchange and information. The feeling is that it should now find ways to participate in the configuration of the ecumenical movement and support the global forum.

SPIRITUAL ECUMENISM, PRAYER, COMMON WITNESS

The Second Vatican Council made it clear that, in the eyes of the council fathers, theological dialogue alone would not lead the Christian churches to unity. They spoke about the need for a change of heart and holiness of life, accompanied by public and private prayer for the unity of Christians. Such "spiritual communion" should be regarded as the very soul of the ecumenical movement (*UR*, 8). Experience over the past forty years has shown just how true this observation is. Ecumenical spirituality calls for churches to create within and among themselves an environment animated by a spirit of repentance, forgiveness, healing, and reconciliation. It calls for an attitude of humbly listening together to God's call for them to foster unity, while working hand in hand to bring about the further proclamation of the good news about Jesus Christ and the coming of the kingdom of God through the power of the Holy Spirit.

In the encyclical letter On Commitment to Ecumenism *(Ut Unum Sint)*, Pope John Paul II gives the primacy in the search for unity to prayer. He sees common prayer, "when brothers and sisters who are not in perfect communion with one another come together to pray," as being "a very effective means of petitioning the grace of unity." Not only does such prayer invite Christ to visit the community of those who call on him, but Christians themselves as they gather in common prayer around Christ "will grow in the awareness of how little divides them in comparison to what unites them" (*UUS*, 21–22).

Almost as a response to the obstacles being encountered along the ecumenical way in the new Christian millennium, the Catholic Church has been placing greater emphasis on "ecumenical spirituality." The 2003 plenary assembly of the PCPCU was dedicated to this topic. In a message to Cardinal Walter Kasper and those taking part in the plenary assembly, Pope John Paul II wrote:

> Only an intense ecumenical spirituality, lived in docility to Christ and in full openness to the suggestions of the Spirit, will help us to live with the necessary energy this intermediate period during which we must take into account our progress and our challenges, the lights and shadows on our path of reconciliation.[69]

Again, on the occasion of the Week of Prayer for Christian Unity 2004, Pope John Paul II spoke about the need for deep spirituality, not only for those directly involved in ecumenical work, but for all Christians. He went on to state: "It is heartening that the search for unity among Christians is expanding more and more thanks to opportune initiatives that interest different aspects of ecumenical commitment."

Among the "signs of hope" he mentioned were the "increase in fraternal charity and the progress made in theological dialogue with various Churches and ecclesial communities" that have brought about "important accords on topics that were very controversial in the past."[70]

Christians have often been reluctant to join together in prayer. Before the Second Vatican Council, Catholics were forbidden to take part in Protestant Church services, while common prayer was severely limited. Today one cannot imagine an ecumenical meeting that does not give a prominent place to common prayer. Prayer is an essential part of ecumenical spirituality, since unity is a gift of the Holy Spirit. Praying together allows Christians from communities that are still divided to enter into a rare and profound moment of communion, without repudiating their own identity. In fact, the shared experience of faith that takes place in common prayer is a basic condition for making progress possible in ecumenical dialogue. Without the living experience of shared faith and communion in prayer, it is difficult for ecumenical dialogue to make real progress. The very reception of dialogue results in a spiritual event.

Perhaps the most universally celebrated act of common ecumenical prayer is the Week of Prayer for Christian Unity, which is usually celebrated in January or around Pentecost. During the nineteenth century various suggestions were made involving prayer for Christian unity and suggesting some form of church unity octave. In 1908, the Anglican (later Roman Catholic) Paul Wattson made a proposal for "a church unity octave," to be held between the feasts of the Confession of St. Peter (January 18) and the Conversion of St. Paul (January 25). In 1926, F&O began publishing "Suggestions for an Octave of Prayer for Christian Unity," and in 1935 Abbé Paul Couturier of France called for the celebration of a "Universal Week of Prayer for Christian Unity," a unity to be achieved "as Christ wishes and by the means he desires." In 1966, the F&O Commission of the WCC and the SPCU began official joint preparation of the material for the Week of Prayer. Since 1975, the two international organs receive suggestions regarding theme and texts from a local ecumenical group.[71]

The Week of Prayer is certainly the most widely observed act of common prayer among Christians throughout the world. While unfortunately little else is done in some places to bring Christians together in prayer, common prayer has become elsewhere a normal ecumenical activity, as we shall see in the section on local ecumenism.

Common prayer at the local level has certainly been fostered and encouraged by the example given by the heads of Christian churches and ecclesial communions. In Jerusalem in 1964, Pope Paul VI and Patriarch Athenagoras I prayed together Jesus' prayer "that they may all be one." Pope John Paul II has made an ecumenical meeting and common prayer with other Christians a regular part of his more than one hundred visits to countries outside of Italy. He took part in the eucharistic liturgy in the Church of St. George at the Ecumenical Patriarchate in November 1979, and was joined by both Patriarch Dimitrios I (1987) and Patriarch Bartholomew I (1995 and 2004) at the Mass in St. Peter's Basilica during visits to Rome. There have been many similar occasions with leaders of other churches over the years of his pontificate.

Two events involving common prayer at the international level deserve special mention. Pope John Paul II was determined to make the Jubilee Year 2000 an occasion for a common Christian celebration of the birth of Christ. In an attempt to bring the leaders of the Christian churches together at the very beginning of that year, the pope invited them all to join him on the first day of the Week of Prayer for Christian Unity, January 16, 2000, for an ecumenical prayer service in St. Paul's Outside the Walls in Rome. The response was exceptional. Representatives came from the Ecumenical Patriarchate and ten other Orthodox Churches, from five Oriental Orthodox Churches, from the Anglican Communion, and from the following:

- The Old Catholic Church—Union of Utrecht
- The Lutheran World Federation
- The World Methodist Council
- The Disciples of Christ
- The Pentecostal Church
- The World Council of Churches[72]

In what was a truly ecumenical service, all the delegations present had a role, while the ceremony included readings from the writings of Russian Orthodox George Florovsky and Evangelical Dietrich

Bonhoeffer. In the minds of many, the moment that stands out as an icon of this celebration and of the progress that has been made in the search for Christian unity is that of Pope John Paul II opening the Holy Door of St. Paul's Basilica together with the archbishop of Canterbury George Carey and Metropolitan Athanasios of the Ecumenical Patriarchate.

A second Jubilee ecumenical gathering took place on May 7, 2000, at the Colosseum in Rome, to jointly commemorate the Witnesses to the Faith in the Twentieth Century. As Pope John Paul II has stated often, the Christian communities in the twentieth century probably experienced more persecution than Christians at any other time since the early persecutions in the Roman Empire. In *Ut Unum Sint*, Pope John Paul II had spoken of "a common *Martyrology*" which, in a theocentric vision, we Christians already share (84). Earlier, in *Tertio Millennio Adveniente*, he made reference to the great sowing of martyrdom in different parts of the world during the twentieth century, and wrote: "The witness to Christ borne even to the shedding of blood has become a common inheritance of Catholics, Orthodox, Anglicans and Protestants.... *This witness must not be forgotten*" (37).

The victims came from different Christian communities, and the service at the Colosseum in May 2000 sought to give common witness to these martyrs and other witnesses to the faith during the Jubilee Year. Representatives of nineteen other churches and ecclesial communions joined Pope John Paul II and a large gathering of Catholic cardinals, bishops, priests, and laity in a joint act of commemoration. This service was also eminently ecumenical, not only bringing those present from other denominations actively into the prayer, but also using readings from a wide range of witnesses to the faith: Russian Orthodox, Armenian, Anglican, Lutheran, Baptist, as well as Catholics of East and West.

Christians throughout the world later in the same year joined the Ecumenical Patriarch Bartholomew I on August 5–6 in a prayer vigil for the feast of the transfiguration, which is celebrated on the same date in East and West. The purpose of this vigil was again to provide an occasion for common prayer and witness during the Jubilee Year. The vigil prayer service in Rome was held in the Basilica of St. John Lateran and presided over in the name of Pope John Paul II by myself in my role as president of the PCPCU.

Among other special occasions for representatives of the Christian churches and ecclesial communions to pray together and give common witness, mention must be made of the Day of Prayer for Peace, held in Assisi on October 27, 1986, and again on January 24, 2002. Representatives of a number of Christian churches and ecclesial communions, as well as ecumenical organizations, joined Pope John Paul II in praying for peace in a troubled world.[73] On both occasions the Christian leaders were joined in giving common witness for peace by representatives of Judaism, Islam, Buddhism, and other world religions. Each group separated for prayer but came together in a moving act of common witness.

A similar, though less representative Assisi meeting in January 1993 was called by Pope John Paul II in response to the tragic situation in Bosnia-Herzegovina at that time. At Pope John Paul's invitation, representatives of the various religious groups from that area, as well as representatives of the Catholic bishops' conferences in Europe, came together for two days of prayer for peace in that troubled land.[74]

The above-mentioned events were not only an occasion for joint worship, but at the same time were examples of common witness. It is important also for the Christian communities themselves and for the world in general to have such examples of the unity that already exists among the followers of Christ. Obviously spiritual ecumenism is more than prayer alone. It may be seen as an entire way of life in which one responds to the inner voice and movement of the Holy Spirit. A spiritual person listens to the abiding Spirit and directs his or her life accordingly, becoming selfless and fully dedicated to expressing this faith in action.

Given the unity that already exists, Christians are called to share every possible form of practical cooperation. The F&O Commission, at the general assembly in Lund, Sweden, in 1952, called on the churches for the sake of Christian unity "to act together in all matters except those in which deep differences of conviction compel them to act separately." Pope John Paul II in the encyclical *Ut Unum Sint* (40) writes that relations between Christians "presuppose and from now on call for every possible form of practical cooperation at all levels, pastoral, cultural and social, as well as that of witnessing to the Gospel message." The Second Vatican Council saw cooperation among all Christians as vividly expressing that bond which already unites them, while it "sets in clearer relief the features of Christ the Servant" (*UR*, 12). Such cooperation is certainly a "school of ecumenism, a dynamic road to unity" (*UUS*, 40).

Regular contacts between the leaders and other representatives of the churches have also proved to be of special value. The PCPCU has sought over the years to enter as far as possible into the life of the other Christian communities at the international level, by accepting invitations to be present at or participate in their assemblies (such as the Lambeth Conferences, the General Assembly of the LWF, the General Council of the WARC, and the World Assembly of the Mennonite World Federation), and by taking part in important meetings and gatherings organized by them. In return, there has been a growing participation of representatives of other churches and ecclesial communions in similar gatherings within the Catholic Church, as for example at the synods of bishops held in Rome from time to time. More informal meetings take place regularly between the PCPCU and the secretariats of the Anglican Communion and the LWF.

The PCPCU is constantly called upon to arrange for delegations from other churches and ecclesial communions to visit Rome and to be received in audience by the pope—something that only a few years ago would have been rare and, for some, quite unthinkable.

The visit of Pope John Paul II to the Nordic countries in June 1989 opened the way for frequent contacts between the Lutheran bishops of those countries and the Roman pontiff. A return visit by the bishops of the Lutheran Churches in those countries in 1991, on the six-hundredth anniversary of the canonization of St. Bridget of Sweden, became the occasion for the first-ever ecumenical celebration in St. Peter's Basilica, as Pope John Paul II and the Catholic bishops of Helsinki and Stockholm were joined in prayer and celebration at the altar of the basilica with the Lutheran archbishops of Turku (Finland) and Uppsala (Sweden).[75]

The seventh centenary of the birth of St. Bridget in 2002 provided a second occasion for a similar ecumenical celebration in St. Peter's Basilica. On October 4, 2002, Catholic bishops from the Roman curia and from various countries were joined by the Lutheran bishops from the Nordic countries in honoring St. Bridget, who had come from Sweden to Rome, where she died on July 23, 1373, and where she was canonized by Boniface IX on October 7, 1391.[76]

On November 16, 2002, Pope John Paul II received in audience Bishop Finn Wagle, Lutheran bishop of the ancient See of Nidaros in Norway (established as an archdiocese in 1152/1153, and known today as Trondheim), together with a delegation from that diocese, which had come to Rome for the feast of St. Olav, patron of Norway. Both the pope and Bishop Finn Wagle recalled that special occasion during the papal visit to the Nordic countries in 1989, when John Paul II was received in the beautiful Cathedral of Trondheim by the then Bishop Kristen Kyrre Bremer.[77] This particular celebration was one of the most significant and memorable events of that papal visit.

Following on the meeting of Pope Paul VI and Patriarch Athenagoras I in Jerusalem on October 28, 1967, there has been a remarkable positive development in Orthodox-Catholic relations. Pope John Paul II visited the Ecumenical Patriarch in Istanbul in November 1979, just one year after his election. Patriarch Dimitrios I, in December 1987, and Patriarch Bartholomew I, in June 1995 and again in June 2004, paid official visits to Rome. For more than twenty-five years, there has been an annual exchange of official delegations between Rome and the Ecumenical Patriarchate. A delegation from the patriarchate takes part each year in the June 29 celebrations in Rome for the feast of Sts. Peter and Paul, while a Catholic delegation from Rome is in Istanbul for the feast of St. Andrew on November 30. These are occasions for prayer together, for an exchange of information, and for discussion of matters of concern to the two partners. On only one occasion has there been a break in this tradition, namely, in June 1997, when a delegation from the patriarchate was not present in Rome for the feast of Sts. Peter and Paul. This action on the part of the patriarch was the result of tensions arising from a proposed meeting between Pope John Paul II and the Russian patriarch in Vienna on the occasion of the Second Ecumenical Assembly in Graz in June of that year. Complications arose when the Ecumenical Patriarch decided also to be in Vienna at the same time. In the end the meeting with the Russian patriarch did not take place and the visit of Patriarch Bartholomew was cancelled.

On January 24, 2002, Patriarch Bartholomew I himself took part in the Assisi Day of Prayer for World Peace, at the invitation of Pope

John Paul II. A few months later, an environmental symposium organized by the patriarch on the theme *The Adriatic Sea: A Sea at Risk—*
Unity of Purpose provided an opportunity for further excellent contacts
between the Vatican and the Ecumenical Patriarchate. Cardinal
Kasper participated in the symposium at the invitation of the patriarch. During a stopover in Ravenna, Patriarch Bartholomew I celebrated a solemn liturgy in the Catholic Byzantine Basilica of St.
Apollinaris in Classe, and on June 10, 2002, Pope John Paul II and
the Ecumenical Patriarch signed a *Common Declaration of Environmen-*
tal Ethics.[78]

As mentioned already, since the beginning of the new millennium
there has been a promising series of exchanges between Rome and
the other Orthodox Churches. Pope John Paul II had visited Romania already in May 1999,[79] and Patriarch Teoctist returned the important ecumenical gesture from October 7–13, 2002.[80] The pope was in
Bulgaria in May 2002[81] and had made a historic visit to the Areopagus
in Athens in May 2001.[82] Only a few months earlier it had seemed
impossible for the head of the Church of Rome to make such a visit.
In fact, relations between the Church of Greece and the Catholic
Church had been, until 1999, rather formal and lacking in substance.
Following on the meeting of Pope John Paul II and Archbishop
Christodulos in Athens, a delegation from the synod of the Church of
Greece made an official visit to Rome in March 2002,[83] and Cardinal
Kasper then led a delegation on an official visit to the Church of
Greece in February 2003.[84]

As president of the PCPCU, His Eminence Cardinal Kasper has
given special attention to developing similar relations with other
Orthodox Churches. In 2002, the cardinal was in Aleppo, Syria, in
March; the Serbian Orthodox Church in May;[85] and Bulgaria[86] and
the Ukraine in October. Various engagements in the Ukraine gave
the cardinal the possibility of meeting representatives of His Beati-
tude Volodymyr, the Metropolitan of Kiev of the Russian Orthodox
Church, who was not in the country at the time.[87] From December
15–18, 2002, Cardinal Kasper visited the Orthodox Church in
Belarus.[88] As a consequence of this activity, a new phase in a dialogue
of friendship and cooperation has opened the way for further
progress in the coming years and the hope of a renewed theological
dialogue.

During the years since Vatican II, succeeding primates of the Anglican Communion have made official visits to Rome. Archbishop Michael Ramsey of Canterbury was the first in March 1966. Archbishop Donald Coggan visited Pope Paul VI in April 1977. In 1982, Pope John Paul II, on his visit to Great Britain, met with Archbishop Robert Runcie in Canterbury and the archbishop made a return visit to Rome in October 1989. During the time that Archbishop George Carey occupied the See of Canterbury, he made quite a number of visits to Pope John Paul II and, as has already been mentioned, joined together the pope in opening the Holy Door of St. Paul's Basilica at the beginning of the Jubilee Year. On January 7, 2001, Archbishop Carey informed the pope of his coming retirement and in June 2002 made a farewell visit to Rome, where he was warmly received by Pope John Paul II, who thanked him for all he had done during his eleven years in office to foster good relations with the Church of Rome. The pope also expressed gratitude to the archbishop for his work in promoting peace and dialogue between Christians, Jews, and Muslims.[89]

Pope John Paul II then sent congratulations to Dr. Rowan Williams on his appointment as archbishop of Canterbury, and Cardinal Kasper was present at his enthronement on February 27, 2003.[90] Within the year, Archbishop Williams was in Rome on an official visit to Pope John Paul II. These visits have indicated and confirmed, in the midst of the new difficulties that have arisen between the two partners, the special nature of Anglican-Catholic relations.

At the international level, the Catholic Church has been closely associated with the Lutheran World Federation in seeking to bring an end to civil conflict in Guatemala and in providing humanitarian relief to troubled areas in Northern Africa. Church organizations in Bangladesh have worked closely together for a number of years in their efforts to assist the Bangladeshi people, the majority of whom are Muslim. National councils of churches offer a valuable opportunity for such practical cooperation among the member churches, and this is producing good results in many parts of the world. Much more could surely be done to develop and expand such cooperation, which after all is itself a form of Christian witness. So one might well ask: What then is holding the churches back from much greater practical cooperation? While many more examples could be given, there is still much hesitation among Christian communities to give up their own good works in favor of cooperation with others.

LOCAL ECUMENISM

In the preceding sections, the emphasis has been on international efforts to promote the search for Christian unity. It is obvious, however, that unless the results achieved at the international level are received and become part of the churches at the local level, progress along the road to unity will not proceed at any great pace. Agreements at the international level bring great joy to those involved, but may remain just beautiful documents unless they become part of the life of the local communities.

The World Council of Churches, together with the PCPCU and other international ecumenical organizations, have constantly emphasized the importance of local ecumenism. Here again there is a great difference between one area and another. The responsibility for action at the local level depends principally on the local church communities themselves. It is in this context that councils of churches and Christian councils can offer valuable opportunities for common prayer, witness, and cooperation. In only a few nations is important theological dialogue possible; however, reception of agreed documents can be effective even at the local parish level. The *Directory for the Application of Principles and Norms on Ecumenism* makes some suggestions in this regard:

> On the local level there are countless opportunities for exchanges between Christians, ranging from informal conversations that occur in daily life to sessions for the common examination in a Christian perspective of issues of local life or of concern to particular professional groups (doctors, social workers, parents, educators) and to study groups for specifically ecumenical subjects. Dialogues may be carried on by groups of lay people, by groups of clergy, by groups of professional theologians or by various combinations of these. (174)

Praying together, giving common witness, and cooperating with other Christians are widespread particularly in North America, Great Britain, Australia, New Zealand, and some European countries. Besides the annual celebration of the Week of Prayer for Christian Unity, churches at the local level have found other ways of bringing members of their communities together regularly for common prayer. The liturgical seasons of Advent and Lent provide opportunities for diocesan or local Christian communities to come together in prayerful preparation for the great feasts of Christmas and Easter. Ash Wednesday, Good Friday, and Pentecost also provide an opportunity for Christians to join together in prayer and common witness to their faith. In the United States, certain memorial occasions—such as Memorial Day honoring the war dead, Thanksgiving Day, Reformation Sunday, and the Black Church Week for the Healing of AIDS—are other opportunities for common prayer. Elsewhere mention is made of the observance of special celebrations of women.

Heads of local churches meet regularly in some areas and prayer together is normal on such occasions. In Pittsburgh, Pennsylvania, the leaders of all denominations come together on Holy Saturday morning to bless the city from a high place overlooking the city. The commemoration of the passion and death of Our Lord Jesus Christ each year brings together members of various Christian communities for common worship, especially on Good Friday. In a number of towns in Australia local churches have a Good Friday Way of the Cross, during which their faithful—often including young people—walk from church to church and reenact scenes from the passion. Bilateral prayer meetings are regularly celebrated in parishes such as Marrickville in Sydney, Australia.

Monasteries and religious orders play a positive role in promoting ecumenical spirituality in several regions, especially by providing opportunities for retreats and studies. Taizé deserves special mention in this regard, together with ecclesial movements such as the Focolare Movement, the Sant'Egidio Community, and Jean Vanier's L'Arche community. Charismatic renewal has also brought members of different ecclesial communities together in prayer to the Holy Spirit.

During the period in which the *Joint Declaration on the Doctrine of Justification* was being prepared and submitted for approval, the LWF and the PCPCU offered Catholic parishes and local Lutheran communities specific Bible studies on justification. The Australian Anglican–Roman Catholic Dialogue Commission (ARC) in 2004 published a discussion resource for Anglicans and Catholics on the ARCIC document *"Church as Communion."*[91] Such common Bible work is highly recommended by the ecumenical directory (183–86). In 1969, the Catholic Church was involved through the PCPCU in establishing in the Catholic Biblical Foundation (formerly the World Federation for the Biblical Apostolate), and it is through this organization that the PCPCU maintains close relations with the United Bible Societies. Together these two have published *Guidelines for Interconfessional Cooperation in Translating the Bible.*[92] This collaboration has yielded good results, as has similar cooperation at the local level in missionary work, catechetics, and religious education.

Other fields in which local ecumenism has contributed to the closer relationship of the Christian communities are in seminary formation, in the preparation of common liturgical texts and scriptural readings for liturgical use, and in theological research and postgraduate studies. The PCPCU has set up a special Catholic Committee for Cultural Collaboration, which includes among its activities the sponsorship of students recommended by their Orthodox Churches to undertake higher studies in Catholic universities in Rome and other European cities. Some university colleges bring together for theological education students from a number of churches. For example, the Brisbane College of Theology in Australia has students from the Catholic, Anglican, and Uniting Church, who have their own special theological formation but are able to study other disciplines together and receive a recognized common university degree.

Even after the Second Vatican Council had completed its work, the Catholic Church was for a time reluctant to join national or regional councils of churches. In recent years there has been a change in this approach. In the ecumenical directory, the following recommendation is given:

> Since it is desirable for the Catholic Church to find the proper expression for various levels of its relation with other Churches and ecclesial Communities, and since Councils of Churches

and Christian Councils are among the more important forms
of ecumenical cooperation, the growing contacts which the
Catholic Church is having with Councils in many parts of the
world are to be welcomed.[93]

More and more, Catholic bishops' conferences are joining such
councils, while others maintain close contacts usually by appointing
observers. Much depends on the constitutions of the councils and the
possibility that members have of maintaining their identity and discipline within such bodies. The experience of the Catholic Church as a
member of such councils has not always been totally satisfactory.
While there have been good opportunities for social and humanitarian cooperation, bishops in some cases would have liked more theological and pastoral discussion.

Churches and ecclesial communions also meet at the regional
level, especially in Europe. The Conference of European Churches
(CEC) and the Council of Episcopal Conferences of Europe (CCEE)
promote cooperation in Europe. In May 2004, an ecumenical meeting
with the theme "All Together for Europe" took place in Stuttgart,
Germany, bringing together representatives from 175 Catholic, Evangelical, Orthodox, and Anglican movements and communities. Pope
John Paul II wrote a letter to the participants in which he emphasized
the importance of the Christian faith for the present and future of
Europe and stated that "ecumenical dialogue decisively contributes to
developing a European identity based on the Christian faith."[94]

Of particular importance are the theological dialogues carried out
at the national level. National dialogues in the United States and
Germany contributed with their own studies to the preparation of the
international *Joint Declaration on the Doctrine of Justification.*

Since its establishment in 1965, the North American Orthodox-
Catholic Theological Consultation has issued twenty-two agreed
statements on various topics.[95] On October 25, 2003, the consultation
unanimously adopted an agreed text on the difficult question of the
Filioque that has divided the two communions for many centuries.
This dispute concerns the creed, which in its original version states
that the Holy Spirit proceeds "from the Father." This was the form
accepted by the First Council of Constantinople in 381, and has been
used ever since by Orthodox Christians. In the West at a later date,

the *Filioque* was added, which states that the Holy Spirit proceeds "from the Father and the Son." This modification appeared in some areas of Western Europe as early as the sixth century, but was accepted by Rome only in the eleventh century. The North American dialogue document will surely contribute to the discussions between Orthodox and Catholics on this question, which has long been considered a church-dividing issue. This statement and all the supporting documents developed over four years of study will be published in one volume.

The Joint Committee for Catholic-Orthodox Theological Dialogue in France released at the beginning of April 2004 an important collection of studies entitled "Catholiques et orthodoxies: les enjeux de l'uniatisme dans le sillage de Balamand" (Catholics and Orthodox: The Stakes of Uniatism in the Wake of Balamand).[96] This is also undoubtedly an important contribution to Catholic-Orthodox theological dialogue, especially in the difficult situation faced by the International Joint Commission caused principally by problems concerning Uniatism. The French publication is the result of more than ten years of reflection on problems related to the Eastern Churches united to Rome and includes contributions of numerous specialists, both French and foreign. Its purpose, according to the press release, is to examine the origins of Uniatism and to reread the pages of its sad and complex history, bringing out its genesis, its development in various forms in the Middle East and in Central and Eastern Europe, and its later theological development. The French joint committee's work points out both the strong points and the limitations of the Balamand document of June 1993, and expresses the hope that this text can inspire and create new momentum in the dialogue between the two Churches.

The Australian Lutheran–Roman Catholic Dialogue has done valuable work for more than twenty-five years. It has published its own study on *justification* and is presently engaged in a study of episcopacy. After overcoming initial difficulties, a particularly interesting dialogue is taking place between the Evangelical Lutheran Churches of Sweden and Finland, and the Catholic Churches in Scandinavia. In this connection, Pope John Paul II spoke to an ecumenical delegation from Finland on January 19, 2004 and, after mentioning the progress made during the years since the signing of the JD, described this dialogue as "a promising sign" of progress on the way to full and visible unity. "It is my hope," he said, "that Lutherans and Catholics will increasingly practice a *spirituality of communion*, which draws on those elements of ecclesial life which they already share and which will strengthen their fellowship in prayer and in witness to the Gospel of Jesus Christ."[97]

These examples indicate what is possible in a field that is difficult, but can be of great importance in the long term in supporting and contributing to the total work of dialogue that is so important to the quest for unity among Christians.

In some cases, local dialogue has brought ecclesial communions into full communion. In Great Britain, the Anglican and Methodist Churches signed a covenant in 2003 committing themselves to "a common life of worship and mission" in the years to come. Unity between the two denominations had been under serious discussion since the 1960s. But proposals to this end failed to gain the required majorities in 1972 and again in 1982. Not all questions have been resolved, and the new covenant commits the two partners "to overcome the remaining obstacles to the organic unity of our two Churches." The three main areas requiring further study are holy communion, episcopacy, and women's leadership.[98]

A great amount of discussion has taken place between churches in North America, with a view to establishing full communion.[99] In the Netherlands, a merger agreement in 2003 brought the Dutch Lutheran Church and the two Dutch Reformed Churches into a union. The question of possible "unions" is much discussed worldwide, especially within the WARC. At the same time there is a tendency in these later days for some churches to prefer an agreement involving full communion, without either party losing its identity or self-direction.

More and more "covenants" are being signed between local churches. This has been taking place particularly in North America. In July 2004, fifteen Australian churches signed a historic "covenant of cooperation." The churches involved are members of the National Council of Churches in Australia. All have agreed to recognize each other's baptism and ministries, and to develop closer relations. Not all joining in the covenant were able to sign every section of the document. Sharing of the Eucharist remains their greatest challenge. For nine of the fifteen members, including the Catholic Church, a common baptismal certificate will be given for all baptisms. The Catholic Church also agreed with nine others to share physical resources such as church buildings and to consult each other before major new developments are undertaken. Along with six other members, the Catholic Church also agreed to explore issues and strategies for mission together.[100] Covenants have also been signed at the local parish level in Australia between Catholic, Anglican, and Uniting churches.[101] In September 2003, four members of churches belonging to the NSW Ecumenical Council (a regional council within Australia)—one from each of the Catholic, Anglican, Uniting, and Lutheran churches—traveled together to Armenia for the seventeen hundredth anniversary of the Armenian Church.

At all levels and in many parts of the world, cooperation between Christians has become normal and quite extensive. The Council of Churches in Birmingham, England, brings together Christians from various local churches in that city in seeking to provide a common response to the grave social problems that affect a significant proportion of the large city population. In the Newcastle area in Eastern Australia, the Anglican and Catholic bishops have their own fund, "The Two Bishops' Fund," which seeks to alleviate unemployment among the young people of the area. Since June 2000 the New South Wales Ecumenical Council (Australia) has been conducting a series of sessions in local communities, both suburban and rural, to encourage growing links between the churches. The workshops begin with an account of the international ecumenical journey as a background to the sharing of stories of cooperation between the churches in their communities. In some large cities, parish councils meet together regularly to plan joint activities in the fields of social justice and humanitarian relief.

These are but a few of the many wonderful initiatives in the ecumenical field being undertaken at the local level. There is no way to know, however, the extent of such cooperation, since these efforts are not always publicized outside the local region.

PART IV

THE STATE OF THE QUESTION

What would the council fathers' verdict be on the way in which their recommendations in *Unitatis Redintegratio* have become part of the life of the Catholic Church? I feel sure that they would experience a sense of joyful satisfaction in seeing how much has actually changed over the past forty years in relations between the Catholic Church and other Christian churches and communions. Under the present pope, the Catholic Church has shown clearly that it is irrevocably committed to the search for Christian unity. Relations between Christians, at every level, have changed radically. As Pope John Paul II stated in the encyclical *Ut Unum Sint:*

> It is the first time in history that efforts on behalf of Christian unity have taken on such proportions and have become so extensive. This is truly an immense gift of God, one that deserves all our gratitude....An appreciation of how much God has already given is the condition which disposes us to receive those gifts still indispensable for bringing to completion the ecumenical work of unity. (N41)

As mentioned before, the "universal brotherhood" of Christians has become a firm ecumenical conviction, a brotherhood that "is not the consequence of a large-hearted philanthropy or a vague family spirit, but rooted in recognition of the one-ness of baptism" (42).

On doctrinal issues considerable progress has been made in all the dialogues, as trust grew among the participants and misunderstandings and old polemics gave way to a genuine desire to seek consensus. The agreements reached in the centuries-old Church-dividing issues of Christology and justification have opened up real possibilities for the future.

The fact that all this has taken place in just forty years, after 1500 years of separation from the Oriental Orthodox Churches and some 450 years since the Reformation, is truly remarkable. Despite the obstacles encountered along the way, the churches have made considerable progress up the mountain that has full communion and eucharistic sharing at the summit.

And yet, many have found the progress far too slow. Even some dedicated ecumenists have become frustrated. The present moment in this ecumenical climb to the summit calls for greater patience and dedication than in the past forty years. New relationships have been established and many old issues of disagreement cleared from the scene, but now the much more difficult task of coming to a consensus on remaining doctrinal issues will naturally be slow; some may even remain insurmountable in the foreseeable future.

Psychological difficulties can also prove to be an obstacle on the way to Christian unity. Christians often find ecumenism to be somewhat threatening. They are very happy in their own Christian community and are worried that they may be asked to give up something that is very dear to them and is often an essential part of their personal or family history. This has been particularly evident when various Protestant churches have come together in a form of a "United" or "Uniting" church. Not all those belonging to the churches involved have made the move. For this reason, more emphasis would seem to be placed now on forms of unity in which the participating bodies, while entering into full communion, maintain their own separate identity.

Again, there is a danger in an endless series of conferences, symposiums, commissions, meetings, sessions, projects, and spectacular events, with the continual repetition of the same arguments, concerns, problems, and lamentations. Some soon grow weary of such initiatives, which seem to lead nowhere.

Closely associated with the above difficulty are, in certain cases, memories of the past. Unfortunately, there have been times in history when one Christian community persecuted or at least treated badly members of other communities. In some places these memories remain strong even after centuries have passed and can constitute a serious obstacle to progress in building trust in the search for greater Christian unity. There has been real progress in Western Europe in the healing of such memories, but less in Central and Eastern Europe. As a consequence, Catholic-Orthodox relations are negatively affected. In Greece, for example, memories of the Crusades seem still to influence negatively ecumenical relations.

In the May 2004 issue of the publication *WARC Update,* Ordair Pedroso Mateus, theology secretary of WARC, writes of a "warning light in the ecumenical boat," in the form of churches not being able to keep up with the financial demands of so many different ecumenical councils and organizations.[102] When funds begin to run short, all too often the ecumenical budget is the first to suffer.

Until recent times, there was a fairly general agreement about the ecumenical goal. For the Second Vatican Council the unity that we seek is unity in faith, sacramental life, and ministries: a visible, organic unity. This teaching is clearly put forward in the *Directory for the Application of Principles and Norms on Ecumenism:*

> The decree *Unitatis Redintegratio* explains how the unity that Christ wishes for his Church is brought about through the faithful preaching of the Gospel by the Apostles and their successors—the bishops with Peter's successor at their head— through their administering the sacraments, and through their governing in love, and defines this unity as consisting of the confession of one faith...the common celebration of divine worship...the fraternal harmony of the family of God. This unity which of its very nature requires full, visible communion of all Christians is the ultimate goal of the ecumenical movement. (*ED,* 20)

A similar definition has been given officially by the World Council of Churches and even more clearly by the F&O Commission of that body. However, not all those engaged today in the ecumenical movement accept this as their goal. The difficulties encountered along the ecumenical way, especially with regard to doctrinal differences, have led some church leaders and ecumenical agents to accept less distant goals. Among the various ideas circulated in this connection, the goal closest to the Catholic vision would be what has come to be known as *reconciled diversity*. Many in the World Council of Churches speak rather of *conciliar fellowship*. Other similar attempts to settle for a goal for Christian unity that falls short of the one proposed by the Catholic Church certainly make the task of seeking doctrinal consensus more difficult. Most of these more recent visions of unity would concentrate on the communion that Christians already share, on greater reconciliation of differences, and on unity in action and witness.

Despite the problems encountered in the search for unity, Pope John Paul II in his encyclical *Ut Unum Sint* once again committed the Catholic Church to the goal of full visible unity among all the baptized (77). This unity, however, is not to be understood as uniformity. In fact, the unity of the Church is realized in the midst of a rich diversity, a diversity that is a dimension of the Church's catholicity. The Second Vatican Council made it clear that the unity that we seek by no means requires the sacrifice of the rich diversity of spirituality, discipline, liturgical rites, and elaboration of revealed truth that has grown up among Christians to the degree that this diversity remains faithful to the apostolic tradition (cf. *UR*, 4 and 15–16; also *ED*, 20). The principle is clear; the application more difficult. Again in his encyclical On Commitment to Ecumenism, Pope John Paul II states that in the journey toward the necessary and sufficient visible unity, in the communion of the one church willed by Christ, ... "one must not impose any burden beyond that which is strictly necessary (cf. *Acts* 15:28)" (*UUS*, 78). During a conference on ecumenism at St. Alban's Cathedral in England in May 2003, Cardinal Kasper spoke about the consequences of this concept of pluriformity within unity:

> It has consequences for our understanding of unity in faith. To confess the same faith does not necessarily mean to confess the same creedal formula. Nor is uniformity required in the sacramental dimension of the Church. It is well known that sacramental life can be expressed through different rites, and that in East and West these rites are indeed quite different. The core challenge for this concept and this vision—and the sticking point in the question of how far pluriformity is possible—is to be found in the question of Church ministry. The ccumenical dialogue seems to be blocked on this issue at

present. Hence, here we touch upon one of the most sensitive points of the current ecumenical debate. This is all the more relevant, as mutual recognition of ministry is fundamental for eucharistic sharing.[103]

When presenting the papal encyclical *Ut Unum Sint*, I indicated the five main doctrinal questions that will need to be studied before a true consensus of faith can be achieved. They are, once again, (a) sacred scripture and tradition; (b) the Eucharist; (c) ordination; (d) authority in the Church and the exercise of the magisterium; and (e) the role of the Virgin Mary as Mother of God and Icon of the Church. Not all these questions remain open in all the dialogues in which the Catholic Church is engaged. With the Orthodox Churches, the main difficulty is the Petrine ministry and questions connected with the exercise of this authority. The difficult problem of Uniatism is directly connected with these. Dialogue with the Anglican Communion has found consensus on the Eucharist and on the nature of ministry, without solving the problem of the validity of priestly ordination. The role of Mary in the Church will in itself not be an insurmountable problem in my opinion, although the Marian dogmas may delay consensus.

It has become increasingly obvious in recent years that the fundamental question to be solved in the dialogue with the Anglican Communion, the Lutheran World Federation, and the churches coming from the Reformation is that of authority in the Church: Where is such authority to be found and how are decisions made that bind the Christian community concerned? This is, of course, intimately connected with the recognition of ministry, and subsequently with eucharistic sharing.

What then is the hope of reaching the summit of the ecumenical mountain? In his homily at the ecumenical vespers service in the Basilica of St. Paul's Outside the Walls in Rome, at the close of the 2004 Week of Prayer for Christian Unity, Cardinal Walter Kasper, president of the PCPCU, spoke of the great progress that has been made in the search for unity. He then indicated the difficult path ahead:

But, if we look at the world with objectivity, we can't pretend that everything is perfect. Sometimes we note feelings of ecumenical exhaustion, signs of new confessionalism, attempts to mine the path to unity. After having filled in the trenches that at one time divided us, we find them opening up anew in the field of ethics.

The cardinal admitted that from a human point of view there are reasons for being concerned and for losing hope. On the other hand, he said, Christians are people of hope. "When the Spirit of God starts something, he always sees it through to completion."[104]

A similar thought is expressed by Pope John Paul II in the exhortation at the end of his encyclical letter on ecumenism, *Ut Unum Sint.* He writes:

> There is no doubt that the Holy Spirit is active in this endeavor and that he is leading the Church to the full realization of the Father's plan, in conformity with the will of Christ. This will is expressed with heartfelt urgency in the prayer which, according to the fourth Gospel, he uttered at the moment when he entered upon the saving mystery of his Passover. Just as he did then, today too Christ calls everyone to renew their commitment to work for full and visible communion. (N102)

To the question "How is the Church to obtain this grace?" Pope John Paul II sets out a program consisting of, in the first place, prayer, accompanied by thanksgiving, and of strong hope in the Spirit, who can banish from us the painful memories of our separation. He then makes a final appeal, first to the faithful of the Catholic Church, and then to "you, my brothers and sisters of other Churches and Ecclesial Communions: *'Mend your ways, encourage one another, live in harmony, and the God of love and peace be with you'* (2 Cor 13:11)."

With these words, Pope John Paul II recalls the well-known words of the Decree on Ecumenism of the Second Vatican Council: "There can be no ecumenism worthy of the name without interior conversion. For it is from newness of attitudes of mind, from self-denial and unstinted love, that desires of unity rise and develop in a mature way" (*UR*, 7). There can be no compromise with truth in matters of faith, and for this reason serious theological dialogue is indispensable in the work for Christian unity. Cooperation in humanitarian and other works also has an important role to play, for as Pope John Paul II has written, cooperation among Christians is a kind of school of ecumenism. But as has already been mentioned, unity is not a human task but a gift of God's Spirit. At this time it would seem that spiritual ecumenism must take pride of place in the quest for unity. Spiritual ecumenism means sharing in spiritual initiatives: in praying together, in reading the Bible together, in exchanging spiritual experiences, in learning to forgive and purify memories. In other words it is an ecumenism of life, by means of which the fruits of dialogue are translated into the real lives of the members of the various Christian communities. Only in fraternal love that excludes rivalry and competition and is truly an exchange of gifts, can the churches overcome the serious difficulties that continue to delay progress.

In a letter addressed to Cardinal Walter Kasper, made public on September 3, 2003, Pope John Paul II wrote that "spirituality creates the suitable psychological context in which to undertake dialogue in an open and trusting fashion."[105]

The experience of the past forty years is indeed proof that God is calling Christians to unity and is ready to provide, through the Holy Spirit, the graces that are required in order to reach the goal of full and visible communion. The big question, however, remains: Are Christians ready to do what is necessary on their part to offer what the pope calls the *sacrifice of unity*? In all his mysterious dealings with human beings there is a constant exchange. God offers grace, but the person is free to accept or neglect the offer. God will not force the child he loves to receive grace against his will. This is, of course, true also with the grace of Christian unity. In the search for that full and visible communion, Christians may be sure that God will not let them down. But can we be sure that the Christians themselves will not let God down? Therein lies the unknown factor in the quest for unity among Christians.

Looking back over the years since the Second Vatican Council, the fruits of God's grace and Christian commitment are evident. Yet, as this period comes to a close there are also signs of a certain reluctance on the part of the churches to want to make the sacrifice of unity. On the one hand, Christian unity does not seem at times to have priority over other more domestic concerns within the churches. And then we have to admit that, while so many obstacles have been removed from the way of unity, decisions have been taken that place new obstacles on that path.

Cardinal Kasper mentioned in his homily for the Week of Prayer for Christian Unity in St. Paul's Basilica in Rome on January 25, 2004, the serious ethical questions that in recent years have come to divide Christians. Only a few years ago Christian leaders could take a common stand on the more serious ethical questions confronting their nations. Today, in parts of the world, there are very few such questions on which they can take a common stand. Catholics and Evangelicals, who remain deeply divided on doctrinal questions, often find themselves together in defending Christian moral values in the public forum, whereas Catholics and Anglicans, for example, are often unable to take such a common position on abortion, homosexuality, euthanasia, or even the nature of marriage.

As has already been mentioned above, the ordination of an active gay person, Gene Robinson, to the episcopate of the Episcopal Church of the United States in 2003 has not only created serious challenges to unity among the provinces of the Anglican Communion, but has brought the work of IARCCUM (International Anglican–Roman Catholic Commission for Unity and Mission) to a standstill. The present challenge to the Anglican Communion is how to find a way to hold together the various provinces as being truly one in faith. Indeed, the earlier decision of several Anglican jurisdictions to ordain women to the priesthood, after such good work by ARCIC on Eucharist and ministry, was seen by many in the Catholic Church as a new insurmountable obstacle to Catholic-Anglican unity. It raised serious doubts about the priority accorded within the Anglican Communion to the search for full communion with the Orthodox and Catholic Churches.

Toward the close of 2003, there were some signs of promise amid the obstacles just referred to. The enthronement of the new archbishop of Canterbury, Rowan Williams, in February of that year had provided an occasion for Cardinal Kasper to speak on behalf of all the invited guests at the banquet immediately following the liturgical celebration and to recall the many important ecumenical bridges that had been built over the past forty years. Pope John Paul II sent greetings to the new archbishop along with the gift of a pectoral cross and received in reply a warm letter of thanks in which the archbishop reflected on their common mission in terms of bearing the cross of Christ. Despite the obstacles that delay the construction of new ecumenical bridges by Anglicans and Catholics, personal and public exchanges at the enthronement reflected clearly that special relationship that exists between the Anglican Communion and the Catholic Church.[106]

This was again evident when, in October 2003, the new archbishop of Canterbury paid his first visit to the Holy See. The Holy Father and Archbishop Williams assured each other of their ongoing commitment to search for full visible unity and to find appropriate ways of engaging, where possible, in common witness and mission. During the visit it was decided to set up a special ad hoc subcommission of IARCCUM to reflect jointly on the ecclesiological issues raised by recent developments within the Anglican Communion in the light of relevant agreed statements of ARCIC. One part of its mandate would be to point to resources from their common tradition, most especially from ARCIC's work on ecclesiology, authority, and morals, which might provide ways forward for the Anglican Communion.

The Catholic Church, for its part, is seen at times to fall into the same temptation of sacrificing the search for unity in order to satisfy internal pressures. This has been particularly evident in respect of relations between the Russian Orthodox Church and the Church of Rome. For Pope John Paul II, fostering ecumenical relations with Moscow has been a priority. Such relations became especially delicate and complicated after the revival of the Eastern Rite Greek Catholic Church in the Ukraine, which Stalin had outlawed. The possibility of Latin-rite bishops and clergy carrying out a ministry to the descendants of Polish, German, Lithuanian, and other Catholic communities in Russia after the fall of Communism has been seen by the Russian Orthodox as proselytism. In an interview with RIA Novosti, December 31, 2003, Patriarch Alexy II stated that "the Russian Orthodox Church cannot reconcile itself to the fact that the Catholic missionary orders, whose activity is aimed at converting the Orthodox believers to Catholicism, continue to function in Russia," and pointed out that the main obstacle on the path to "friendly and unhypocritical dialogue" between the two churches is "the Catholic proselytism in Russia and other countries of the Commonwealth of Independent States (CIS) and also the conflict between the Orthodox believers and the Greek Catholics in the Ukraine."[107]

In such a delicate situation, one would expect the legitimate demands of the Ukrainian Greek Catholic Church for the freedom to reestablish its communities and institutions, and of the Latin-rite Catholic communities in Russia to rebuild its church structures and carry out its ministry in conformity with canon law and the normal practice in other places, to be weighed against the desire for better relations and greater unity. In that case, the ecumenical priority would have called for decisions that were not absolutely necessary, to be delayed while greater trust and better relations were established. Unfortunately this was not done, with the result that relations between Moscow and Rome reached a particularly low ebb.

The decision of the Vatican to raise the status, on February 11, 2002, of the four apostolic administrations in the Russian Federation to the rank of dioceses and so create a normal metropolitan province of the Catholic Church was the latest and most serious in a number of similar choices made by the Catholic Church. That the Vatican had the right to do this is not in question. The Russian authorities certainly overreacted. The organization of the dioceses into a metropolitan province was perceived by the Moscow Patriarchate as creating, on the national level, a parallel church to the Russian Orthodox Church. As a consequence, a planned meeting of the delegations of the Holy See and the Moscow Patriarchate scheduled to take place just ten days later was postponed until a more favorable date. In fact, it did not take place until mid-February 2004.

The question is: Would it not have been better, in view of building better relations with Moscow, for the Vatican to delay this move, since it was obvious that there would be such a reaction? Many committed ecumenists would reply in the affirmative. Others within the Catholic Church, however, feel that the only way to deal with Orthodox objections of this nature is to reject them openly, pointing out that the moves in question are simply normal Catholic principles at work, not intended to do harm at all to the Orthodox Church. For instance, with regard to the decision to elevate the apostolic administrations in Russia to the status of dioceses, these people would point out to the Russians that the Moscow Patriarchate has placed metropolitans in Western Europe wherever they have wished. In Vienna, for instance, where there has been a Catholic see since the first millennium, the Russian Orthodox have a metropolitan not just "in" Vienna but "of" Vienna. It is doubtful if there are more than 5,000 Russian Orthodox in all of Austria. While the Russian Orthodox complain that their land is the canonical territory of the Russian Orthodox Church, they do not accept the same law for what would then be the canonical territory of the Church of Rome. There are over 3,000,000 Catholics in Russia, 65,000 of them living in Moscow alone. There is also no common definition of just what is meant by proselytism. Archbishop Tadeusz Kondrusiewicz of Moscow has condemned proselytism, by which he means "efforts to win Orthodox converts." He has stated, "We are condemning proselytism because there is no sense in it. The Russian Orthodox and other Orthodox Churches have the same means of salvation as we Catholics have. I am a Catholic bishop, but for me the Orthodox Church is our sister church. I kneel with equal reverence when I enter their places of worship."[108]

A further source of Russian Orthodox–Catholic tension is the strong claim of the Greek Catholic Church in the Ukraine to have its own patriarch. At present, this Church has at its head a major archbishop, while other much smaller Eastern-rite Catholic Churches, such as the Catholic Copts of Alexandria, have their own patriarch. The situation in the Ukraine is particularly difficult for the Russian Orthodox because of the division there of the Orthodox into three groups, only one of which is recognized by Moscow. Another is led by a patriarch not in communion with Moscow, but resident in Kiev where the Russian Church was born a little over a thousand years ago. In quite an unprecedented move, all the Orthodox Churches have made it clear to the Holy See that a decision by Rome to approve the establishment of a Greek Catholic Patriarchate in the Ukraine would have alarming repercussions, damaging interchurch relations for many years to come. The decision of the Ukrainian

Greek Catholic Church in 2004 to move the see of the major archbishop from Lvov in the Western Ukraine to Kyiv, the capital of the
Ukraine and the traditional birthplace of Russian Christianity, has
only added to the tension.

The dialogue between the Russian Orthodox Church and the
Church of Rome is of importance, not only in itself, but also for the
future of all Catholic-Orthodox relations. In an interesting article,
published in *The Tablet* on November 29, 2003, Archpriest Sergis
Hackel of the Russian Orthodox Church in Great Britain suggests a
way forward that is very close to that indicated already by Pope John
Paul II: "What we need is a love so active and generous that it can
encompass others as they are. Diversity is something to be treasured."

Archpriest Hackel reminds the reader that there was *communio in
sacris*—communion and confession—between the Latins and Greeks
even in the seventeenth century, regardless of the fact that there had
been mutual condemnations of the Christian East and West since 1054.
Metropolitan Nikodim of Leningrad (1929–78) did much to create
understanding and build relations between his church and the Church
of Rome during the Communist times, and he opened up the Orthodox altars to Catholics who had been dispersed throughout the Soviet
Union by the persecutions of the wartime years. Under his auspices in
1969, the Russian synod made the sacraments available to any Catholic
who was seeking to receive them. No conversion was required. This
practice is something the Catholic Church applied to Orthodox in certain circumstances, but this was abandoned later by the Russians under
the influence of other Orthodox Churches. It indicates, nevertheless,
the depth of agreement in faith that already binds together Orthodox
and Catholics.

During 2004, there were signs of a reduction in tension between
Rome and the Orthodox Churches. From all reports it would appear
that the question of a patriarchate for the Ukrainian Greek-Catholic
Church has been put aside at least for the present. Then on February
22, 2004 Cardinal Kasper was able to visit Russia and meet with Russian patriarch Alexy II. Three days earlier Cardinal Kasper and Metropolitan Kirill of Smolensk and Kalingrad agreed to set up a joint
working group for the solution of specific issues in relations between
the Russian Orthodox and Catholic Churches. Representatives of

both churches would meet to examine such questions and make proposals for their solution.[109] A spokesman for the Russian Orthodox
Church, Vsevolod Chaplin, suggested at the close of this visit that the
Vatican was returning to its former view of Orthodoxy as "a sister
church rather than an enemy organization."[110]

The working group set up as a result of Cardinal Kasper's visit
met in Moscow on May 5–6, 2004, to examine a number of situations
of tension between Orthodox and Catholics in Russia, the Ukraine,
Kazakhstan, and Uzbekistan.[111]

Pope John Paul II has taken a further decision that should contribute to better Vatican-Russian relations. In 1993, His Holiness was
able to obtain possession of a precious icon of Our Lady of Kazan
that had been secretly brought out of Russia during the Communist
period and had become the property of a Catholic organization in the
United States. This organization agreed to hand the icon, which was
then at the Fatima shrine in Portugal, to Pope John Paul II so that he
might personally return it to the Russian Orthodox Church in due
course. The Holy Father had for long hoped to hand this precious
icon over to Patriarch Alexy II during a visit to Moscow. Since there
seemed little likelihood of such a visit taking place at least in the foreseeable future, the pope decided to wait no longer but to appoint a
special delegation, led by Cardinal Walter Kasper, to travel to Moscow and present the icon, together with a personal papal message to
the patriarch.

The icon was handed over to Cardinal Kasper in a beautiful,
moving ceremony in the *Aula Paolo VI* during the public audience on
August 25, 2004. Three days later, the cardinal handed the icon to
Patriarch Alexy II in a ceremony at the Kremlin's Dormition Cathedral after a service to mark the Orthodox feast of the assumption. In
receiving the icon, the patriarch told the Vatican delegation:

> Now Russia is welcoming one of the most venerable images
> of the Mother of God of Kazan. This icon has passed a long
> and difficult route over many countries and cities. Orthodox
> and Catholic faithful, Christians of other denominations
> prayed before it. For a long time this icon was carefully kept
> in the Vatican and warmed up the love of the Most Holy

Mother of God, to Russia, to her culture and her cultural heritage in the heart of numerous Catholics. According to the Divine Providence, this holy image is coming home.

Patriarch Alexy II asked Cardinal Kasper "to pass to His Holiness Pope John Paul II our warmest gratitude for this gift," and expressed the hope that "this would testify the firm intention of the Vatican authorities to come back to sincere and respectful relations between our Churches, relations which would be deprived of unkind competition and would be filled with the desire to brotherly help one another."[112]

The presence in Rome of the Ecumenical Patriarch Bartholomew I for the feast of Sts. Peter and Paul, on June 29, 2004, also provided an opportunity for a significant improvement in Orthodox-Catholic relations. The Ecumenical Patriarch had visited Rome for the same feast in 1995, but returned on this occasion to receive the Church of St. Theodore on the Palatine Hill for the use of the Greek Orthodox Archdiocese of Italy. Pope John Paul II explained that he had offered this beautiful, ancient church in the heart of Rome to the Ecumenical Patriarch "to allow the faithful of the Greek Orthodox Archdiocese to have a significant and continuing presence close to the tomb of Peter."[113]

During his stay in Rome, the Ecumenical Patriarch was present and addressed the large gathering in St. Peter's Square during the solemn liturgy for the feast of Rome's patronal saints. On the final morning of the visit, the two church leaders signed a common declaration, dated June 29, 2004, in which they renewed "their firm determination to continue on our way toward full communion with one another in Christ."[114] They recalled with gratitude the historic embrace just forty years earlier between their respective predecessors, Pope Paul VI and Ecumenical Patriarch Athenagoras I on the Mount of Olives, and traced briefly the positive development of relations following that event.

With reference to the Joint International Commission for Theological Dialogue between the Catholic Church and the Orthodox Churches, the two dignitaries expressed their determination to reopen the work of the commission as soon as possible, since "it is

still a suitable instrument for studying the ecclesiological and historical problems that are at the root of our difficulties, and for identifying
hypothetical solutions to them."

The patriarch and the pope expressed the hope that, "in a Europe
moving in the direction of higher forms of integration and expansion
toward the East of the Continent...collaboration between Catholics
and Orthodox may grow," and indicated several fields of activity calling for such cooperation, among them healing with love the scourge
of terrorism and building true dialogue with Islam. They declared:

> Before a world that is suffering every kind of division and
> imbalance, today's encounter is intended as a practical and
> forceful reminder of the importance for Christians and for
> the Churches to coexist in peace and harmony, in order to
> witness in agreement to the message of the Gospel in the
> most credible and continuing way possible.

They then concluded by asking God "to give peace to the Church
and to the world, and to imbue our journey toward full communion
with the wisdom of his Spirit, *"ut unum in Christo simis"* (so that we
may be one in Christ).

The traditional exchange of messages between the two heads of
churches on this occasion, and other interventions during the visit,
were characterized by the same spirit of warm fraternity and hope,
giving the impression that each was making a special effort to ensure
that the meeting would contribute positively to the relationship
between the two churches.

Another source of misunderstanding that has led to doubts being
expressed about the commitment of the Catholic Church to the ecumenical task is to be found in certain documents or statements made
by authorities in Rome that, to say the least, confuse dedicated ecumenists in other churches. The publication, on the eve of the celebration of the second Christian millennium, of a document of the
apostolic penitentiary in Rome restating Catholic tradition on the
question of indulgences to be granted during the Jubilee Year resulted
in the representative of the World Alliance of Reformed Churches
declining the invitation to take part in the ceremonies at St. Paul's
Basilica in Rome on January 16, 2000. On September 5 of the same

Holy Year 2000, the Congregation for the Doctrine of the Faith published a declaration, approved by the Holy Father, entitled *Dominus Jesus: Declaration on the Unicity and Salvific Universality of Jesus Christ and the Church*.[115]

The document received wide publicity, much of which unfortunately was not always accurate and often very polemical. In several quarters the document was not interpreted correctly and such misunderstandings resulted in disappointment and at times pain within other Christian churches and communions, who saw in the declaration a new and negative approach to the ecumenical movement on the part of the Catholic Church, in contrast with that of the Second Vatican Council and subsequent dialogue achievements.

In preparing this declaration, the Congregation for the Doctrine of the Faith had in mind primarily "the dialogue between the Christian faith and the other religious traditions" (3). The declaration stresses a traditional teaching of the Church, contained in the Nicene Creed, confirmed by the Second Vatican Council, and shared with other Christian communities; namely, that Jesus Christ—the Word made flesh and Son of the Father—has an absolutely unique role in the salvation of the world. On this there was no disagreement within Christian ecumenical circles. In the polemical atmosphere that followed the publication of the declaration, this great consensus of Christian affirmation of our basic common understanding of the unique role of Our Lord and Savior Jesus Christ in the work of salvation was mostly overlooked by the media in general, and given little importance in subsequent discussions.

In fact, the heated debates that followed the publication of *Dominus Jesus* centered almost entirely—at least in the Western hemisphere—on the fourth chapter of the document, entitled "Unicity and Unity of the Church." Again, the difficulties were not so much directed at the main thesis exposed by the document, but rather at what seemed to other Christians as the unnecessary negative tone of the statements made and the lack of any recognition of the work done and progress made in the ecumenical field over the past thirty-five years. Reformed Communions in particular objected to the statement that "ecclesial communities which have not preserved the valid Episcopate and the genuine and integral substance of the Eucharistic mystery, are not Churches in the proper sense; however, those who are baptized in these communities are, by Baptism, incorporated in Christ and thus are in a certain communion, albeit imperfect, with the Church" (17). For the Catholic Church, only those churches that are united to her by apostolic succession and a valid Eucharist "are true particular Churches" (17). The Orthodox and Oriental Orthodox Churches, while not existing in perfect communion with the Catholic Church, come into this category.

As mentioned above, ecclesiology is very much at the center of ecumenical theological dialogue. The position of the Catholic Church is certainly not new, but for a Christian community to be denied the title of "church" is bitterly resented. Even the use of the expression "ecclesial communities" creates difficulties in Catholic-Reformed documents.

Coming as it did in the midst of the celebrations for the Jubilee Year, during which other Christian communities had so enthusiastically participated in the Roman celebrations, discussions regarding *Dominus Jesus* dominated for some time almost every ecumenical gathering, with chapter IV the center of attention.

Agreement among Christians on the nature of the church, as founded by Jesus Christ, is of course a matter for intense theological debate. In view of this, some asked the question if the publication of *Dominus Jesus*, containing this chapter especially, was opportune in a year dedicated in a particular way to fostering better relations among all the Christian churches and ecclesial communions.

From these various examples, it seems obvious that much has still to change before the priority and commitment of the Christian communities to what John Paul II has called the *"noble goal"* (*UUS*, 3) of Christian unity, becomes fully accepted by all those responsible for decision-making within these communities. God the Father, in the Son Jesus Christ, is calling Christians to unity. The Holy Spirit is active within the Christian communities, urging Christ's followers forward along the ecumenical path. The coming years will show to what extent those disciples are ready to make the *sacrifice of unity* required for the divine plans to become a reality.

Although most of the details given in this attempt at revisiting Vatican II's teaching on ecumenism are from the period of the pontificate of Pope John Paul II, the foundation for the advances made were already laid during the pontificate of Pope Paul VI during and immediately after the council (1963–78). He established the Secretariat for Christian Unity and gave its members constant support. Moreover, he himself made a particular contribution to Orthodox-Catholic relations. It is perhaps opportune then to complete this study with an understanding of ecumenism as this pope expressed it on March 8, 1964: "Ecumenism—Not constituting a frontier, but opening a door; not closing a dialogue, but keeping it open; not blaming for errors, but seeking virtue; not waiting for those who have not come for four centuries, but going to look for them in a brotherly way."[116]

(Further reading for this section and the next is at the end of the book).

Section II
Interreligious Dialogue

Nostra Aetate

PART I

THE DOCUMENT

BACKGROUND

Having dealt with the decree *Unitatis Redintegratio*, which brought the Catholic Church into the modern ecumenical movement in such a striking and lasting way, I now turn to the contribution that the Second Vatican Council made to interreligious dialogue. Before the council, "interreligious dialogue" was not high on the agenda of the Catholic Church. It was once again Pope John XXIII who wanted the council to make a statement on relations with the Jews, and Cardinal Bea who was entrusted with preparing a document. The story that unfolded proved to be one of the most dramatic of the council, and attracted the attention of the world's press and communications' media.[1]

Christian-Jewish relations have always been an important component of Christian history from the very beginning, and one cannot fully understand the church without appreciating the intimate relationship between Christianity and Judaism. Christianity not only traces its origin to the Jewish community, into which Jesus Christ was born of a young Jewish girl of Nazareth, the Virgin Mary, but it is also built upon the revelation entrusted over the centuries by God to the Jewish people.

In the first two millennia of the modern era, Catholic-Jewish relations were frequently part of a troubled area in the story of Christianity. Unfortunately, the history of these relations is not one of which the Catholic Church can be proud, since all too often it is a story of official oppression and discrimination, as the church gradually considered the Jewish people guilty of "deicide" and consequently rejected by God. In Christian tradition, the Jewish people were considered, with the coming of Christ, to have lost their special place as the people of God. This place had been taken over, as it were, by those who had accepted Christ as their savior, and Christians believed themselves to be the new people of God. Myths and legends that painted the Jews in a terrible light grew over the centuries, and were often portrayed publicly in sculpture, painting, and literature. In Christian understanding, salvation for the Jewish people lay in conversion to Christianity, and at times conversion was the only way that Jews could survive. Yet survive they did, even after six million of their people had been victims, during the Second World War, of the Nazi attempt to eliminate them altogether from the face of Europe. The *Shoah*, or the *Holocaust* as it became known, brought the sad history of Christian-Jewish relations to the attention of council fathers in a way they could not ignore or put aside, despite attempts to do so even within the council.

Other religions were in a quite different situation. In Christian tradition they were often considered pagan, or even the fruit of Satan's presence in the world. Christian mission was primarily addressed to them, or to people of more primitive spiritual beliefs, in the hope of saving the souls of their followers. Dialogue with these religions did take place at times, but it was rare and directed principally at conversion. Some Christian scholars came to appreciate the positive contribution that these great religions made to the spirituality of their followers, but the work of these scholars was often looked upon officially with skepticism and even some concern.

AT THE COUNCIL

The first document to come before the Second Vatican Council dealing with interreligious relations was a schema entitled "Relationship of the Church to Non-Christian Religions." The first three chapters dealt with relations with other great world religions—in particular Hinduism, Buddhism, and Islam—while the fourth chapter was dedicated to Catholic-Jewish relations. Cardinal Bea, in presenting the schema to the council on November 19, 1963, stated that this fourth chapter had been prepared at the express wish of Pope John XXIII before his death. The impression was given that the Holy Father had even approved the basic lines of the document.[2] The reception within the council was not very enthusiastic. Some of the council fathers expressed particular concern at having the Jews mentioned at all in this particular document, preferring that there be a separate statement on Catholic-Jewish relations. Others, including the patriarchs of the Eastern Churches, simply did not want the council to make any statement at all on the Jews. They were deeply concerned that Arab nations would see in such a declaration a political move favoring the State of Israel, and feared that the Christian minorities in these countries might well have to suffer as a consequence. The council fathers voted on the first three chapters of the schema, but no vote was taken on the fourth during the second session of the council.

Between the second and third sessions, the secretariat headed by Bea prepared a new draft on the Jews and other non-Christians, which reached the press and so became widely known. Particular attention was given to a statement in this document that removed from the church's teaching the centuries-old accusation of "deicide" against the Jewish people. This draft, however, was modified somewhat by the coordinating committee before being presented to the council fathers during the third session: the statement removing the charge of "deicide" was no longer there, and the section on non-Christians other than the Jews had been extended, with special attention given to Islam.

A remarkable debate followed that not only saw the restoration of the statement removing "deicide," but the addition of another statement to the effect that scripture could not be invoked to justify persecution or hatred of the Jews. Led by cardinals from France, Germany, Canada, and the United States, a call was made during the debate for all persecutions to be condemned and for insertion of a request for forgiveness from those who had been wronged by Christian persecution. There was still uneasiness in some circles. Cardinal Tappouni and four other Eastern patriarchs wanted the whole document dropped on grounds that it would impede the pastoral work of the church.

More dramatic days passed before the final text was submitted to the council fathers. Reports appeared that the whole document was to be shelved, or that the section on the Jews would be reduced to a single sentence. In the end, the Declaration on the Relationship of the Church to Non-Christian Religions (*Nostra Aetate*) was approved. The proposition that the Jews were not to be regarded as repudiated or cursed by God was accepted on October 28, 1965, by a great majority: of the 2,080 who voted, 1,821 were in the affirmative, 245 negative, and there were 14 invalid votes. However, no reference was made in the final text asking for forgiveness from those who had been persecuted by Christians down through the centuries. Another thirty-five years were to pass before Pope John Paul II would do this on behalf of the church during the Jubilee Year Day of Pardon, March 2000.

During the council, a remarkable change had taken place in Catholic teaching on the Jewish people, and a new era had opened for relations with other world religions. For many of the bishops present at the council, this declaration was the fruit of a new understanding and wider horizons. For the council fathers coming from Europe and North America, relations with the Jewish people were of particular interest, especially as a consequence of their treatment by the Germans during the Second World War. Bishops from other parts of the world at first found it difficult to understand what the fuss was all about, since many of them had very few Jews in their countries and only a vague knowledge of the horrors of the *Shoah*. On the other hand, relations with other world religions were of particular concern to bishops from Asia and Africa, but far less to those from Europe and the Americas.

This was the first time that a council of the church had attempted to deal with questions like these in a positive manner.[3] Yet, in the end, a large consensus had been achieved. Perhaps, looking back, we might find the declaration rather general and abstract in dealing with religions other than the Jewish religion, but as we shall see, the foundation had been laid for future dialogue that has produced good fruit. While the statement on Jewish relations formed only a fifth of the final declaration, it was this chapter that was to have the greatest influence on the church's relations with other non-Christian religions in the coming forty years.

PART II

Major Points

The Declaration on the Relationship of the Church to Non-Christian Religions (*Nostra Aetate*) is a very short document, consisting of just five sections. The opening section explains the motive for making such a statement, together with an explanation of the principles that allow the council to approach this subject. Coming from all over the world, the council fathers were well aware that isolation and barriers between different peoples and nations were gradually disappearing as new forms of social communication brought people closer together. They observed that every day people "are being drawn closer together and the ties between various peoples are becoming stronger" (*NA*, 1). Moreover, the church teaches that "one is the community of all peoples, one their origin, . . . one also is their final goal" (*NA*, 1). The council expressed the hope that this declaration would contribute to greater understanding among people and foster fellowship among nations. The stress placed by the council on what all men and women have in common is a reflection of one of the basic principles of Pope John XXIII's own approach. While not denying or playing down the important differences that exist, emphasis is placed on seeking out and highlighting the positive, shared understandings.

In the second section, the declaration notes that, irrespective of their origin, people ask themselves similar questions about the meaning of life, the existence of good and evil, sorrow and happiness, and similar matters of deep human concern. "From ancient times down to the present, there is found among various peoples a certain perception of that hidden power which hovers over the course of things" (*NA*, 2), and often results in peoples developing a profound religious sense. Some have come to the recognition of a Supreme Divinity and even of a Supreme Father.

This is illustrated then by reference to Hinduism and Buddhism. The declaration indicates certain basic elements of each of these religions that indicate deep spiritual insights, without, however, entering into details or attempting to present a complete introduction. Other religions, too, strive to counter the restlessness of the human heart, each in its own manner, by proposing "ways" and comprising teachings, rules of life, and sacred rites (*NA*, 2).

Then follows an important statement that will greatly influence the church's relationship with other world religions in the postconciliar years:

> The Catholic Church rejects nothing that is true and holy in these religions. She regards with sincere reverence those ways of conduct and of life, those precepts and teachings which, though differing in many aspects from the ones she holds and sets forth, nonetheless often reflect a ray of that Truth which enlightens all men. (*NA*, 2)

The declaration exhorts the members of the church that "through dialogue and collaboration with the followers of other religions, carried out with prudence and love and in witness to the Christian faith and life, they recognize, preserve and promote the good things, spiritual and moral, as well the sociocultural values found among these men" (*NA*, 2). This was a completely new approach to interreligious dialogue on the part of the church. Rather than stress and condemn what is to be found there that is not compatible with Christian teaching and understanding, dialogue and cooperation are proposed. In this way a promising field for fruitful collaboration with other great religions is prepared.

A special third section is dedicated to relations with Islam. It points out the special links that exist between Christians and Muslims: Muslims "adore the one God, living and subsisting in Himself, merciful and all-powerful, the Creator of heaven and earth, who has spoken to men; they take pains to submit wholeheartedly to even His inscrutable decrees, just as Abraham, with whom the faith of Islam takes pleasure in linking itself, submitted to God" (*NA*, 3). They revere Jesus as a prophet and honor Mary his virgin mother, to whom they turn to at times with devotion. They await the day of judgment when God will give each man his due after raising him up, and consequently they prize the moral life while giving worship to God, especially through prayer, almsgiving, and fasting. Even today, many Christians are surprised to learn that they have so much in common with Muslims. The invocation of the Koran to justify acts of terrible violence by fundamentalist Muslims continues to create a false understanding of the teaching of that holy book. The council does not ignore the fact that in the course of centuries "not a few quarrels and hostilities have arisen between Christians and Muslims," but it urges all "to forget the past and to work sincerely for mutual understanding" (*NA*, 3). For the good of all mankind, Christians and Muslims are called upon "to promote together for the benefit of all mankind social justice and moral welfare, as well as peace and freedom" (*NA*, 3).

The fourth section of the declaration is dedicated to relations with the Jewish people. It was this that Pope John XXIII had in mind when he invited Cardinal Bea to prepare a document for the presentation to the council. It was here the declaration had its beginning, and this section has had a life of its own in the postconciliar period, as we shall see later.

Finally, a concluding fifth section moves from specific religions to a statement embracing all peoples. In a strong affirmation, the council points out that Catholics "cannot truly call on God, the Father of all, if we refuse to treat in a brotherly way any man, created as he is in the image of God" (*NA*, 5). When it comes to human dignity, there is no ground in theory or practice for distinctions between peoples. As a consequence "the Church reproves, as foreign to the mind of Christ, any discrimination against people or harassment of them because of their race, color, condition of life, or religion." The document concludes with an appeal to all the Christian faithful to "maintain good fellowship among the nations" (1 Peter 2:12), and if possible "to live for their part in peace with all men (Cf. Rom 12:18), so that they may truly be sons of the Father who is in heaven (Cf. Matt. 5:45)" (*NA*, 5).

PART III

Implementation

In the immediate postconciliar period, relations with the Jewish people came under the competence of the Secretariat for Christian Unity, while relations with the other non-Christian religions were entrusted to the Secretariat for Non-Christians. This arrangement was decided by Pope Paul VI, on the advice of Cardinal Bea. Having carried the responsibility for the documents on Christian unity and non-Christian religions through the council sessions, Bea then became the first president of the Secretariat for Christian Unity. A longtime scripture professor, he was well aware of the special relationship between the Christian and Jewish religions. As a consequence of the decision to entrust Catholic-Jewish relations to a commission within the Secretariat for Christian Unity, the study of developments regarding the declaration *Nostra Aetate* begins at this point to follow two distinct paths: first, relations with non-Christian religions other than Judaism, and then developments based on section 4 of *Nostra Aetate*.

RELATIONS WITH NON-CHRISTIAN RELIGIONS, OTHER THAN JUDAISM

The Secretariat for Non-Christians

On Pentecost Sunday, 1964, Pope Paul VI instituted a special department of the Roman curia for relations with peoples of other religions. Known at first as the Secretariat for Non-Christians, in 1988 it was renamed by Pope John Paul II as the Pontifical Council for Interreligious Dialogue (PCID). Already during the discussion of the Second

Vatican Council, Pope Paul VI realized that the work done by the council would need a special organ of the curia to carry forward and develop the decisions of the council fathers in what would be a new field of activity for the Catholic Church. A great deal of effort would have to be made in order to bring the renewal called for by the council into the life of the particular churches. Above all, age-old mentalities would have to change. Millions of people all over the world would be affected. The Roman curia would obviously be deeply involved in this process and for that purpose would have to be expanded.

In announcing the establishment of the Secretariat for Non-Christians, Pope Paul VI expressed the hope that in the future "no pilgrim, no matter how distant the country from which he comes may be by geography or religion, will be a complete stranger in this Rome, which remains faithful still today to the historical program that the Catholic faith conserves as 'Patria communis.'"[4] The new dicastery for relations with non-Christians, under the presidency of Cardinal Paolo Marella, would have a small number of officials based in Rome, supported in their task by members and consulters chosen from among the bishops, clergy, religious, and laity from all over the world.

The way in which the secretariat would carry out its work of coming to a loyal and respectful dialogue with all those "who believe in God and worship him" was given as follows:

- First, by establishing a new relationship in the *psychological* order, by breaking down barriers resulting from misunderstandings, calumny, prejudice on the part of both sides, intolerance and hurtful insults to the other partner, and by promoting attitudes inspired by truth and brotherliness. In other words, by an approach on the human level.

- Second, by seeking reciprocal understanding on an *ideological* plain through greater and more intimate knowledge of the religions and clarity on what they have in common with the Christian faith and where we differ; also, by offering members of other religions the possibility of obtaining a better knowledge of Christianity and its way of life.

- Third, by making contacts and encouraging personal encounters to facilitate understanding and cooperation between Christians and non-Christians, as desired by the council.

"Through the Secretariat, the Church extends a hand to our brothers and sisters on their way to God, who is the end of every human life."[5]

On August 6, 1964, Pope Paul VI issued the encyclical *Ecclesiam Suam* to explain and promote the work of the council throughout the church.[6] In this document, there are special considerations on dialogue with Jews and other non-Christians. In a section dedicated to "Worshippers of the One God," after having read about dialogue with non-believers, we then read:

> Then we see another circle around us. This too is vast in extent, yet not so far away from us. It comprises first of all those men who worship the one supreme God, whom we also worship. We would mention first the Jewish people, who still retain the religion of the Old Testament, and who are indeed worthy of our respect and love.
>
> Then we have those worshipers who adhere to other monotheistic systems of religion, especially the Muslim religion. We do well to admire these people for all that is good and true in their worship of God. And finally we have the followers of the great Afro-Asiatic religions.
>
> Obviously we cannot agree with these various forms of religion, nor can we adopt an indifferent or uncritical attitude toward them on the assumption that they are all to be regarded as on an equal footing, and that there is no need for those who profess them to enquire whether or not God has Himself revealed definitively and infallibly how He wishes to be known, loved, and served. Indeed, honesty compels us to declare openly our conviction that the Christian religion is the one and only true religion, and it is our hope that it will be acknowledged as such by all who look for God and worship Him.
>
> But we do not wish to turn a blind eye to the spiritual and moral values of the various non-Christian religions, for we desire to join with them in promoting and defending common ideals in the spheres of religious liberty, human brother-

hood, education, culture, social welfare, and civic order. Dialogue is possible in all these great projects, which are our concern as much as theirs, and we will not fail to offer opportunities for discussion in the event of such an offer being favorably received in genuine, mutual respect. (107–108)

The secretariat approached this difficult task by a twofold path: first, by promoting within the Catholic Church the radically new understanding of the relation of the church to the other great world religions as set out in *Nostra Aetate*; and then by making a constant effort to establish contact and develop dialogue with these religions, with the aim of building trust and breaking down barriers. The methodology of this dicastery of the Holy See has been explained as follows:

1. Dialogue is a two-way communication. It implies listening, giving, and receiving, for mutual growth and enrichment. It includes witness to one's own faith as well as openness to that of the other. It is not a betrayal of the mission of the church, nor is it a new method of conversion to Christianity. This has been clearly stated in the encyclical letter of Pope John Paul II *Redemptoris Missio*.

2. Although the secretariat is the central office for dialogue in the Catholic Church, dialogue is to be carried out mainly in and through the local churches. Local churches were to set up dialogue commissions, both at the national and regional level. This would take some time, but it was the desire of the Roman dicastery from the beginning to work in close collaboration with such commissions, and encourage their formation where they did not yet exist.

3. The ecumenical dimension of interreligious dialogue is kept in mind. From very early on, the secretariat entered into an ongoing relationship with the corresponding office of the World Council of Churches.

4. The secretariat would restrict itself to religious questions. Its brief does not extend to sociopolitical issues, which are the competence

of other dicasteries. Broader issues are discussed in interdepartmental meetings.[7]

The activities of the secretariat, and later of its successor, the Pontifical Council for Interreligious Dialogue, have centered around studies and publications; participation of staff members in meetings, conferences, and other interfaith gatherings; and also the organization of similar meetings, on both the bilateral and multilateral level. Visits to the local churches have helped the dicastery officials to become more familiar with the situations in different parts of the world and to encourage dialogue at the local level. An important activity has been that of welcoming visitors from the local churches, but also representatives of the other world religions, to the secretariat.

Pope Paul VI received Cardinal Marella and a group of consulters of the secretariat on January 16, 1967, in a private audience, during which he expressed thanks for the work being done by this new office of the Roman curia, and encouraged those present not to lose heart in the face of the difficulties before them. He spoke of boundless horizons on the one hand, but also noted the limits to their competence on the other. He urged them to be patient and remain docile to the Spirit, even should they find themselves working as if groping in the dark.[8]

The First Ten Years of the Secretariat

The first publication to come from the secretariat was a kind of guidebook, setting out general principles for dialogue: *Vers la recontre des Religions* (Toward a Meeting of the Religions), published in 1967. The first of a series of publications on specific religions appeared in 1969: *A la recontre des Religions Africanes* (Toward a Meeting with African Religions) and *Orientations pour un Dialogue entre chrétiens et musulmans* (Indications for a Dialogue between Christians and Muslims). *Toward a Meeting with Buddhism* followed in 1970.

As early as 1967, we find representatives from the secretariat taking part in an interreligious congress in Kandy, Sri Lanka. But in the early years, the emphasis was mostly on promoting understanding within the Catholic Church, while making first contacts with some representatives of other religions. By the close of the first ten years of its existence, the secretariat was receiving visits from important leaders of other world religions. From September 29 to October 1, 1973, the Dalai Lama made his first visit to the office; in June of the same year, the Buddhist patriarch of Laos, Somdeth Phra Buddganjinorot, was received there.

Looking back on these first ten years, the secretariat offered an overview of its activities to the synod of bishops that was meeting in 1973 to discuss reconciliation and penitence. The following is a summary of the presentation made by the pro-president of the secretariat, Archbishop Jean Jadot:

1. Interreligious dialogue is carried out at different levels: it begins with a *dialogue of life* that is directed toward a friendly coexistence that enriches the partners by living out the human and spiritual values of the respective faiths. Then there is the *cultural dialogue*, consisting of exchanges and collaboration that foster knowledge and reciprocal understanding. Then there is *religious dialogue on the doctrinal level* and spiritual experience.

2. The second of these levels concerns preeminently the local churches since they live together and are in contact with non-Christians, sharing with them the same culture and social conditions. The secretariat seeks to make the local churches aware of this possibility, and to cooperate with them by promoting communion and information among them.

3. Interreligious dialogue is closely linked with the process of inculturation, and assists the church in its task of being present and giving Christian witness.

4. Interreligious dialogue is an essential dimension of the whole church, since in these years the presence of various religions is increasing in all the continents and countries. A particular problem is being caused by the sects or new religious movements[9] that seem to be on the increase everywhere.

5. Islam merits particular attention because of its monotheistic faith, as well as for its increasing presence in traditional Christian countries, and for its reawakening and sociopolitical implications. Evangelical motivations and attitudes should guide our initiative toward ever more constructive relations with Muslims, even when a certain intransigence violates the rights of religious minorities.

Archbishop Jadot then offered a number of recommendations to the episcopal conferences represented at the synod:

• The setting up, support, and effective commitment of bishops' commissions for interreligious dialogue
• The creation of scientific study centers of the religions at the national level and for large cultural regions
• The offering of study courses on the non-Christian religions in seminaries, theological faculties, and centers of religious and pastoral formation

In conclusion, he assured the bishops that the secretariat is at the service of the Holy See and of the local churches.

The early efforts of the secretariat in the first ten years of its existence, in seeking to bring alive throughout the Catholic Church the principles and hopes set out in *Nostra Aetate*, have continued along the same lines in the thirty years following that beginning. For the purpose of this study, I believe that we can now concentrate on the important publications that have been prepared by the secretariat and on some major international gatherings that are an indication of the progress made in the forty years since the Second Vatican Council.

Interreligious Gatherings of Importance

Tripoli, 1976

Of the many interreligious meetings in which the secretariat played an important role, the Christian-Islam Congress in Tripoli, Libya,[10] from February 1–5, 1976, deserves particular attention. It was a meeting of two official delegations, to which observers were invited. Some five hundred were present and came from all over the world. Cardinal Sergio Pignedoli, who had taken over as president of the secretariat in 1973, led the Catholic participation.

The program set out to consider the following:

- A common basic approach to faith and morals
- Religion as providing an ideology for life
- Social justice as the fruit of faith in God
- Means of eliminating the misunderstandings and hostility between Christians and Muslims that have multiplied over the centuries

Unfortunately, some discrepancy between the Arabic and English texts signed at the close of this meeting greatly embarrassed Cardinal Pignedoli, since his signature appeared on the Arab document though it contained statements of which he was not aware. Despite this regrettable incident, the secretariat considered the Congress a success, as can be seen from the following conclusions published at the time. The Catholic delegation agreed upon these points:

- Dialogue with Islam is necessary and urgent. The Muslim presence, which makes up such a large section of the world population, is becoming daily more visible both on the political and economic horizons. If we wish to make known something of the Gospel in this world, the only way open is that of dialogue in its early forms of listening and accepting, and eliminating hostility and prejudice. In this sense, the Catholic delegation was convinced that valuable work was done at Tripoli, and sincerely hoped that its fruits would not be lost.

- It must be recognized that dialogue with Muslims is difficult. There is a great difference between Christian and Muslim understanding of history, culture, social development, and religious mentality, and it is only now that Christians are beginning to understand this more fully.

- The most valid methodology for future Christian-Muslim dialogue is the one currently being followed, namely, personal contact and welcome, by which we seek to consider ourselves, and hope to be accepted, as friends in the name of the one God, while offering Muslims an example of humility and unselfish generosity.

Day of Prayer for Peace, Assisi, 1986

This very special event in the post–Vatican Council period has already been mentioned in the section on ecumenism. A number of Christian churches and ecclesial communions took part in this event, but it was considered predominantly an expression of interreligious dialogue, and it was the Secretariat for Non-Christians that was mainly responsible for its preparation and organization. The gathering of religions in Assisi was an initiative of Pope John Paul II, who early in 1986 at the close of the Week of Prayer for Christian Unity had launched a special appeal for prayer for peace. His Holiness noted in so doing that the United Nations Organization had proclaimed 1986 as an International Year for Peace. His Holiness announced that he was

> initiating opportune consultations with the leaders, not only of the various Christian churches and Communions, but also of the other religions of the world, to organize with them a special meeting of prayer for peace, in the city of Assisi, a place which the seraphic figure of St. Francis has transformed into a center of universal brotherhood.[11]

As Pope John Paul II had expected, the choice of Assisi proved to be particularly auspicious. It is one of the few places in the world in which all Christian communities and representatives of other world religions are able to gather without hesitation. His Holiness took the occasion of his Angelus address on September 21, 1986, to thank all those who had accepted his invitation and to make it clear that "each one present at Assisi will pray to God according to his own religious tradition."[12]

The meeting in Assisi took place on October 27, 1986, with the following format:

- The "Welcoming Encounter" consisted of a greeting to all the participants by the pope at the door of the Basilica of St. Mary of the Angels, and a brief allocution by His Holiness explaining the purpose of the encounter and of the entire day.

- From there, all proceeded to the place stipulated for prayer by each religion in the city of Assisi.

- In the third part of the day, all came together in the Lower Square of Saint Francis for common witness and prayer. Each religious tradition offered its own proper prayer for peace in the presence of all the assembly: Buddhist, Hindu, Jainist, Muslim, Shinto, Sikh, Traditionalist African, Traditionalist Amerindian, Zoroastrian, Jewish, and Christian. By raising an olive branch in a symbolic gesture in reply to questions proposed by young people, those present committed themselves "1) to making peace a central aim of our prayer and action, as religious men and women; 2) to building peace in our families, in our countries, among the religions we profess and among the nations of the world; 3) to overcoming injustice with justice, hate with love, resentment with forgiveness, violence with meekness, division with unity."[13]

This first Assisi meeting was attended by thirty-four representatives of non-Christian religions: twelve from Islam; nine from Buddhism; four from Hinduism; five from Traditional Religions of Africa and America; and one each from Shintoism, Jainism, Sikhism, and Zoroastrianism.

At the end of 1986, Pope John Paul II in his annual Christmas address to the Roman curia, referred to the Day of Prayer at Assisi as "the *religious event* that attracted the greatest attention in the world in this year which is drawing to a close." He continued:

Indeed, on that day, and in the prayer which was its motivation and its entire content, there seemed for a moment to be even a visible expression of the hidden but radical unity which the Divine Word, "in whom everything was created, and in whom everything exists" (Col 1:16; John 1:3), has established among the men and women of this world, both those who now share together the anxieties and the joys of this portion of the twentieth century and those who have gone before us in history, and also those who will take up our places "until the Lord comes" (Cf. 1 Cor 11:26). The fact that we came together in Assisi to pray, to fast and to walk in silence—and this in support of the peace that is always fragile and threatened, perhaps today more than ever—has been, as it were, a clear sign of the profound unity of those who seek in religion spiritual and transcendent values that respond to the great questions of the human heart, despite the concrete divisions (Cf. *Nostra Aetate*, 1).[14]

In this comment on the Assisi meeting, Pope John Paul II expressed a basic approach that characterizes the path that he and the Catholic Church have taken in respect to interreligious dialogue. As we shall see in the major document published later by the PCID, this dialogue is not to be considered just as a means to promoting peace and harmony among religions and peoples, but is demanded of the church by the mystery of unity. "There is but one plan of salvation for all mankind, with its center in Jesus Christ, who in his Incarnation has united himself in a certain manner to every person" (*Redemptor Hominis* [*RH*], 13).

Assisi Day of Prayer for Peace in Bosnia-Herzegovina, 1993

On December 1, 1992, a meeting of the presidents of the European episcopal conferences with Pope John Paul II in Rome made an appeal for peace in Bosnia-Herzegovina, a part of the former Republic of Yugoslavia that was in the throes of a terrible civil war. It was decided to call for a special day of prayer again at Assisi the following month. The appeal was directed in the first place to the Catholic churches in Europe, but a cordial invitation was issued at the same time to other churches and Christian communities of Europe, as well as to Muslims and Jews.

Forty-seven delegations were present in Assisi for this event on January 9 and 10, 1993. The opening ceremony on Saturday evening, January 9, was in two parts: The first was held in the Franciscan convent next to the Basilica of St. Francis and consisted of testimonies from the war zone in Bosnia-Herzegovina, including those of two Muslim representatives from the Islamic Center, Sarajevo. This was followed by separate prayer services for the Christian, Jewish, and Muslim participants, after which a procession went forth through the streets of Assisi.

On the morning of January 10, ceremonies concluded with a Mass in the Basilica of St. Francis, followed by a special address by the pope to the Muslim delegation. This was not strictly an interreligious gathering, but a day of special prayer for the Catholic communities of Europe, to which other Christians, Muslims, and Jews were invited. A number of the Muslim representatives, however, were present at their own request at the Mass on Sunday morning.[15]

Interreligious Assembly, Vatican, 1999

As the Jubilee Year 2000 was approaching, the Pontifical Council for Interreligious Dialogue expressed concern that other religious traditions might interpret as triumphalistic and perhaps even threatening such an extraordinary celebration by the Christian world. Pope John Paul II had sought in his apostolic letter On the Coming of the Third Millennium (*Tertio Millennio Adveniente*) to allay such fears. Number 53 of this document states:

> On the other hand, as far as the field of religious awareness is concerned, the eve of the year 2000 will provide a great opportunity, especially in view of the events of recent decades, for *interreligious dialogue*, in accordance with the specific guidelines set down by the Second Vatican Council in its declaration *Nostra Aetate* on the relationship of the church to non-Christian religions. In this regard, the Jews and the Muslims ought to have a preeminent place. God grant that as a confirmation of these intentions it may also be possible to hold *joint meetings* in places of significance for the great monotheistic religions.... However, care will always have to be taken not to cause harmful misunderstandings, avoiding the risk of syncretism and of a facile and deceptive irenicism.[16]

A new millennium, even though it may not have the same significance for others as for Christians, is nevertheless a threshold to cross, a significant goal to reach. It was hoped that the participation of non-Christians in the joy of the Christian community would provide a tangible sign of the reciprocal sharing and understanding that are essential elements of interreligious dialogue.

In this context, an interreligious assembly was held in the Vatican from October 25–28, 1999. Representatives of various religious traditions joined Catholic and other Christian leaders in a four-day meeting with the theme *"On the Eve of the Third Millennium, Collaboration between Different Religions."* There were approximately two hundred participants from sixty countries, half of whom were Christian and half members of other religions. In all, eighteen traditions were represented.

The meeting consisted of three days of discussion in the synodal hall within the Vatican, where the principal address was given by Teresa Ee Chooi of Malaysia, president of the Catholic Press Union. Discussions followed in groups, and the results were presented to the assembly. A concluding report and an appeal were approved and then read during the closing ceremony in St. Peter's Square on October 28. On the previous day, which was the anniversary of the 1986 Assisi Day of Prayer for Peace, the participants went on pilgrimage to Assisi.

The concluding ceremony took place in St. Peter's Square with Pope John Paul II presiding. Earlier each group had offered prayers according to its own tradition in different locations nearby. Six people who were engaged in interreligious dialogue gave significant and encouraging testimonies. The appeal that had been approved in the synodal hall was read, and each of those participating in the assembly received a candle that was lit from a five-branch brazier, symbol of the five continents (Africa, America, Europe, Asia, and Oceania). The ceremony concluded with an address from Pope John Paul II.

This event received widespread coverage in many geographical and religious contexts as a result of the publication of the acts or proceedings of the assembly in three languages and of the distribution of a videocassette on the event and on the spirit of interreligious dialogue.[17] During the Jubilee year that followed, and undoubtedly linked to the experience of this assembly, significant numbers of members of other religions were present at various Jubilee events. Many came from Italy, but there were Buddhists from Japan and Muslims from the United States, and these were present not as tourists but with the desire to be spiritually part of events that seemed important also for them. A large group of young people of other religions joined Catholic youth from all over the world for the 2000 World Day of Youth in Rome in August. For this celebration, the Focolare movement had invited a good number of friends from the Jewish, Buddhist, Hindu, and Muslim communities.

The acts of this assembly have been published by the Central Committee for the Great Jubilee of the Year 2000 and the PCID under the title *Toward a Culture of Dialogue*.

Day of Prayer for Peace, Assisi, 2002

In the aftermath of the events of September 11, 2001, world peace was once again being threatened. In particular, tension had grown between the rest of the world and certain Muslim countries. Fears were being expressed in the Vatican of a possible deterioration that could lead to a great conflict. On November 18, 2001, in a Sunday Angelus address, Pope John Paul II referred to "worrisome tensions" that continued to disturb the international scene, a situation "made dramatic by the ever present threat of terrorism." He called on Catholics to observe a special day of prayer and fasting on December 14, and then announced his intention "to invite the representatives of the world religions to come to Assisi on January 24, 2002, to pray for the overcoming of opposition and the promotion of authentic peace." In particular, he hoped "to bring Christians and Muslims together to proclaim to the world that religion must never be a reason for conflict, hatred and violence."[18]

Again, the response was particularly encouraging and on this occasion Pope John Paul II traveled by special train from Vatican City to Assisi with the other participants. Apart from Jewish representatives, roughly one hundred members of the following non-Christian religions participated: Islam, Buddhism, Hinduism, Jainism, Traditional African Religions, Sikhism, Zoroastrianism, Shintoism, Confucianism, Tendai, Rissho Kosei-Kai, Myochikai, and Tenrikyo.[19] On the day preceding the Assisi journey, the PCID organized a forum of religious participants on contributions that the various religions can make toward creating a climate of peace. The acts of this forum were published by the PCID in 2002 under the title *Peace: A Single Goal and a Shared Intention*. This volume includes also a full report on the actual World Day of Peace in Assisi.[20]

This celebration in Assisi was notable for the serene, fraternal climate of prayer in which it was held. The program for the day consisted of a welcome, testimonies for peace, prayer in different locations, a fraternal meal in the Franciscan convent, an act of commitment to peace, and a conclusion.

The first act after arrival in the morning took place in the Piazza San Francesco, where testimonies for peace were given by Christian leaders, including Ecumenical Patriarch Bartholomew I, the archbishop of Canterbury, and the secretaries general of the Lutheran World Federation and the World Alliance of Reformed Churches. Testimonies from other religions were given by Geshe Tashi Tsering (Buddhism), Chief Amadou Gassetto (African Traditional Religion), Didi Talwalkar (Hinduism), Sheik Al-Azhar Mohammed Tantawi (Islam), and Rabbi Israel Singer (Judaism).

Prayer was then offered in ten separate locations by the various religious communities represented at the meeting. After a fraternal meal that celebrated agape, the delegates assembled again in the Piazza San Francesco. A common commitment to peace was read in different languages by representatives of the religions taking part in the day of prayer, and concluded with the following declaration by Pope John Paul II:

> Violence never again!
> War never again!
> Terrorism never again!
> In the name of God,
> may every religion bring upon the earth
> justice and peace,
> forgiveness and life, love!

The Holy Father then made his way to a specially prepared pedestal and placed a lighted candle-lamp there. The representatives of other religions did the same after him. All present then exchanged a sign of peace, and Pope John Paul II concluded the meeting with a word of thanks to those who had taken part.

On the following day, the participants had lunch with Pope John Paul II and took home with them the peace lamp that each one had lit in Assisi.

World Religions Congress, Astana, 2003

The First Congress of Leaders of World and Traditionally National Religions was held from September 23–24, 2003, in Astana, the capital of the Republic of Kazakhstan. The Catholic Church was invited and was represented by a delegation headed by Cardinal Josef Tomko.[21]

Pope John Paul II sent a message to the president of the congress, His Excellency Mr. Nursultan Nazarbayev, and all the participants, in which he affirmed that "the Catholic Church, on the basis of the revealed teaching living within her, is committed to support every sincere effort in favor of a genuine peace based on truth, justice, love and freedom."[22] In wishing the congress every success, the pope saw this initiative of the Kazakhstan authorities as being "in the spirit of Assisi" and able to promote respect for human dignity, the defense of religious freedom, and the growth of mutual understanding among peoples, "convinced as we are that religion, properly understood, shows itself to be a solid instrument for the promotion of peace." A Franciscan delegation from Assisi participated in the congress.

The declaration at the close of the congress stated that "extremism, terrorism and other forms of violence in the name of religion have nothing to do with genuine understanding of religion, but are threats to human life and should be rejected." Similarly, the congress affirmed "that interreligious dialogue is one of the key means for social development and the promotion of the well-being of all peoples, fostering tolerance, mutual understanding and harmony among different cultures and religions, and operating to bring an end to conflicts and violence." A commitment was made to strengthen cooperation in promoting spiritual values and the culture of dialogue with the aim of ensuring peace in the new millennium. Educational programs and the means of social communication were seen as essential elements for promoting positive attitudes toward religions and cultures. The participants looked forward to joint actions to ensure peace and progress for humanity and declared themselves "ready to strain every effort not to allow the use of religious differences as an instrument of hatred and discord, in order to save mankind from a global conflict of religions and cultures."

It was agreed that the congress should be convened at least once every three years under the title "The Congress of Leaders of World and Traditional Religions." A secretariat will be set up and the second congress will also be held in Astana, the Republic of Kazakhstan.[23]

Publications by the Vatican Secretariat

Dialogue and Mission

After a plenary session of the Secretariat for non-Christians dedicated to considerations on mission and dialogue, the secretariat published at Pentecost 1984 a short document with the title *The Attitude of the Church Toward the Followers of Other Religions: Reflections and Orientations on Dialogue and Mission*.[24] This document has become known simply as *Dialogue and Mission (DM)*. Remaining faithful to the teaching of *Nostra Aetate*, Dialogue and Mission evaluates, broadens, and consolidates the commitment of the Catholic Church to dialogue with other religious traditions. The Dogmatic Constitution on the Church (*Lumen Gentium*) speaks about the people of other religious traditions as being "related" to the people of God (*LG*, 16). *Dialogue and Mission* takes this principle forward by placing dialogue within the very mission of church, which is oriented toward the realization of the kingdom of God.

Dialogue and Mission is divided into three parts: (I) Mission, (II) Dialogue, and (III) Dialogue and Mission. In the first section, the document explains its purpose. "It intends to encourage behavior formed by the Gospel in its encounters with believers of other faiths with whom Christians live in the city, at work, and in the family" (*DM*, 6). It sees dialogue as a way of relating to others, and the accent is on positive and constructive relations with communities and individuals of other faiths. This dialogue becomes an exchange of gifts, promoting mutual understanding.

In an important second section, *Dialogue and Mission* states that dialogue with people of other faith traditions is situated within the very mission of the church. This section recalls the teaching of the Second Vatican Council which declared that other religious traditions contain "elements that are true and good...elements of truth and grace." In them God has sown the "seeds of the Word." *Dialogue and Mission* affirms that interreligious dialogue is not something that is left to the choice of a Christian, but is an obligation for every member of the church. Four forms of dialogue are open to Christians: *dialogue of life*, by a true Christian witness of charity, mercy, pardon, reconciliation, and peace; *dialogue of collaboration or deeds*, by common efforts in the fields of humanitarian, social, economic, and political activity, directed toward the liberation and advancement of mankind; *dialogue of reflection*, by which the Christian, without ignoring the differences that exist among religions, recognizes the treasures of other religious traditions; *dialogue of religious experience*, through prayer and contemplation.

> It must first be kept in mind that every quest of the human spirit for truth and goodness, and in the last analysis for God, is inspired by the Holy Spirit.... In every authentic religious experience, the most characteristic expression is prayer. Because of the human spirit's constitutive openness to God's action of urging it to self-transcendence, we can hold that every authentic prayer is called forth by the Holy Spirit, who is mysteriously present in the heart of every person. (*DM*, 285)

The third and final section of the document deals with the relationship between mission and dialogue. Here the emphasis is on the fact that the apostolate of interreligious dialogue is one way of building God's kingdom.

Dialogue and Mission is certainly a positive development in the church's understanding of her relationship with other religious traditions. While being firmly rooted in the council declaration *Nostra Aetate*, the document strengthens the church's commitment to interreligious dialogue by pointing out the link between dialogue and mission, and then by affirming dialogue as an essential element of the church's mission (*DM*, 13). This official declaration makes it clear that, contrary to widespread thinking in the church in the years following the Second Vatican Council, interreligious dialogue cannot be reserved to specialists. Since every Christian is called to mission, every member of the church is by that very fact expected to participate in promoting interreligious dialogue.

Dialogue and Proclamation

By inserting dialogue into the mainstream activities of the church, or rather by recognizing its legitimate place in these activities, *Dialogue and Mission* raised for many the question of how such dialogue was to be related to the duty of the church to proclaim Jesus Christ to the world. Did this mean that proclamation was now obsolete, as some missionaries were saying? Had dialogue become the new name of mission? Or was dialogue simply another way of bringing about conversion to the Christian church? "These were important questions which could not be eluded. On the one hand lay the danger of sapping the missionary vitality of the Church, and on the other the risk of arousing the suspicions of people of other religions with regard to the purpose of dialogue."[25]

The decision was therefore taken by the Secretariat for Non-Christians to publish a new document that would study the relationship between dialogue and proclamation. This document, *Dialogue and Proclamation: Reflection and Orientations on Interreligious Dialogue and the Proclamation of the Gospel of Jesus Christ*[26] (*DP*), was prepared under the authority of both the prefect of the Congregation for the Evangelization of Peoples and the president of the Secretariat for Non-Christians. The text remains the responsibility of the secretariat, and was endorsed by the plenary assembly of that dicastery in 1990. With the approval of the Congregation for the Doctrine of the Faith, it was published at Pentecost, May 19, 1991.

As this text was in its final stages of preparation for publication, Pope John Paul II gave the church his encyclical *Redemptoris Missio*, in which he addresses, among other questions, the relation of dialogue and mission. The document of the Secretariat for Non-Christians spells out in greater detail the teaching of the encyclical on dialogue and its relationship to proclamation, and should therefore be read in the light of the encyclical.

It was obvious that precise definitions were needed of the terms being used in this context, and *Dialogue and Proclamation* begins by stating clearly what is meant by *evangelization, dialogue,* and *proclamation* (*DP*, 8–10). The term *evangelization* can refer to the mission of the church in its totality, including, of course, efforts "to convert solely through the divine power of the message she proclaims both the personal and collective consciences of people, the activities in which they engage, their ways of life, and the actual milieu in which they live" (*Evangelii Nuntiandi* [*EN*], 18). But it can also include "the clear and unambiguous proclamation of the Lord Jesus" (*EN*, 22). In *Dialogue and Proclamation,* the first of these actions is referred to as *evangelization,* the second as *proclamation.*

The first section of the document is dedicated to an in-depth study of "interreligious dialogue," examining the scriptural basis for a theology of dialogue, as well as briefly presenting the views of the fathers of the church on this question. More space is given then to the teachings of Vatican II and developments in the subsequent magisterium. The document strongly emphasizes that the unique way of salvation is in Jesus Christ. At the same time it recalls Pope John Paul II's teaching on the mystery of the unity of all mankind. God has created all men and women in his own image and as a result of this common origin, the whole of humankind forms one family. All are called to a common destiny, the fullness of life in God. Moreover, there is but one plan of salvation for humankind, with its center in Jesus Christ, who in his incarnation "has united himself in a certain manner to every person" (*RH*, 13; cf. *Gaudium et Spes* [*GS*], 22.2). This mystery of unity, according to Pope John Paul II, was manifested clearly at Assisi in 1986, "in spite of differences between religious professions" (*DP*, 28). "From this mystery of unity it follows that all men and women who are saved share, though differently, in the same mystery of salvation in Jesus Christ through his Spirit.... The mystery of salvation reaches out to them, in a way known to God, through the invisible action of the Spirit of Christ" (*DP*, 29). Those who are not Christian remain unaware that Jesus Christ is the source of their salvation. How they enter into this mystery of salvation is left open, though it is suggested that "concretely it will be in the sincere practice of what is good in their own religious traditions and by following the dictates of their conscience" (*DP*, 29).

The document stresses again the understanding of interreligious dialogue as forming part of the church's evangelizing mission:

> The Church's commitment to dialogue is not merely anthropological but primarily theological. God, in an age-long dialogue, has offered and continues to offer salvation to

humankind. In faithfulness to the divine initiative, the Church too must enter into a dialogue of salvation with all men and women. (*DP*, 38)

Dialogue and Proclamation acknowledges that interreligious dialogue can be difficult, and mentions some of the more important obstacles that may affect the process of dialogue. Some of these arise from insufficient grounding in one's own faith or a lack of preparation for dialogue with members of other religious traditions. Other difficulties come from intolerance, which can be associated with political or racial factors, but can also be grounded in religious prejudice. A correct attitude is needed if one is to initiate and remain in dialogue: a balanced approach, neither ingenuous nor overly critical; rootedness in one's own faith conviction, yet receptiveness to the value of others; and finally openness to the truth (*DP*, 47).

The second part of *DP* (55–76) is concerned with proclaiming the message of Jesus Christ. There is not much that is new in this section of the document, which consists rather of a statement of the church's understanding of the urgency of proclamation, based on the teaching of the New Testament and documents such as *Evangelii Nuntiandi* (December 8, 1975). The mandate given by Jesus, the Risen Lord, to the first disciples is recalled. Reference is made to the role of the church in proclaiming the kingdom of God established on earth in Jesus Christ, as God's decisive and universal offer of salvation to the world. An explanation is given of the content of proclamation, which is essentially the message that the Risen Christ is Lord and Savior. Much emphasis is placed on the role of the Holy Spirit, who empowers the disciples of Jesus to give witness. Finally, several numbers are dedicated to the manner of proclamation (68–71) and to obstacles to proclamation (72–74).

The third and final section of *the document* seeks to bring together

interreligious dialogue and proclamation, [which,] though not on the same level, are both authentic elements of the Church's evangelizing mission. Both are legitimate and necessary. They are intimately related, but not interchangeable: true interreligious dialogue on the part of the Christian supposes the desire to make Jesus better known, recognized and loved; proclaim-

ing Jesus Christ is to be carried out in the Gospel spirit of dialogue. The two activities remain distinct, but as experience
shows, one and the same local Church, one and the same person, can be diversely engaged in both. (*DP,* 77)

Anyone who has experience of the mission of the church in areas
where the great majority of people belong to a religion other than
Christianity will readily understand this dual presence.

The theological justification for this twofold approach is to be
found in the fundamental importance of God's universal salvific will,
and in the vision of the church as universal sacrament. If God wills
the salvation of all, then surely God must provide the means for this
salvation. Both dialogue and proclamation have a role to play in
bringing those who do not know Christ into the paschal mystery,
which is the way to salvation. *Dialogue and Proclamation* explains the
church's commitment to this one mission in the following paragraph:

All Christians are called to be personally involved in these
two ways of carrying out the one mission of the church,
namely proclamation and dialogue. The manner in which
they do this will depend on the circumstances and also on
their degree of preparation. They must always bear in mind
that dialogue, as has already been said, does not constitute the
whole mission of the church, that it simply cannot replace
proclamation, but remains orientated toward proclamation in
so far as the dynamic process of the church's evangelizing
mission reaches in it its climax and fullness. As they engage in
interreligious dialogue they will discover the "seeds of the
Word" sown in people's hearts and in the religious traditions
to which they belong. In deepening their appreciation of the
mystery of Christ they will be able to discern the positive values in the human search for the unknown or incompletely
known God. Throughout the various stages of dialogue, the
partners will feel a great need both to impart and receive
information, to give and to receive explanations, to ask questions of each other. Christians in dialogue have the duty of
responding to their partners' expectations regarding the contents of the Christian faith, of bearing witness to this faith

when this is called for, of giving an account of the hope that is within them (1 Pet 3:15). In order to be able to do this, Christians should deepen their faith, purify their attitudes, clarify their language and render their worship more and more authentic. (*DP*, 82)

At the end of the day of prayer, fasting, and pilgrimage for peace in Assisi in 1986, Pope John Paul II said: "Let us see in it [this day] an anticipation of what God would like the developing history of humanity to be: a fraternal journey in which we accompany one another toward the transcendental goal which he sets for us."[27] These words are quoted in *DP* 79, and would seem to describe well the spirit in which we can understand the close connection between interreligious dialogue and the proclamation of Jesus Christ as the Savior of all people.

Jesus Christ, The Bearer of the Water of Life

A short paragraph in *Dialogue and Proclamation* mentioned "new religious movements," and explained that they would not be considered in that document "due to the diversity of situations which these movements present and the need for discernment on the human and religious values which each contains" (*DP*, 13). Also, the Pontifical Council for Interreligious Dialogue, in collaboration with Pontifical Councils for Christian Unity, for Non-Believers, and for Culture, had already published in 1986 a document on sects or new religious movements titled *Phenomenon of the Sects and New Religious Movements—Pastoral Challenge.*[28] These new religious movements are of concern to all four of the dicasteries of the Roman curia just mentioned, but the PCID is the one that directs and organizes their study. The papal constitution *Pastor Bonus* indicates that the PCID "fosters and supervises relations with members and groups of non-Christian religions *as well as those who are in any way endowed with religious feeling.*"[29]

Jesus Christ, the Bearer of the Water of Life[30] is addressed to pastors, spiritual directors, committed laypeople, and those who accompany others who are searching for common spiritual values. While recognizing that persons who are influenced by New Age spirituality have a true "religious sense," the document makes a distinction between the form of dialogue entered into with traditional religions, and the manner of approach to these new religious movements. In the first case, dialogue includes meetings and reciprocal understanding, collaboration for peace and development, and a discussion of shared spiritual values. The dialogue with new religious movements, on the other hand, seeks simply to accompany the individual follower of such movements in his or her spiritual search.

Jesus Christ, the Bearer of the Water of Life presents in chapter 2 a very thorough overview of New Age spirituality (2.1–2.4), and indicates some of the factors that have contributed to its rapid growth (2.5). Two approaches are suggested for making a comparison of the fundamental ideas of New Age and the Christian faith. The first, considered in chapter 3 of the document, is that of spirituality.

> While recognizing the aspects of authentic spiritual searching which are found in the best expressions of *New Age*—as a search for harmony, unity, and an experience of the divine— the text [of Jesus Christ, the Bearer of the Water of Life] points out the dialogical character of the Christian life that is founded on the eternal dialogue at the heart of the Trinity and shapes from within the conversation between God and the human creature, giving a new shape to interpersonal relations.[31]

Chapter 4 of the document lists fundamental questions of a doctrinal nature to which Christians and followers of the New Age movement respond differently. The document makes it clear, however, that

> it is difficult to separate the individual elements of New Age religiosity—innocent though they may appear—from an overarching framework which permeates the whole "thought-world" of the New Age movement. The Gnostic nature of this movement calls us to judge it in its entirety. From the point of view of Christian faith, it is not possible to isolate some elements of *New Age* religiosity as acceptable to Christians, while rejecting others. Since the *New Age* movement makes much of a communication with nature, of cosmic knowledge of the universal good—thereby negating the

revealed contents of Christian faith—it cannot be viewed as positive or innocuous. (4)

The fundamental questions to which Christians and New Agers respond differently are as follows:

- Is God a being with whom we have a relationship or just something to be used or a force to be harnessed?
- Is there just one Jesus Christ, or are there thousands of Christs?
- Is there one universal "human being" or are there many individuals?
- Do we save ourselves or is salvation a free gift from God?
- Do we invent truth or do we embrace it?
- Are we talking to ourselves or to God in prayer and meditation?
- Are we tempted to deny sin or do we accept that there is such a thing?
- Are we encouraged to reject or accept suffering and death?
- Is social commitment something shirked or positively sought after?
- Is our future in the stars or do we help to construct it?

Chapter 4 of the document explains the title, namely *Jesus Christ, the Bearer of the Water of Life.* In his encounter with the Samaritan woman by Jacob's well in the fourth chapter of St. John's Gospel, Jesus offers the stranger the water of life. This is given as a model for the way Christians can and should engage in dialogue with anyone who does not know Christ:

> The gracious way in which Jesus deals with the woman is a model for pastoral effectiveness, helping others to be truthful without suffering in the challenging process of self-recognition ("he told me everything I have done," verse 39). This approach could yield a rich harvest in terms of people who may have been attracted to the water-carrier (Aquarius) but who are genuinely still seeking the truth. They should be invited to listen to Jesus, who offers us not simply something that will quench our thirst today, but the hidden spiritual depths of "living water." It is important to acknowledge the sincerity of people searching for the truth; there is no question of deceit

or of self-deception. It is also important to be patient, as any good educator knows. (5)

A lengthy chapter 6 is dedicated to pastoral issues, which do not directly concern our study. They are seen by the pontifical councils as being an important means of exchange with the local churches and with the centers for formation and culture, with the aim of achieving a better understanding of the religious scene and discerning new possibilities of dialogue and witness. The Pontifical Council for Interreligious Dialogue points out that it is at the local level that one can study and give useful responses to those who are searching, and it affirms: "This is not only a duty of pastors, but of all who are actively involved in the mission of the Church."[32]

The appendix to this document contains information for anyone studying the New Age phenomenon. The glossary should also prove useful to students of New Age or similar currents of thought.

The phenomenon of the New Age continues to occupy the attention of various Vatican dicasteries. A three-day international consultation on this subject took place in the Vatican, June 14–16, 2004, as a follow-up to the document just dealt with. Delegates from twenty-two episcopal conferences met with members of the Roman curia and a representative of the General Union of Superiors in what was described as a study session.

In preparation for this meeting, episcopal conferences had been asked to study the document *Jesus Christ, the Bearer of the Water of Life* on the basis of a questionnaire that had been forwarded to them. Their answers were examined by this gathering, which also considered two fundamental aspects of the phenomenon: the discernment of techniques and finalities in the New Age, and the comparison between Christian spirituality and the mystical experiences proposed by the New Age. The discussion resulted in pastoral indications to be sent to the Episcopal conferences so that they may respond in "a rich and articulate way to the silent request for help made by so many people faced with the phenomenon of the New Age which is so complex in its ideas and manifestations."[33]

The question of sects and new religious movements has been prominent in discussions between the PCID and the WCC over the years. As already mentioned, within the Roman curia, this phenomenon is studied by the PCID together with the Pontifical Councils for Christian Unity, Non-Believers, and Culture. In cooperation with FUCI (International Federation of Catholic Universities), international seminars were organized in Omaha, Nebraska, and in Vienna in 1991, and then in Quito, Ecuador, in 1992.

Other Publications

The PCID has published several books to assist those engaged in interreligious dialogue. In *Journeying Together,* the pontifical council gives a brief introduction to the religious tradition of each of its partners in dialogue, adding at the end of each chapter a selected bibliography for the use of those who wish to look more deeply into a particular religious tradition.[34]

The acts, or proceedings, of an interreligious colloquium organized by the PCID in Rome from January 16–18, 2003, have been published as *Spiritual Resources of the Religions for Peace: Exploring the Sacred Texts in Promotion of Peace.*[35] This colloquium was held as a follow-up to the 1999 interreligious assembly in the Vatican and to the 2002 Assisi Day of Prayer for Peace, to which reference has already been made. The published acts of this colloquium contain presentations on the theme of peace according to Hindu, Buddhist, Jain, Muslim, Sikh, Zoroastrian, and Jewish traditions, together with a Catholic perspective on religions for peace as seen from the experience in the United States of America and the Middle East.

On the occasion of the seventieth birthday of Cardinal Francis Arinze, who was still at that date president of the PCID, a "Reading of Selected Catholic Church Documents on Relations with People of Other Religions," in the form of essays by various authors, was published under the title *Milestones in Interreligious Dialogue.*[36] In this publication, a number of Vatican II documents are studied in reference to interreligious dialogue, together with encyclicals and postsynodal exhortations. There are comments on documents of the PCID and a very interesting reading of the document of the Congregation for the Doctrine of the Faith *Dominus Jesus*[37] by the present secretary of that dicastery, Bishop Angelo Amato. The PCID publishes three times a year the bulletin *Pro Dialogo*, which gives an account of its activities and contains significant church texts on dialogue, articles, and news of dialogue activities throughout the world. An interreligious dialogue directory has also been published.

Finally, mention must be made of the various messages that the PCID addresses to peoples of other religious traditions yearly, on the occasion of a religious celebration of particular importance to the religion in question. The PCID has published, under the title *Meeting in Friendship*, the messages sent to Muslims from 1967 to 2002.[38] The occasion chosen in this case is the feast of *'Id al-Fitr*, that brings to a close the period of Ramadan, a special time of fasting, prayer, and sharing for followers of Islam. Similar messages are addressed each year to Hindus on the feast of Diwali, and to Buddhists for the feast of Vesakh.[39]

The yearly reports of the Holy See on the activities of the pope and the Roman curia (Attività della Santa Sede) give in summary form an account of the various initiatives of the PCID. It is there that one can get an overview of the participation of the president and other members of the council in various encounters with representatives of other religions both in Rome and in many parts of the world. Reference is made to visits by council officials to regional and national bishops' conferences, to dioceses, and of course to leaders of other world religions. Little by little, these visits were repaid, as it were, by more and more frequent encounters within the council offices.

As already indicated, an important aspect of the work of the PCID has been the encouragement it gives to the local churches to engage in interreligious dialogue. As president of the council, Cardinal Arinze was particularly active in this task. To take just one year, 1985, the twentieth anniversary of *Nostra Aetate*, His Eminence visited eight countries in order to meet with the local churches and encourage them in their work of promoting interreligious dialogue. In 1985, the PCID stated that collaboration with the local churches was considered "a priority for the secretariat."

One feature of the activity of the PCID has been the close collaboration it has established over the years with the WCC. Officials of the PCID and the corresponding office of the WCC meet annually for discussions. Already in 1988 we find the participants in these meetings considering together the problem of fundamentalism in religion.[40] On March 24, 1995, six members of Unit II of the WCC visited the offices of the PCID for discussion on the Christian approach to sects and new religious movements, on the relationship between interreligious dialogue and evangelization, and on interreligious formation in the field of education. In recent years the PCID and the WCC have also been working together on two projects: prayer and interreligious worship, and mixed marriages of Christians and members of other religions, with the intention of providing churches and ecclesial communions with pastoral assistance in these two delicate areas of interreligious relations. The document on interreligious marriages was concluded and published in *Pro Dialogo* in 1997. From December 8–14, 2002, the PCID and the Office for Interreligious Relations of the WCC organized a joint seminar in Senegal on the theme "The African Person," as part of a common project on the contribution of Africa to the religious heritage of the world. As secretary of the PCID, Bishop Fitzgerald served for several years on the Joint Working Group of the WCC and the Catholic Church. The PCID has also maintained regular contact with the Middle East Council of Churches.

CATHOLIC–JEWISH RELATIONS

Commission for Religious Relations with the Jews

In 1966, Pope Paul VI approved the setting up of a special office for Catholic-Jewish relations within the Secretariat for Promoting Christian Unity. It was obvious that section 4 of the Second Vatican Council's declaration *Nostra Aetate* would need to be followed up, and this was done by providing a central office to bring the teaching outlined by the council fathers to the knowledge of the universal church, and to promote within the worldwide Catholic community this new understanding of the Catholic-Jewish relationship. The experience of the council itself showed that a great deal of work would have to be done within the church to dispel the widespread prejudices about the Jewish tradition, and at the same time to remove the well-founded mistrust in the Jewish community of the church and its intentions.

Although it may have seemed strange at the time, there were very good reasons for not entrusting this task to the Secretariat for Non-Christian Religions:

- *psychologically*, since it would have been unsuitable to put Jews on the same level as Buddhists, Hindus, and others, because Jews truly believe in the God revealed uniquely in the books of the Old Testament;
- *historically*, since the great majority of Jews have, since the time of Christ, lived among Christians and for better or worse feel themselves linked with Christianity in one way or another; and
- *theologically*, since the church considers the Old Testament a sacred work inspired by God and part of the basis of her own faith. This forms an essential link between her and Judaism that recognizes the Old Testament as the reason of its existence.[41]

With the 1967 reform of the curia, the Secretariat for Promoting Christian Unity is given "competence also in questions concerning the Jews under their religious aspect." The apostolic constitution *Regimini Ecclesiae* of Pope Paul VI defines the scope of this task and its proper character.[42]

Already in the same year, it was possible to refer to cooperation between Catholics and Jews "in several countries" within Christian-Jewish organizations, and to mention special commissions that had been set up as part of episcopal conferences in the United States, Canada, France, England, and Holland. Contact had been made between the office in Rome and the Committee on Church and the Jewish People within the "World Mission and Evangelism" division of the WCC.

In view of the difficulties encountered by the dialogue in the years to come, it is interesting to note the following evaluation given by the office within the SPCU in 1967:

There are different branches of Judaism which are at variance in their contacts with Christianity. All of them can be said to favor cooperation in the social field. But the same cannot be said of the directly religious and theological field. Here one finds, especially among Orthodox Jews, great reserve or even

open opposition. It is here then that contact is most important. Social work in common can develop, but the time for
true religious dialogue, especially on a large scale, has not yet
arrived. A good deal of work has to be done first in eliminating prejudices and providing serious information; there must
be profound study and changes of attitude...progress must
be slow and will call for a great deal of understanding.[43]

As we shall see, this consideration proved to be exact, and it was to be
many years before a dialogue in the "directly religious and theological
field" could be undertaken.

In his report to the 1972 plenary of the SPCU, President Cardinal Johannes Willebrands stated, "For my part I am astounded to
realize how poorly Christians and Jews know each other." He added:

This is not an obstacle that can be overcome by mere books.
A *religious* dialogue is needed here. Catholics will not come to
understand what Judaism is, especially in its religious experience, except by meeting Jews who are trying to grasp what is
at the heart of Christianity. The converse is obviously true.
The task demands that both should be on the same wave-
length. Dialogue with Jews appears as a duty within the
framework of our mission. It is sustained by that hope which
resounds through the biblical texts that Jews and Catholics
use in their liturgies.

Cardinal Willebrands also pointed out that, with regard to this dialogue, "there is no lack of unknown factors and difficulties." Among
those he mentioned is the difference between Christians and Jews in
the way they see the relation of people and religion, with the consequence that "the distinction between the political and religious
domains is especially difficult for the Jews." In addition, he emphasized the disparity between dialogue between Christians and Christian dialogue with Jews. While the Catholic Church has already been
for some time involved in dialogue with other Christians, Catholic-
Jewish dialogue "is in its beginnings."[44]

Despite these difficulties, the dialogue soon gained momentum
both at the local and the international levels. At the local level, groups

of Jews and Catholics were coming together to foster friendship, and mention was made of common action and collaboration between them. Moreover, on the local level some studies and research were being carried out with the intention of making catechetics more faithful to the principles outlined by the Second Vatican Council.

At the international level, a very important development occurred that was to have a determining influence on Catholic-Jewish relations in the coming years. The positive response of the Jewish world to the hand of friendship offered by the Second Vatican Council in *Nostra Aetate, no. 4,* is often taken for granted today. Yet one could easily have understood a less positive attitude on the part of a people who had suffered so greatly over the centuries, especially at the hands of members of the church, even, at times, those in the highest positions. Fortunately, there were some courageous Jewish leaders willing to grasp the hand of friendship. As a result of informal discussions between some of these courageous Jewish leaders and authorities of the Roman curia, an official meeting in Rome on December 20–23, 1970, took place in which the decision was made to set up the International Catholic-Jewish Liaison Committee between the Catholic Church and important Jewish organizations.

Taking into account these encouraging developments, Pope Paul VI on October 22, 1974, raised the status of the office for Jewish relations within the SPCU to the Commission for Religious Relations with the Jews (CRRJ) and gave it "the scope of promoting and fostering relations of a religious nature between Jews and Catholics." The commission would be responsible for developing "true and proper relations with Judaism on a worldwide plane" and would be at the disposal of all interested bodies or those concerned with Jewish-Catholic relations, "in order to supply them with information or receive information from them, and in order to help them to pursue their goals in conformity with the directives of the Holy See." It would endeavor to promote "the effective and just realization of the orientations given by the Second Vatican Council, particularly in section four of the declaration *Nostra Aetate.*"[45] The CRRJ would have as president and vice president the cardinal president and the secretary respectively of the SPCU. It would have its own full-time secretary, who would be attached to the SPCU staff, and would be assisted by eight consulters.

Let us now look at two documents issued by the Commission for Religious Relations with the Jews.

Guidelines and Suggestions for Implementing the Conciliar Declaration **Nostra Aetate, *No. 4***

Under the signature of its president, Cardinal Johannes Willebrands, the new commission issued on December 1, 1974 a document entitled *Guidelines and Suggestions for Implementing the Conciliar Declaration* Nostra Aetate, *No. 4 (Guidelines)*.[46]

This very practical document is aimed at promoting dialogue, without any attempt to present a background of a Christian theology of Judaism. The preamble recalls the principal teachings of the council on the obligation of the church to foster reciprocal understanding and mutual esteem, while condemning anti-Semitism and all forms of discrimination.

In the first section on dialogue, the document points out that such relations as there have been until then between Jew and Christian "have scarcely risen above the level of monologue." The time has now come for the establishment of real dialogue. For this, competent people will be encouraged to meet and study together the many problems deriving from the fundamental convictions of Judaism and Christianity. Dialogue demands respect for the other as the other is; above all, respect for the faith and religious convictions of the other. The document also envisages the possibility, in certain circumstances, of "a common meeting in the presence of God, in prayer and silent meditation, a highly efficacious way of finding that humility, that openness of heart and mind, necessary prerequisites for a deep knowledge of oneself and of others."

A second section of *Guidelines* is dedicated to liturgy. Mention is made of the links between the Christian and Jewish liturgies. "The idea of a living community in the service of God, and in the service of men for the love of God, such as it is realized in the liturgy, is just as characteristic of the Jewish liturgy as it is of the Christian one." Biblical texts show the continuity of the Catholic faith with that of the earlier covenants. While Christians believe that the promises then made were fulfilled with the first coming of Christ, "it is none the less true that we still await their fulfillment in his glorious return at the end of time." Particular attention is to be made in homilies to avoid anything that would distort passages that show the Jewish people as such in an unfavorable light. The Christian faithful should be instructed so that they will understand the true interpretations of such texts and their meaning for the contemporary believer.

A third section briefly illustrates the progress already made within the Catholic Church in preceding years to develop a better understanding of Judaism itself and of its relation to Christianity. Further research and study by specialists are encouraged, and so too is the establishment of chairs of Hebrew studies.

Then a final section refers to the common understanding of the value of the human person, the image of God. "In the spirit of the prophets, Jews and Christians will work willingly together, seeking social justice and peace at every level—local, national and international."

The document concludes by admitting that "there is still a long road ahead," and by calling on the bishops throughout the world to do whatever they see as best to promote Jewish-Christian relations. It is suggested that they create "some suitable commissions or secretariats on a national or regional level, or appoint some competent person to promote the implementation of the conciliar directives and the suggestions made above." The problem of Jewish-Christian relations concerns the church as such, since it is when "pondering her own mystery" that she encounters the mystery of Israel.

These guidelines and suggestions were meant as a help and encouragement to the local churches, and can be considered from a certain point of view as the new commission's first step in the realization of its mandate to promote religious relations with the Jews.

In his presidential address to the plenary session of the SPCU, February 17–24, 1975, Cardinal Willebrands recalled the setting up of the CRRJ and the publication of *Guidelines*. The plenary was informed that the latter document had been generally well received: "The welcome given to this text by the Catholics engaged in dialogue with Jews and especially by the Jewish circles receptive to the idea of such a dialogue has been in general very favorable and even warm, in spite of certain reserves (which were foreseeable)." The Secretariat then explained that unfortunately the reservations expressed "have been transformed into bitter criticism in certain more intransigent, more traditional and more activist Jewish circles."[47]

There were three main criticisms directed to the document. We note them here, as they will be repeated in the case of other statements by the commission in future years:

- The text is silent on the spiritual bond existing between the Jewish faith, the people, and the land of Israel.
- The document's statement reminding the church of her duty to proclaim Jesus Christ encourages proselytism and contradicts what is also said in the document about respect for the faith of the Jews.
- Certain formulas in *Guidelines* regarding the relationship between the Old Testament and the New are not acceptable to Jews, as they express the Christian understanding of that relationship; for example, "the New Testament brings out the full meaning of the Old, while both Old and New illumine and explain each other" (*Guidelines*, II).

Orthodox Judaism also found the mention of the possibility of prayer in common totally unacceptable.

Replying to these reservations, Cardinal Willebrands explained that the *Guidelines* had been drawn up by the Catholic Church for Catholics, and was not intended as a dialogue document. In fact, the scope of the document is obviously first and foremost practical. He also pointed out that "dialogue between Catholics and Jews presupposes respect for the Jewish faith on the part of Catholics, but also on the part of Catholics fidelity to all the essential components of their own faith. It is quite certain that there could be no dialogue if mutual respect and fidelity on both sides were not practically compatible."

Notes on the Correct Way to Present Jews and Judaism in Preaching and Catechesis in the Roman Catholic Church

A new document on a similar theme as *Guidelines* was made public by the CRRJ on June 24, 1985, under the title *Notes on the Correct Way to Present Jews and Judaism in Preaching and Catechesis in the Roman Catholic Church (Notes)*.[48] The document itself explains its purpose:

Religious teaching, catechesis, and preaching should be a preparation not only for objectivity, justice, and tolerance but also for understanding and dialogue. Our two traditions are so related that they cannot ignore each other. Mutual knowledge must be encouraged at every level. There is evident in particular a painful ignorance of the history and traditions of Judaism, of which only negative aspects and often caricature seem to form part of the stock ideas of many Christians.

This is what these notes aim to remedy. This would mean that the council text and *Guidelines and Suggestions* would be more easily and faithfully put into practice.

From this comment, made twenty years after the Second Vatican Council, it is obvious that the teaching on Judaism proposed by the council fathers had still quite some way to go before being satisfactorily received by the Catholic worldwide community. Pope John Paul II, who had succeeded Paul VI and John Paul I on October 16, 1978, brought this problem to the attention of delegates of episcopal conferences and other experts in Jewish-Catholic relations who were meeting in Rome on March 6, 1982. He called for a catechesis that "presents Jews and Judaism in an honest and objective manner, free from prejudices and without any offences, but also with full awareness of the heritage common to Jews and Christians."[49] The commission therefore set out in *Notes* to present clearly the principles on which sound preaching and catechesis on Jews and Judaism should be based, according to the teaching of the Second Vatican Council.

Though eminently practical, *Notes* considers it necessary to provide also the theological explanation for its statements. The document is divided into six sections:

I. Religious Teaching and Judaism
This first section refers to the council teaching on "the spiritual bonds" linking Jews and Christians. With a clear reference to the low interest shown in many places to this relationship, the commission quotes Pope John Paul II in stating that Jewish-Christian relations are "founded on the design of the God of the Covenant," and should not therefore "occupy an occasional and marginal place in catechesis.

Their presence there is essential and should be organically integrated" (I, 2). Just two years earlier, Pope John Paul II had made an historic address in Mainz to the Jewish community of West Germany during which he referred to "the meeting between the people of God of the Old Covenant, never revoked by God (cf. Rom 11:29), and those of the New Covenant."[50]

The document admits that the need to balance certain ideas makes this dialogue difficult and gives it a singular character. Teaching about Judaism has to explain that *promise* and *fulfillment* throw light on each other; that *newness* lies in a metamorphosis of what was there before; that the *singularity* of the people of the Old Testament is not exclusive, but open in the divine vision to a universal extension; and that the *uniqueness* of the Jewish people is meant to have the force of example (I, 5).

But to avoid any misunderstanding about its mission, *Notes* also makes it clear that Christianity and Judaism cannot be seen as two parallel ways of salvation. The church must of its very nature proclaim Jesus Christ as the redeemer of all people (I, 7).

II. Relations between the Old and New Testament

What then is the relationship between the Old and New Testaments, keeping in mind the unique status of biblical revelation? Already from apostolic times (cf. 1 Cor 10:11; Heb 10:1) and then constantly in tradition, the church has had recourse in this regard to "typology." Thus the events of the Old Testament are not seen as concerning only Jews but also as touching Christians personally. Singular happenings recounted there certainly concern a particular nation but are destined, in the sight of God who reveals his purpose, to take on a universal and exemplary significance.

The danger in this approach is that the transition from the Old Testament to the New might be seen as a rupture, by which the old simply ends and a new begins. The document warns against this possibility and against a form of dualism. It points out that there is a Christian reading of the Old Testament that does not necessarily coincide with the Jewish reading, but states that this does not detract from the value of the Old Testament in the church. Neither does it hinder Christians from profiting from the traditions of Jewish reading, recognizing, however, their essential difference. And, of course, it is clear that the New Testament itself demands to be read in the light of the Old.

In concluding these thoughts, the commission enters into an important eschatological reflection that helps to relate the Christian and Jewish traditions and will demand much future consideration:

> Typology further signifies reaching toward the accomplishment of the divine plan, when "God will be all in all" (1 Cor 15:28). This holds true also for the church which, already realized in Christ, yet awaits its definite perfecting as the Body of Christ.
>
> Furthermore, in underlining the eschatological dimension of Christianity we shall reach a greater awareness that the people of God of the Old and New Testament are tending toward a like end in the future: the coming or return of the Messiah—even if they start from two different points of view. It is more clearly understood that the person of the Messiah is not only a point of division for the people of God but also a point of convergence. Thus it can be said that Jews and Christians meet in a comparable hope, founded on the same promise made to Abraham (cf. Gen 12:1–3; Heb 6:13–18). (II, 8 and 10)

This section concludes with a call to Christians and Jews to accept, in view of this eschatological vision, a common responsibility "to prepare the world for the coming of the Messiah by working together for social justice, respect for the rights of persons and nations and for social and international reconciliation" (II, 11). Similar appeals were to appear frequently in future interventions of Pope John Paul II and the CRRJ.

III. Jewish Roots of Christianity
Though Jesus was born for peoples of all nations and died for all, he was nevertheless Jewish by birth and always remained a Jew. He was fully a man of his times in Palestine. While he showed great liberty with regard to the biblical law as then practiced in Palestine, he showed constant respect for this law, submitted to its prescriptions and was trained in its observance (III, 1–2).

Jesus taught in the synagogues and in the Temple. For the supreme act of the gift of himself, he chose the setting of the domestic liturgy of the paschal festivity (III, 3).

His relation with the Pharisees, though complex, must not be seen as wholly polemical (III, 5). All of this, according to *Notes*, helps to explain what St. Paul writes in the Letter to the Romans (11:16ff) about the "root" and the "branches": "The church and Christianity, for all their novelty, find their origin in the Jewish milieu of the first century of our era, and are deeply still in the "design of God" (*Nostra Aetate*, no. 4), realized in the Patriarchs, Moses and the Prophets, down to the consummation in Christ Jesus" (*Notes*, III, 9).

IV. The Jews in the New Testament

Having established these basic considerations, the document then takes up the delicate subject of the Jews in the New Testament, which so often has figured prominently in a catechesis used to condemn the Jews of deicide. The *Guidelines* had already pointed out that sometimes in the New Testament the formula "the Jews" refers to the leaders of the Jews or to the adversaries of Jesus, and not to the whole nation. In preaching and catechesis, every effort should be made to achieve an objective presentation of the role of the Jewish people in the New Testament (IV, 1).

Such a presentation must take account of various facts:

- The Gospels are the outcome of long and complicated editorial work, accomplished in various stages. Some of the references hostile or less than favorable to the Jews may well have their context in the conflicts that soon rose between the nascent church and the Jewish community (IV, 1A)
- At the same time, it is clear that already from the early days of his ministry there were conflicts between Jesus and certain categories of Jews of his time, among them the Pharisees (IV, 1B).
- The majority of the Jews did not in fact accept Jesus, nor did their Jewish authorities believe in him (IV, 1C).
- As the Christian mission developed, especially among the pagans, a rupture occurred and this is undoubtedly reflected in the texts of the New Testament, and particularly in the Gospels (IV, 1D).

Together with these considerations, there is the clear teaching of the Second Vatican Council declarations *Nostra Aetate*, no. 4, and *Dignitatis Humanae*, no. 2, which make it clear that "what happened in (Christ's) passion cannot be blamed upon all the Jews then living without distinction or on the Jews of today" (IV, 1E–F and 2).

V. The Liturgy

This section of *Notes* reminds the reader that it is in the same Bible that Jews and Christians find the very substance of their respective liturgies. This is particularly evident at the time of the great feasts of the liturgical year.

VI. Judaism and Christianity in History

While pointing out that the history of Israel and of the Jewish people did not end in AD 70, *Notes* states that "the existence of the State of Israel and its political options should be envisaged not in a perspective which is in itself religious, but in their reference to the common principles of international law." The relationship between the Jewish people and the land of Israel was to prove a far more complicated problem in Christian-Jewish relations in the years following the publication of this document.

There is, however, a mystery in the permanence of Israel, while so many ancient peoples have disappeared without trace. The Jewish people remain a chosen people, "the pure olive on which are grafted the branches of the wild olive which are the Gentiles" (John Paul II alluding to Rom 11:17–24, on March 6, 1982[51]). The document concludes with the following recommendation:

> We must remember how much the balance of relations between Jews and Christians over two thousand years has been negative. We must remind ourselves how the permanence of Israel is accompanied by a continuous spiritual fecundity, in the rabbinical period, in the Middle Ages and in modern times, taking its start from a patrimony which we long shared, so much so that "the faith and religious life of the Jewish people as they are professed and practiced still today, can greatly help us to understand better certain aspects

of the life of the Church" (John Paul II, March 6, 1982). Catechesis should on the other hand help in understanding the
meaning for the Jews of the extermination during the years
1939–1945, and its consequences.

International Catholic-Jewish Liaison Committee

As already mentioned, on December 20–23, 1970, a meeting took
place in the premises of the Secretariat for Christian Unity that was
to have an all-important positive influence on future Catholic-Jewish
relations. This was jointly organized by the International Jewish
Committee for Interreligious Consultations (IJCIC) and the Vatican's
Office for Catholic-Jewish Relations. IJCIC had just been set up and
was intended specifically for contact with the Catholic Church. The
original members were the World Jewish Congress with constituents
in sixty-five countries; the Synagogue Council of America, acting on
behalf of Orthodox, Conservative, and Reform Judaism in the United
States; and the American Jewish Committee, which had been active
since 1906 in interreligious activities and in the fields of the civil and
religious rights of Jews in any part of the world. This meeting in
Rome opened up for study and action a vast range of matters of common interest and proposed the setting up of joint working groups and
study commissions to follow up the discussions. The office for
Catholic-Jewish relations noted at the time that "only in a few countries have Christians begun to realize the importance of this question.
And even in most countries where Jews and Christians live together
almost everything must still be done."[52]

It was hoped that serious collaboration on the international level
might begin in the course of the coming year, and to further this project the International Catholic-Jewish Liaison Committee (ILC) was
set up, consisting of five members from each side. The Catholic side
would be headed by the archbishop of Marseilles, the Most Reverend
Roger Etchegaray, who later was to become a prominent member of
the Roman curia, whilst among the Jewish members were leaders
whose names would figure prominently in future Jewish-Catholic
relations: Rabbi Arthur Hertzberg, Dr. Gerhart Riegner, Rabbi
Henry Siegman, and Rabbi Marc Tanenbaum.

The aim of the committee was defined as follows: the improvement of mutual understanding between the two religious communities, as well as the exchange of information and possible cooperation in areas of common responsibility and concern. The ILC met for the first time in "an atmosphere of frankness and cordiality" in the Jewish Consistory in Paris on December 14–16, 1971. From the outset it became clear that while it would be desirable in certain fields for a common position to be reached, in other fields the principal aim should be to clarify both similarities and differences with a view to attaining genuine mutual understanding.

Already it was foreseen that some difficulty would be experienced as a consequence of the separation within the Vatican of responsibility for religious relations with the Jews (the Office for Catholic-Jewish Relations) and responsibility for all that concerns relations with civil governments (Council for the Public Affairs of the Church). On the Jewish side it was noted that such a division of competence would almost certainly create a difficulty, since in Jewish eyes all questions concerning Jews and Judaism have a religious aspect. Small mixed commissions made up of experts were consequently asked to study two questions concerning relations between the Catholic Church and Judaism: the way in which the relationship between the religious community, people, and land is conceived in the Jewish and Catholic traditions; and the promotion of human rights and religious freedom.[53]

Over the next fifteen years, the ILC met almost annually (with the exception of 1980 and 1983) in various European cities and once in Jerusalem.[54] These meetings provided the participants and the organizations they represented with an opportunity of exchanging information regarding matters of shared interest and of discussing questions of common concern. Among other matters, attention was given to anti-Semitism, the situation in the Middle East, human rights, and religious freedom.

The ILC gatherings were of special value in developing a spirit of trust at the international level between the church and the Jewish people. When the CRRJ was established in 1974, it was officially stated that this had occurred principally at the suggestion of the ILC.[55] By the time of the fourth meeting of the ILC in Rome from January 10–17, 1975, the document *Guidelines* had also been published. Unanimously the ILC felt "that a new stage in relations between Jews and Catholics may well have begun."[56] On this occasion, Pope Paul VI received the committee in his private library where the tone of the official addresses, the attitude of the personalities present, and the private exchanges between the Holy Father and the participants "were marked by mutual warmth and an atmosphere of *détente*, simplicity and frankness which impressed all taking part."[57]

The fifth meeting of the ILC was held in Jerusalem, March 1–3, 1976, and had as its theme "Evaluation of the Ten Years of Relations between the Catholic Church and Judaism." Reports from Rabbi Henry Siegman, executive vice president of the Synagogue Council of America for the Jewish delegation, and the Rev. Laurentius Klein, abbot of the Abbey of the Dormition in Jerusalem, introduced the theme.

Rabbi Siegman stated that the publication of *Guidelines* "constituted a significant forward step." He then outlined, among other things, the differing approach of the two parties to the dialogue, the Jews taking more of a historical viewpoint and the Catholics stressing on the other hand theological aspects. Abbot Klein indicated various difficulties encountered in the attempt to find mutual understanding between Catholics and Jews, including those stemming from the different cultural and philosophical positions from which the concept of religion is seen on each side.

Discussion on the two reports showed the need to probe further the themes that had been handled, beginning with examination of the concepts of "mission" and "witness" and their implications for Jewish-Christian dialogue. The meeting also exchanged information and views on topics of common interest, including the possibilities opening up for promoting religious liberty and other human rights, on the basis of the Helsinki Conference and the United Nations convention on civil and political rights. The participants at this meeting spent a day in the religious kibbutz of Lavi, near Nazareth, and held a ceremony at Yad Vashem, the Holocaust memorial.

The vital question of mission and witness figured prominently at the 1977 meeting in Venice, Italy, where the ILC had before it the study paper "The Mission and Witness of the Church." While this was a Catholic document dealing with Catholic theological issues, it

nevertheless made a significant contribution to Catholic-Jewish relations by setting out the following fundamental principles concerning
the Catholic understanding of mission and witness:

- The Catholic Church is bound by divine command to make known
  the name of the One God among all the people of the earth in
  every age.

- In doing so, the Catholic Church feels closely connected to the
  task of the Jewish people in the world. "It is becoming clearer in
  the Catholic Church today, despite any temptation which may
  exist to the contrary, that the mission she received from her mas-
  ter is above all to live in faithfulness to God and man; it is unity
  in love, respect for all brothers, service without distinction of persons, sacrifice, goodness."

- This understanding of the church's mission precludes proselytism. It excludes "any form of witness and preaching that in any
  way constitutes a physical, moral, psychological or cultural
  restraint on the Jews, both individuals and communities, such as
  might in any way destroy or even simply reduce their personal
  judgment, free will and full autonomy of decision at the personal
  or community level."

- "Also excluded is every sort of judgment expressive of discrimination, contempt or restriction against the Jewish people as such,
  and against individual Jews as such or against their faith, their
  worship, their culture, their past and present history, their existence and its meaning."

The paper rejects hateful forms of comparison that exalt the religion
and fact of Christianity by throwing discredit on the religion and fact
of Judaism. Finally, it rejects all "attempts to set up organizations of
any sort, particularly educational or welfare organizations for the *conversion* of Jews."

Responding to this paper, Rabbi Henry Siegman saw the unquali-
fied condemnation in the document of proselytism and the rejection
of organizations aimed at the conversion of Jews as representing "a

significant development in the Catholic Church that is bound to con-tribute to a deeper understanding between the two faiths."

During the meeting, information was exchanged on issues of common concern, including Catholic-Jewish study programs in vari-ous countries, development of national and regional cooperation between Catholics and Jews, and the status of human rights. A pre-liminary exchange was held on the presentation of Judaism and Christianity in their respective educational programs.[58]

The 1979 meeting was particularly significant, since it was held at Regensberg in the Federal Republic of Germany, October 22–25. This was underlined in a telegram sent for the occasion by Chancel-lor Helmut Schmidt, expressing gratitude for the fact that such a meeting was being held for the first time since the Second World War in Germany.

Two main subjects were discussed: "Religious Freedom" and "Education for Dialogue in a Pluralistic Society." The two papers presented on religious freedom revealed convergences of basic ideas and many problems similar to the two religious communities.

On the subject of "Education for Dialogue in a Pluralistic Soci-ety," three Catholic papers expressed the need for developing new teaching methods and curricula in the area of Catholic-Jewish dia-logue at all levels of education. A Jewish paper analyzed the phenom-enon of pluralism in contemporary society and its implications for dialogue in the field of education. The author, Dr. David Silverman of New York's Jewish Theological Seminary of America, discussed the problems and opportunities for dealing creatively with pluralism.

The meeting also considered current trends of anti-Semitism and was informed of the joint efforts being made by the German Confer-ence of Catholic Bishops, the Central Committee of German Cath-olics, and the Council of the Protestant Church in Germany to counteract anti-Semitism, to promote Christian-Jewish relations in Germany, and to foster scholarly research in this field.[59]

The meetings from 1981 to 1984 were dedicated to the study of various themes:

- "The Challenge of Secularism to Our Religious Commitments" (London, 1981).[60]

- "The Sanctity and Meaning of Human Life in the Present Situation of Violence" (Milan, 1982).[61] On this topic it proved easy to find large areas of agreement.
- "Youth and Faith, and the Reaction of Youth to the Social Problems of Our Times" (Amsterdam, 1984).

The twelfth ILC meeting in Rome, October 28–30, 1985, merits special consideration. Over the years the IJCIC had been enlarged to include among its members the B'nai B'rith Anti-Defamation League and the Israel Jewish Council for Interreligious Dialogue, in addition to the three original members. The participants came together on October 28, 1975, which was to the very day the twentieth anniversary of the proclamation of the council declaration *Nostra Aetate*, and on that day they were received in a special audience by Pope John Paul II. The pope reaffirmed the church's commitment to *Nostra Aetate* and the uniqueness of the sacred "link" between the church and the Jewish people, a relationship that the church has with that religious community alone, "stemming from the mysterious will of God." Speaking for the Jewish delegation, Rabbi Mordecai Waxman, chair of IJCIC, hailed *Nostra Aetate* and subsequent papal statements as documents that had revolutionized Christian-Jewish relations and created new opportunities for dialogue.

This meeting looked back over the twenty years following the council. Dr. Gerhart Riegner of the World Jewish Congress noted areas of remarkable progress and other areas where further efforts toward understanding were needed. Regional reports were given on the status of relations between Catholics and Jews in Latin America, Europe, Israel, Africa, and North America. Sisters from the Congregation of Our Lady of Sion presented a report on the work in Rome of SIDIC (Service International de Documentation Judeo-Chrétienne).

The atmosphere once again was very positive and on this occasion the ILC committed itself to a program of action for the immediate future, consisting of six points:

1. to disseminate and explain the achievements of the past two decades to the two religious communities;

2. to undertake an effort to overcome the residues of indifference, resistance, and suspicion that may still prevail in some sections of the two communities;
3. to work together in combating tendencies toward religious extremism and fanaticism;
4. to promote conceptual clarifications and theological reflection in both communities and to create appropriate forums acceptable to both sides, in which this reflection can be deepened;
5. to foster cooperation and common action for justice and peace;
6. to undertake a joint study of the historical events and theological implications of the extermination of the Jews of Europe during World War II.

A steering committee was to be established to work out the details of this program.

Both Pope John Paul II and Cardinal Johannes Willebrands made comments that indicated confidence in the future of this relationship. The pope spoke of the "rich, varied, and frank relationship" that had been achieved within the ILC over the fifteen years of its existence, "despite the normal difficulties and some occasional tensions," and gave the following advice:

> In order to follow along the same path, under the eyes of God and with his all-healing blessing, I am sure you will work with ever greater dedication for constantly deeper mutual knowledge, for ever greater interest in legitimate concerns of each other and especially for collaboration in the many fields where our faith in one God and our common respect for his image in all men and women invite our witness and commitment.

Cardinal Johannes Willebrands also spoke in encouraging terms, referring to the "link" or "bond" that for the Catholic Church flows from her identity as church, and then suggested:

> Let us try to see very clearly where we are going, how we should move to get there and in which way we can already

translate our relationship into concrete forms of collaboration toward all men and women in a world torn by hate, violence, discrimination and also indifference for the poor, the sick, the elderly and the oppressed.[62]

While the dialogue was achieving good results, Catholic participants were experiencing a certain frustration at not being able to enter into serious discussions on questions of faith of particular interest to both sides. *Nostra Aetate* had stated: "Since the spiritual patrimony common to Christians and Jews is so great, this sacred synod wants to foster and recommend that mutual understanding and respect which is the fruit, above all, of biblical and theological studies as well as of fraternal dialogue" (*NA*, 4). Orthodox Jews, however, were not open to "biblical and theological studies," and other members of the ILC were not willing to go against this opposition, being themselves quite satisfied just to concentrate on fraternal dialogue with a view to responding to practical concerns and improving relationships.

Certain Jewish organizations, however, were ready to consider theological discussions with the CRRJ outside of the ILC. In April 1985, a colloquium was held in Rome organized by the theological faculty of the Pontifical University of St. Thomas Aquinas, the Anti-Defamation League of B'nai B'rith, the Roman *Centro Pro Unione*, and SIDIC. A second colloquium organized by the same group took place in Rome from November 4 to 6, 1986. The subject chosen was "Salvation and Redemption in the Jewish and Christian Theological Tradition and in Contemporary Theology." While there is no published report of the discussions, the closing remarks of Cardinal Johannes Willebrands and the addresses delivered during the audience granted to the participants by Pope John Paul II indicate the value and serious nature of the meeting.[63]

Cardinal Willebrands considered the subject chosen for this colloquium to be central for theological studies between Christians and Jews. He noted that it was "a delicate theme." On the one hand, the two faith traditions followed similar patterns and used similar terms in expressing their understanding of "salvation" and the action of a saving God. On the other hand, there were serious divergences characteristic to each tradition. The cardinal indicated other themes that, in his opinion, merited similar joint study: messianism, the Word of God, prayer, exegesis and in particular the *Typos* and the covenant.

In a meeting of the participants with Pope John Paul II, Mr. Nathan Perlmutter, Director of the Anti-Defamation League, referred to the determined defense on the part of both the Catholic Church and the Jewish community of their faith and tradition, and commented: "To profess caring concern for Catholicism without respect for its faith and tradition is to love it less. So too do Jews look to their neighbors' approbation for the bedrock of their faith, Jerusalem as the spiritual and recognized capital of Israel." Pope John Paul II, for his part, spoke of theological reflection as being "part of the proper response of human intelligence." As such "it gives witness to our conscious acceptance of God's gift." He continued: "Honoring our respective traditions, theological dialogue based on sincere esteem can contribute greatly to mutual knowledge of our respective patrimonies of faith and can help us to be more aware of our links with one another in terms of our understanding of salvation."

Though there was no follow-up to these two theological colloquiums, they were an important beginning. It would be some years before the Catholic desire for such dialogue would again find a positive Jewish response, but eventually this was bound to happen.

Fifteen Years of Catholic-Jewish Dialogue—1970–85

In 1988, the ILC published a book of selected papers under the title of *Fifteen Years of Catholic-Jewish Dialogue—1970–1985*, referring to the first fifteen years of official Jewish-Catholic dialogue up to the 1985 Rome meeting of the ILC.[64] The publication contains a historical note on the ILC by Monsignor Pier Francesco Fumagalli of Milan, who was at the time secretary of the CRRJ. The selected papers were chosen from those presented to the various meetings of the ILC and so came to complete the information given above. There is also an appendix of "The Most Important Documents of the Catholic Church on Catholic-Jewish Relations" in the same period.

This book was presented to the public during a symposium held at the Lateran University in Rome on March 22, 1988. The rector of the university, Bishop Pietro Rossano, introduced the topic, and addresses were given by Cardinal Johannes Willebrands and Dr. Gerhart M. Riegner of the World Jewish Congress.

In his address, Cardinal Willebrands spoke of the development in Catholic-Jewish relations after the Second Vatican Council as being "so rich and dynamic." Looking to the future, he suggested five points for reflection and hopefully concrete action:

- A commitment against anti-Semitism
- A reflection on the *Shoah*
- A mature dialogue
- A common religious basis and hope, mutually recognizing each other's essential characteristics and substantial differences
- A common commitment for justice and peace

In his address, Dr. Riegner spoke of the publication of *Fifteen Years* as being a happy moment, "because one can say that we see in the publication of this book the formalization of our relations." He too had some thoughts on the future dialogue that merit special mention, not only for their own significance, but also for the very special position of their author in the task of fostering Jewish-Christian relations. Dr. Riegner remained right from the beginning until his death in 2001 a trustworthy friend of the dialogue and a valuable contributor to its work. His program for the future included these points:

1. It's a necessity to make known and to spread among the masses of the faithful the new theology of the church about the Jewish people and Judaism. This new teaching, he claimed, is still an affair of a small elite, known practically only by the leaders of our respective communities.

2. Some important concepts need to be deepened through reflection and study, such as the Catholic teaching that the covenant with Israel, "the Old Covenant," has not been abolished and is still valid. What are the theological consequences of this affirmation?

3. Common action for justice and peace must be encouraged. Dr. Riegner laments the fact that, despite previous statements calling

for common action in the social and humanitarian fields, little has been done at the international level. He stated his conviction that there is a great deal in common in the social teaching of the church and in that which comes from the great prophets of Israel.[65]

Pope John Paul II and Catholic-Jewish Relations—1979–87

As already mentioned, it was Pope Paul VI who promulgated the Second Vatican Council's declaration *Nostra Aetate*, and made the decision to entrust Catholic-Jewish relations to the Secretariat for Promoting Christian Unity. Again it was Pope Paul VI who created within the SPCU in 1974 a special commission for religious relations with the Jews. During his visit to Bogotá, Colombia, in August 1968, Pope Paul VI received representatives of the Jewish community and recalled for them the riches of the great common inheritance shared by Christians and Jews.[66] On January 10, 1975, he addressed the participants of the ILC meeting in Rome.[67]

Pope John Paul II not only continued this special interest in Jewish-Catholic relations, but from the very beginning of his pontificate began to contribute in an extraordinary way to the development of this dialogue. It is simply not possible to write of this relationship over the past forty years without paying tribute to Pope John Paul II for the difference that he personally has made during his pontificate.

This story begins with the audience that the pope gave on March 12, 1979, to representatives of several Jewish organizations forming part of the ILC. The audience, to which reference has already been made, took place in a very cordial atmosphere and, reading through the papal address for this occasion, one can see that John Paul II was delighted to have this opportunity so early in his pontificate of meeting the Jewish leaders. The Holy Father acknowledged "the friendly response and good will, indeed the cordial initiative, that the Church has found and continues to find among your organizations and other large sections of the Jewish community." For someone coming from Poland, the friendly response to the outstretched hand from the Second Vatican Council was certainly not something that would have been presumed. John Paul II expressed his own intention to promote the teaching of *Nostra Aetate* and to pursue the steps set out in the *Guidelines*, following in the footsteps of Paul VI. The pope concluded by turning to prayer:

> To God, then, I would like to turn at the end of these reflections. All of us, Jews and Christians, pray frequently to him with the same prayers, taken from the Book which we both consider to be the Word of God. It is for him to give to both religious communities, so near to each other, that reconciliation and effective love which are at the same time his command and his gift (cf. Lev. 19:18; Mk. 12:30). In this sense, I believe, each time that Jews recite the "Shema' Israel," each time that Christians recall the first and second great commandments, we are by God's grace, brought nearer to each other.[68]

Pope John Paul II was to make a meeting with the local Jewish representatives a normal feature of his many visits abroad, and in the course of a papal visit to Mainz in West Germany on November 17, 1980, he took the occasion to address Jewish representatives. Referring to a "Declaration on the Relationship of the Church with Judaism" by the bishops of the Federal Republic of Germany in April of that year, he began by making his own the following words: "Whoever meets Jesus Christ, meets Judaism."

The papal address is remembered particularly for the statement that the first dimension of the dialogue between Christians and Jews consists of "the meeting between the people of God of the Old Covenant, never revoked by God, and that of the New Covenant." The phrase "never revoked by God," referring to Romans 11:29, opened up new possibilities of dialogue on the two covenants and their relationship.

The pope stressed the importance for Christians to aim at understanding better the fundamental elements of the religious tradition of Judaism, and at learning what fundamental lines are essential for the religious reality lived by the Jews according to their own understanding. He concluded with an appeal that he would continue to repeat many times in the years to come:

Jews and Christians, as children of Abraham, are called to be a blessing to the world (cf. Gen 12.2 ff.), by committing themselves together for peace and justice among all men and peoples, with the fullness and depth that God himself intended us to have, and with the readiness for sacrifices that this high goal may demand. The more our meeting is imprinted with this sacred duty, the more it becomes a blessing also for ourselves.[69]

Pope John Paul II during his pontificate has frequently expressed the belief that actions are more effective than words in getting a message across to the modern day world. A perfect example of this was the historic visit that the pope paid, on April 13, 1986, to the synagogue of Rome. Even though the synagogue is only a couple of kilometers from the Vatican, no pope is known ever to have set foot there. Pope John XXIII did stop his car to bless Jewish worshippers leaving the synagogue one Sabbath, but John Paul II took an initiative that was to contribute greatly to better worldwide Jewish-Catholic relations when he set foot within the precincts of the Roman synagogue.

There he was warmly received by the chief rabbi of Rome, Prof. Elio Toaff, by the president of the Jewish community of Rome, and by numerous members of that community. In his welcoming address, the chief rabbi expressed "intense satisfaction" at the papal initiative, destined, as he said, to be remembered throughout history.

We find ourselves at a true turning point in Church policy. ...We cannot forget the past, but today we wish to begin, with faith and hope, this new historical phase, which fruitfully points the way to common undertakings finally carried out in a plane of equality and mutual esteem in the interest of all humanity.

In words that closely reflected ideas expressed by Pope John Paul II, Rabbi Toaff spoke of the common task incumbent on Jews and Christians in society to strive together to affirm man's right to freedom and the inalienable human rights that flow from it, "like the right to life, to freedom of thought, conscience and religion."[70] Chief Rabbi Toaff subsequently became a close personal friend of Pope John Paul II and of many officials of the Roman curia. He willingly joined with members of the *Comunità San Egidio*, whose headquarters are only a hundred meters or so from the synagogue, in a number of initiatives to cement Catholic-Jewish relations in the city of Rome.

In a cordial and moving reply to the chief rabbi, the pope gave thanks and praise to the Lord

> because it has been His good pleasure, in the mystery of Providence, that this evening there should be a meeting in this your "Major Temple" between the Jewish community that has been living in this city since the times of the ancient Romans and the Bishop of Rome and universal pastor of the Catholic Church.

His Holiness saw himself as taking up in this way the heritage of Pope John XXIII, and considered the gathering taking place as in a way bringing "to a close...a long period which we must not tire of reflecting upon to draw from it the appropriate lessons."

The pontiff spoke of his visit to the concentration camp at Auschwitz in 1979 and took the occasion to express "a word of abhorrence for the genocide decreed against the Jewish people during the last war, which led to the *holocaust* of millions of innocent victims." He referred to the riches of paragraph four of *Nostra Aetate* and in this context made a statement that would serve as a sound theological basis for future Christian-Jewish dialogue:

> The Church of Christ discovers her "bond" with Judaism by "searching into her own mystery." The Jewish religion is not "extrinsic" to us, but in a certain way is "intrinsic" to our own religion. With Judaism therefore we have a relationship which we do not have with any other religion. *You are our dearly beloved brothers and, in a certain way, it could be said that you are our elder brothers* [emphasis mine].
>
> [The pope went on to say that he meant his visit] to make a decisive contribution to the consolidation of the good relations between our two communities, in imitation of the example of

so many men and women who have worked and are still working today, on both sides, to overcome old prejudices and to
secure ever wider and fuller recognition of that "bond" and
that "common spiritual heritage" that exists between Jews and
Christians.

He recognized that the path undertaken was still at the beginning
and that there would be difficulties to overcome. Yet, in the light of
the common heritage of Jews and Christians drawn from the Law and
the prophets, the possibilities of collaboration are various and important. The pope mentioned collaboration "in favor of man, his life
from conception until death, his dignity, his freedom, his rights, his
self-development in a society that is not hostile but friendly and
favorable, where justice reigns and where, in this nation, on the various continents and throughout the world, it is peace that rules, the
shalom hoped for by the lawmakers, prophets and wise men of Israel."
He also wished to promote a common reflection and collaboration on
the problem of morality in a society that is often lost in agnosticism
and individualism, and which is suffering the bitter consequences of
selfishness and violence.

Finally, with reference to the problems of the city of Rome, their
common home, the pope called for common action and expressed the
hope that "from this visit of mine and the harmony and serenity that
we have attained may there flow forth a fresh and health-giving
spring like the river that Ezekiel saw gushing from the eastern gate of
the Temple of Jerusalem (cf. Ezek 47:1ff.), which will help to heal the
wounds from which Rome is suffering."[71]

The Difficult Years of Dialogue—1987–90

In the first half of 1987, Pope John Paul II made a pastoral visit to
Argentina, and again visited the Federal Republic of Germany and
Poland. On each occasion he met with Jewish representatives, and
while in Cologne he beatified Edith Stein on May 1, 1987.

This latter act had already caused some negative reaction in Jewish
circles and this became considerably greater when it was announced
that the recently elected president of Austria, Kurt Waldheim, was to

be received in official audience by the pope on June 25 of that same year. For the Jewish people, Kurt Waldheim was an unrepentant Nazi, guilty of involvement in Nazi atrocities.

As president of IJCIC, Rabbi Mordecai Waxman wrote to Cardinal Johannes Willebrands on June 22, 1987, "with a heavy heart." He saw the twenty-year dialogue, with its "enormous historical meaning," endangered by this event and expressed dismay that "the underlying principles of dialogue are being set aside. Dialogue, we believe, involves consideration for the feelings and attitudes of one's dialogue partners, as well as preliminary discussion of potentially troubling problems. Valued partners should not be presented with a *fait accompli*." Rabbi Waxman expressed the view that "what is happening this week is a terrible blow to the future of Vatican/Jewish relations" and reported that "there is an outcry in Jewish communities around the world asking what has the Vatican/Jewish dialogue achieved and why should it be continued." Rabbi Waxman sees in this issue a consequence of not addressing political issues regularly within the ILC and concludes:

> You are surely aware that the Vatican's failure to establish full and formal diplomatic relations with the State of Israel and also to come to face the realties of the extermination of the Jewish people in Christian lands is considered by the Jewish community as a great injustice. Only a truly meaningful and momentous gesture toward the Jewish people by the Vatican might help to advance Catholic-Jewish relations.

To this cry from the heart, Cardinal Willebrands could only reply "with absolute certainty" that "the convictions fostered by the Council are alive in the heart of the Holy Father, Pope John Paul II," and by insisting on the distinction between the religious relations of the Holy See, on the one hand, and the political and social relations on the other. They should not be, he wrote, confused and one cannot decide over the other, although progress in one field can be of decisive importance for the other.[72]

One can sympathize with the reaction of the Jewish community, who perceived the action of the Vatican in the case of Waldheim as casting doubt on the sincerity of the Catholic Church in pursuing dialogue with the Jews. The Holy See, for its part, found itself in a very difficult situation. Kurt Waldheim had been democratically elected as president of a traditionally Catholic country and, as Cardinal Willebrands pointed out, he had never been formally accused or convicted of any crime. In these circumstances, it was virtually impossible for the Holy Father to refuse such a state visit.

Whatever the merits of the case, the dialogue had been seriously affected. Pope John Paul II was due to visit the United States of America in September 1987, and as usual a meeting with Jewish representatives had been planned for Miami, Florida. For a time, it seemed that as a consequence of the Waldheim affair this event might not take place. The situation was saved by a papal audience with the IJCIC representatives at the summer residence of the pope in Castelgandolfo, just one week before the scheduled visit to the United States.

The representatives had gone to Rome to meet with the CRRJ on August 31, 1987, in an attempt to get the dialogue back on track. On the following day the Jewish delegation was received by Cardinal Agostino Casaroli, the secretary of state, who listened carefully to their concerns and agreed that, as occasions require, in areas which are of concern to the world Jewish community and where religious and political issues intertwine, future exchanges between IJCIC and the secretariat of state would be possible from time to time. As the question of formal diplomatic relations with Israel was entering more and more into the dialogue, the cardinal pointed out that while diplomatic relations with the State of Israel have not been "perfected," good relations at various levels did exist, including official visits to the Holy See by Israeli leaders.

The vital meeting, however, that was to clear the way for the Miami encounter came at noon on that day, when Pope John Paul II received the participants at Castelgandolfo. From all reports, a free and open conversation took place among those present and this allowed the Jewish participants to express themselves fully on the issues that had been discussed the previous day with the CRRJ. Two important decisions on the part of the Holy See were made in the course of this meeting: (1) A Catholic document would be prepared on the *Shoah* and anti-Semitism;[73] (2) The commission would encourage a more regular series of consultations with the Jewish partners (IJCIC), even dealing with complex subjects.[74]

These decisions cleared the way for the meeting in Miami to take place on September 11, 1987. In the circumstances the pope's words were awaited with great interest. Rabbi Waxman welcomed His Holiness on behalf of all the Jewish participants, which included representatives of all the main Jewish organizations in the United States. In his address, he spoke of the transformation that had taken place in Catholic-Jewish relations throughout the world as a result of the declarations of the Second Vatican Council and subsequent directives from the Holy See, and stated, "this positive change is especially evident here in the United States." While reporting on the wide range of activities that Jews and Catholics throughout the United States carry out in concert with one another, he noted that Jews particularly cherished their relationship with the National Conference of Catholic Bishops and its Secretariat for Catholic-Jewish Relations. Rabbi Waxman reminded the pope that the differences discussed at the meeting a week earlier had not been resolved, but looked forward to a common commitment to "the sacred imperative of *tikkun olam*, the mending of the world." He added: "But before we can mend the world, we must mend ourselves." Rabbi Waxman concluded with the reminder that "whenever Christians and Jews meet in serious conversation, Israel is at the center of that encounter," and expressed concern at the absence of full diplomatic relations between the Holy See and the State of Israel.

In his reply, Pope John Paul II also spoke at some length on the relationship between Catholics and Jews in the United States: their very similar experience as poor immigrants facing prejudice and discrimination in the early days of the new nation, and the contribution that together they had made to the development in the United States of the basic principles of freedom and justice, of equality and moral solidarity, affirmed in the Torah as well as in the Gospel.

The pope then turned to a reflection on the *Shoah*, recalling the "strong, unequivocal efforts of the popes against anti-Semitism and Nazism at the height of the persecution against the Jews." He encouraged "joint collaboration and studies by Catholics and Jews on the *Shoah*," and repeated the affirmation that "a Catholic document on the *Shoah* and anti-Semitism will be forthcoming, resulting from such serious studies."

The pope then made a strong appeal for Catholics in every diocese to implement, under the direction of the bishops, the statement of the Second Vatican Council and the subsequent instructions issued by the Holy See regarding the correct way to preach and teach about Jews and Judaism.

Without making a direct reference to the question of diplomatic relations between the Holy See and the State of Israel, Pope John Paul II stated that "Catholics recognize among the elements of the Jewish experience that Jews have a religious attachment to the land, which finds its roots in Biblical tradition," and agreed that after the tragic extermination of the *Shoah*, the Jewish people have a right to a homeland, as does any civil nation, according to international law. The same, he said, applies to the Palestinian people, so many of whom remain homeless and refugees, and called on all concerned— Muslims no less than Jews and Christians—"to forge those solutions which will lead to a just, complete and lasting peace in that area."[75]

For a short time it seemed that the dialogue was back on track and that the ILC would meet soon to take up the study of the *Shoah*. It was not to be, for a new dark cloud had already appeared on the horizon. It had suddenly come to the notice of the Jewish people that a cloistered Carmelite convent had been established within the precincts of the extermination camp at Auschwitz. In setting up this place of prayer, the Carmelite Order and the church in Poland had no intention of offending the Jews or of claiming Auschwitz as a Polish war memorial. A large number of Poles had in fact died in that camp, including the Catholic priest and martyr Maximilian Kolbe, and it seemed right and just to have the sisters there pray for the victims and for the great sin itself of the extermination camp. Moreover, the convent was not within the actual prison compound, but in a building known as the "Old Theater" which had been used by the Nazis for storing extermination gas on the outskirt of the camp, but was nevertheless part of it.

For the Jewish world, however, the convent was seen as an attempt to move the emphasis away from the place of Auschwitz within the *Shoah*, and turn it rather into a place of suffering and death for the Christian victims of Nazism. The large cross in the convent grounds was considered particularly offensive to Jews.

Once the problem caused by the convent became known, efforts were made to find a solution. Explanations given by the church in Poland and the CRRJ in Rome did not achieve their purpose and, as

Cardinal Willebrands admitted in the course of a reception given for him by IJCIC in New York on May 16, 1989, "even today we are facing together the tension arising from the presence of a Carmelite convent at Auschwitz."[76]

Meetings were held between Jewish representatives and leading members of the European Catholic Hierarchy in Geneva in 1986 and 1987. At this second meeting in February 1987, Cardinal Macharski, within whose territory the Auschwitz camp was situated, promised that a new educational and spiritual center would be built away from the precincts of the extermination camp, and that the convent would move to that location. Pope John Paul II expressly supported this solution on June 24, 1988, during a visit to Poland, and on September 6, 1989, Bishop Henryk Muszynski, president of the Polish Episcopal Commission for Dialogue with Judaism, stated clearly that it was the intention to proceed with the center as proposed in the Geneva agreement. On September 18, 1989, the CRRJ noted this "with satisfaction" in a special Vatican statement.[77] An article that appeared in Italian in *L'Osservatore Romano* of September 30 the same year informed the public of these moves and expressed the hope "that the matter has now been clarified and will no longer give rise to feelings of bitterness."[78]

Unfortunately this was not to be the case, especially as there was strong resistance on the part of the prioress (superior) of the convent and some members of the Carmelite community there to any such move. As a result the planned meeting of the ILC to discuss the *Shoah* did not take place and Catholic-Jewish relations continued to be rather tense.

It was most unfortunate that the term of Cardinal Johannes Willebrands as president of the Pontifical Council for the Promotion of Christian Unity and of the CRRJ should conclude at just this time. On September 4, 1989, the cardinal had celebrated his eightieth birthday. He had been associated with Cardinal Bea during the Second Vatican Council and immediately afterwards as the first secretary of the Secretariat for Christian Unity. During the next thirty-five years, and especially after the death of Cardinal Bea in 1968, he had guided Vatican efforts to bring about a radical transformation in Catholic-Jewish relations. Much of the progress made was due to his wise direction and untiring personal endeavor. As his presidency came to a close, he could state without fear of contradiction: "For many years, I have worked to build up better knowledge of the Jews among Catholics, and to foster a new relationship with the Jews on the basis of the Declaration *Nostra Aetate*."[79] In a special tribute to Cardinal Johannes Willebrands on the occasion of his ninetieth birthday, September 4, 1999, the quarterly journal *Information Service* of the PCPCU published a special issue dedicated to the cardinal and his work for Christian unity and Catholic-Jewish reconciliation. An article there by Archbishop (later Cardinal) Jorge Maria Mejia, a former secretary of the CRRJ, describes well the special contribution that the cardinal made to Catholic-Jewish relations from the time of the Second Vatican Council until his retirement in 1989.[80]

The building of the new center and transfer of the convent dragged on for some time. The transfer of the sisters to the new convent eventually took place in 1995, but only after a very personal intervention of Pope John Paul II. The successful conclusion of this unfortunate episode was due in no small measure to the dedication and hard work of Rev. Stanislaw Musial, a Polish Jesuit priest and, from 1986 to 1997, secretary of the Polish Bishops' Commission for Dialogue with Judaism. Rev. Musial was responsible for the construction of the new buildings and for raising the necessary finances.

A New Phase in the Dialogue

In November 1989, Pope John Paul II appointed me to succeed Cardinal Willebrands as president of the PCPCU and president of the CRRJ. In view of the situation described above, I was greatly encouraged when the then chairman of IJCIC, Seymour Reich, requested a meeting with the new president of the commission. He visited Rome in early 1990, accompanied by several other Jewish leaders, including Dr. Gerhart Riegner. During the meeting, it was clear that both sides were anxious to return to the dialogue. For my part, having just come from service as substitute (or under-secretary) for general affairs in the Secretariat of State, I was able to assure the Jewish leaders of the Holy See's determination to resolve the Auschwitz problem and of the Holy Father's complete support for the ILC.

As a result of this assurance it was agreed that the ILC finally resume its work. After a break of five years, *the thirteenth ILC meeting* took place in Prague, Czechoslovakia, in September 1990. Prague had been the home for centuries of a large and influential Jewish community that had almost been wiped out during the *Shoah*. The extermination camp of Theresienstadt was situated not far from the capital city.

Before the Prague meeting, Pope John Paul II received in audience representatives of the American Jewish Committee, led by their president. The American Jewish Committee had in the meantime been working with good results in Poland with the Polish Episcopal Commission for Dialogue with the Jews. His Holiness expressed the hope that the initiatives taken might be "a hopeful sign of genuine brotherhood between Christians and Jews in Central and Eastern Europe and thus contribute to the process of peaceful and democratic development taking place there."[81]

The Prague meeting of the ILC proved to be a remarkable success, keeping in mind the background situation of the preceding years. Both the Jewish and Catholic delegations were widely representative and of the highest quality. The presence among the Jewish members of such influential delegates as Dr. Gerhart Riegner, Rabbi Marc Tanenbaum, Rabbi Mordecai Waxman, Rabbi Jack Bemporad, and Rabbi Israel Singer, secretary-general of the World Jewish Congress, made a significant impact on the meeting.

The general topic for this meeting had been chosen in 1987: "The Historical and Religious Dimensions of Anti-Semitism and Its Relations with the *Shoah* (Holocaust)." Before beginning their discussions, the delegates made a visit to the concentration and extermination camp of Theresienstadt, where Rabbi Feldman recited the Qaddish and Fathers Dubois and Fumagalli read Psalm 130.

In my opening presidential address, I sought to direct the thoughts of the meeting to the future. With the fall of the Berlin Wall, new possibilities were being offered by developments in Europe for the creation of a true "civilization of love," based on the values taught in the Torah and the Gospel. At the same time we were being called to consider the great tragedy of the *Shoah*, and in this connection I opened my heart to declare something of which I was deeply convinced:

Indeed, it seems to me that as Christians, we have a particular obligation to take the initiative in this regard, for the faith that we profess is in a God of love, Who reconciles man to God and man to man. If we are to serve him we must love each and every one of those He has created; and we do that by showing respect and concern for our neighbor, by promoting peace and justice, by knowing how to pardon. That anti-Semitism has found a place in Christian thought and practice calls for an act of *teshuva* and of reconciliation on our part as we gather in this city, which is a witness to our failure to be authentic witnesses to our faith at times in the past.

On September 6, 1990, after many hours of discussion and hard work, the meeting approved a remarkably positive statement.[82] It "acknowledged the monumental role of the Second Vatican Council Declaration *Nostra Aetate*, as well as of later efforts by the popes and church officials, to bring about a substantive improvement in Catholic-Jewish relations." The delegates present in Prague called for a "deepening of this spirit in Catholic-Jewish relations, a spirit that emphasizes cooperation, mutual understanding and reconciliation; goodwill and common goals to replace the past spirit of suspicion, resentment and distrust."

Jewish speakers pointed out, in relation to the *Shoah*, how this past spirit had unfortunately contributed to the creation of anti-Semitism in Western society. The new spirit presupposes repentance and "would also manifest itself in the work that the two faith communities could do together to respond to the needs of today's world." The participants recognized the "trail-blazing" work being done in a number of communities in various parts of the world, making special reference to the United States, to the establishment of joint Jewish-Christian liaison committees in Czechoslovakia and Hungary, and to the diffusion in their own language by Polish church authorities of official documents concerning Catholic-Jewish relations.

With regard to the special problems of anti-Semitism in Eastern and Central Europe, the ILC made a number of recommendations concerning dissemination in the local languages of all relevant church documents on relations with Judaism: the inclusion of the teaching of these documents in the curricula of theological seminaries; the monitoring of all trends and events which threaten an upsurge of anti-Semitism, with a view to countering promptly such developments; ongoing actions aimed at guaranteeing freedom of worship and religious education for all citizens (Christians, Jews and others); active support of general legislation against discrimination on grounds of race or religion; and support of general educational programs that could favor these recommendations.

The statement concludes with the following hopeful vision of the future:

> After two millennia of estrangement and hostility we have a sacred duty as Catholics and Jews to strive to create a genuine culture of mutual esteem and reciprocal caring. Catholic-Jewish dialogue can become a sign of hope and inspiration to other religions, races and ethnic groups to turn away from contempt, toward realizing authentic human fraternity. The new spirit of friendship and caring for one another may be the most important symbol that we have to offer to our troubled world.

After Prague, the ILC continued to meet regularly every second year until 2001.

Shortly after the close of the 1990 ILC meeting, Jews and Catholics joined in celebrating *the twentieth-fifth anniversary of Nostra Aetate*, in Sao Paolo, Brazil, November 4–5, 1990, and in Rome, December 5–6, 1990. On both occasions Jews and Catholics expressed gratitude for the council declaration and for the change that it had brought about in Catholic-Jewish relations.

The Sao Paolo gathering was organized by Cardinal Paulo Evaristo Arns, archbishop of Sao Paolo, and Rabbi Henry I. Sobel, of the Latin American Jewish Congress, who had been from the years immediately following the Second Vatican Council a constant supporter of the reconciliation process between Jews and Catholics, not only in Latin America but also at the wider international level. In Sao Paolo, I had the opportunity of delivering an address that looked back in some detail over the past twenty-five years, but also reflected on the future of this important relationship.[83]

At the Rome gathering, which was sponsored by the CRRJ and IJCIC, Cardinal Franz Koenig, the former archbishop of Vienna, spoke at the Lateran University on "Catholic-Jewish Relations: Perspectives and Guidelines."[84] While recalling the "common elements of our religious patrimony," the cardinal indicated some of the questions "which keep arising from the Jews":

- Does the church continue to recognize the Jewish people as "the people of God" and in what sense, when compared with the church's understanding of itself as "the people of God"?
- Has the church given up on its mission toward Israel for its "conversion"?
- Does the church recognize a spiritual significance to the land of Israel and to her State?
- Does the church attribute some providential theological meaning to the *Shoah*?
- Does the church give an autonomous value to Hebrew Scriptures, or simply a typological value?

Cardinal Koenig then laid out a set of guidelines for future Jewish-Catholic dialogue, the first of which suggested the following approach to beginning joint theological research:

> In the global context of a solid systematic theology, those that should be encouraged are exegetical researchers and theologians so that they might better expand the role of the Jewish People in the mystery of redemption. God reveals himself as Savior "in history," and the character of "revealed religions" applies to Judaism and Christianity, and to a certain extent to Islam as well, the sons of Abraham through Ishmael.

This theme also formed part of the address given by Pope John Paul II to the participants in the Rome gathering when he received them in a special audience on December 6, 1990. He affirmed that the church is fully aware that Sacred Scripture bears witness to the Jewish people, "this community of faith and custodian of a tradition thousands of years old," as an intimate part of the mystery of revelation and of salvation. Then follow words that the Jews present at this audience will not easily forget:

> When we consider Jewish tradition we see how profoundly you venerate the *Torah*. You live in a special relationship with the *Torah*, the living teaching of the living God. You study it with love in the *Talmud Torah*, so as to put it into practice with joy. Its teaching on love, on justice and on the law is reiterated in the Prophets—*Nevi'im*—and in the *Ketuvim*. God, the holy *Torah*, the synagogal liturgy and family traditions, the Land of holiness, are surely what characterize your people from the religious point of view. And these are things that constitute the foundation of our dialogue and of our cooperation.[85]

His Holiness added that "no dialogue between Christians and Jews can overlook the painful and terrible experience of the *Shoah*," and in support of the decisions taken by the Prague meeting, urged that the declarations on "the religious and historical dimensions of the *Shoah* and of anti-Semitism...be implemented wherever human and religious rights are violated."

While in Rome, the representatives of the five member organizations of IJCIC met with the CRRJ. The meeting reaffirmed the principles agreed to in Prague, and underscored in particular the need for creating a joint mechanism at the grass roots level to disseminate these teachings throughout the Jewish and Catholic communities. This would include, among other things, education at all levels, textbook revision, popular literature, use of mass media, and conferences.[86]

In the Special Assembly for Europe of the Synod of Bishops a few days later, I had the possibility of informing the European bishops and other members of the synod, including the ecumenical delegates, of the above developments and future hopes. The synod devoted a major section of its final declaration to the issue.[87]

The fourteenth meeting of the ILC took place in Baltimore, May 4–7, 1992. It built upon the work done in Prague, taking as its theme: "*Shoah*, Anti-Semitism, Cooperation." The meeting was exceptionally well attended—thirty-four Jewish and twenty-two

Catholic delegates, and sixteen guests. The Baltimore statement emphasized again the common duty of Catholics and Jews to build together a new world: "This would be a world in which the problems which have plagued the past will be considered abnormal rather than normal, in which differences are addressed in quiet and constructive dialogue rather than fractious accusations, in which there is an ever-expanding basis for hope despite the evil that threatens our ancient faiths."[88]

Between the Prague and Baltimore meetings, in February 1992 members of the ILC had made visits to Poland, the Federation of the Czech and Slovak Republics, and Hungary. A visit to Auschwitz allowed the Jewish representatives to see for themselves the progress that was being made with the building of the new center to house the convent and other buildings clearly outside the limits of the extermination camp. Pope John Paul II had also been to these countries in this period, and on April 6, 1993, sent a special message to Jews from around the world who had gathered in Warsaw to commemorate the fiftieth anniversary of the uprising of the Warsaw Ghetto. Recalling those terrible days, he stated: "It is with profound grief that we call to mind what happened then, and indeed all that happened in the long night of the *Shoah*. We remember, we need to remember, but we need to remember with renewed trust in God and in his all-healing blessing."

Pope John Paul II referred to the pastoral letter of the Polish bishops of November 30, 1990, which stated: "The mutual loss of life, the sea of terrible suffering and of wrongs endured should not divide but unite us. The places of execution, and in many cases the common graves, call for this unity." Continuing this thought, the pope developed the idea he had first expressed in Mainz in 1980: "As Christians and Jews, following the example of Abraham, we are called to be a blessing to the world (cf. Gen 12:2ff.). This is the common task awaiting us. It is therefore necessary for us, Christians and Jews, to be first a blessing to one another."[89]

Another major event that was to prove extremely beneficial for this relationship was the establishment, on December 30, 1993, of diplomatic relations between the State of Israel and the Holy See, put forth in the statement *Fundamental Agreement between the Holy See and the State of Israel.* From what has already been mentioned, it is clear that the implementation of *Nostra Aetate* had been impeded to some extent by the absence of such formal official relations. The preamble to the *Fundamental Agreement* makes specific reference to the "unique nature of the relations between the Catholic Church and the Jewish people, the historical process of reconciliation and understanding and the growing mutual friendship between Catholics and Jews." In presenting his credential letters to the pope, the first Israeli ambassador to the Holy See saw the establishment of these diplomatic relations as "a new and constructive dimension in which to bring together in dialogue the Catholic Church and the Jewish People."[90]

The truth of these words became immediately apparent when the ILC met for the fifteenth time in Jerusalem from May 23–26, 1994.[91] The cochairs in their opening presentations noted that the warmth of the encounter was enhanced by its new and encouraging setting in the context of the *Fundamental Agreement.* The theme of the meeting was "The Family: Traditional Perceptions and Contemporary Realities." In addition, two papers were presented on ecology with the recommendations that a statement be drawn up in the future. The gathering noted with keen interest the fact that, although there had been no consultation between the Catholic and Jewish authors of these two papers, they proved to be remarkably similar in both content and background scriptural inspiration.

During the meeting and in the framework of an exchange of information, Prof. Hans Herman Henrix of Aachen reported on progress in drafting a statement on anti-Semitism and the *Shoah* by a working group of German Catholics at the request of the CRRJ. This was intended to serve as preparation for the promised statement to be issued by the Vatican. The report was introduced as being strictly confidential, especially as the English translation distributed to the participants was not precise in regard to certain important expressions used in the document. Nevertheless, the contents became immediately known to the press, much to the displeasure and annoyance of the Catholic representatives.

The sixteenth meeting of the ILC was due to be held in Buenos Aires in 1996, but was cancelled at the request of the Jewish partner for internal reasons that had nothing to do with the dialogue.

In 1998, the actual state of the Catholic-Jewish relationship was well summed up in a report of the CRRJ to the plenary that year of the PCPCU.[92] Among the particular concerns being addressed by the CRRJ, emphasis was placed on the need for "education" about developments in Catholic-Jewish relations within both the Catholic and Jewish communities. Greater attention to this problem was necessary in the formation of those who are destined to be leaders and teachers in the respective communities.

It was pointed out in this presentation that much remains to be done, especially at the national and local levels if the work of the ILC and other international organizations is to be effective. What has been achieved "all too often remains unknown." Once again the CRRJ returned to the question of a real Catholic-Jewish theological dialogue: "In order to move away from the hostility and misunderstandings of the past and to give a deeper meaning to our relationship, we must move on from the constant examination of difficulties to joint action in favor of the moral values which as faith communities we share."

The report also mentioned the need for a healing of memories, and in this connection noted with satisfaction the declarations that had been made in the previous two or three years by the German, Polish, American, Dutch, Swiss, Hungarian, and French Catholic hierarchies on anti-Semitism and the Holocaust.

We Remember: A Reflection on the Shoah

Introduction to the Document

On March 16, 1998, the CRRJ published the document on the *Shoah* that had been promised by Pope John Paul II in 1987 and had been eagerly awaited by the Jewish world community, especially after the press reports on the Jerusalem meeting of the ILC. The document is *We Remember: A Reflection on the Shoah*.

In the years following the decision to prepare such a statement, the CRRJ had engaged in a process of consciousness-raising and of reflecting on the *Shoah* at various levels in the Catholic Church. It was clear that this would be an important contribution to Catholic-Jewish relations, but the CRRJ was also well aware that the subject to be dealt with was not only delicate, but seen in a quite different light by various local churches.

In an address to the American Jewish Committee,[93] I explained that the CRRJ had begun in January 1990 with the idea of a single document that would be able to present all that the Catholic Church throughout the world might wish to state on this great tragedy of the twentieth century. As the work proceeded, however, it had become clear that the experience and involvement of the local churches throughout the world in relation to the *Shoah* were very different. What the church in Germany or in Poland, for instance, might wish to say in this regard might well not be identical, and even their statements quite inappropriate for particular churches in other continents. The bishops' conferences in Germany, Poland, the Netherlands, Switzerland, Hungary, and France had gone ahead and had each issued their own particular statement that, while dealing with the same general topic, referred in a special way to the experience of the people in the country concerned. The Catholic bishops of Italy followed by presenting on March 16, 1998, a formal letter to the Italian Jewish community strongly condemning anti-Semitism and deeply regretting the past treatment of Jews in Italy. In studying these various texts, one can note a variety in the tone and in the emphasis placed on certain aspects of the question, due naturally to the context in which they were issued and to the audience being addressed.[94]

Accordingly, the CRRJ felt that the way was thus open for the Holy See to speak to the Jewish people on behalf of the universal church. Obviously, then, it is important not to consider that document in isolation from the other statements made by local Catholic churches or from the numerous statements on this question by Pope John Paul II in the course of his pontificate.

The statement *We Remember*, published on March 16, 1998, is addressed to "our brothers and sisters of the Catholic Church throughout the world." At the same time it asks "all Christians to join us in meditating on the catastrophe which befell the Jewish people." In the final paragraph, an appeal is made to "all men and women of goodwill to reflect deeply on the significance of the *Shoah*," stating that "the victims from their graves, and the survivors through the vivid testimony of what they have suffered, have become a loud voice calling the attention of all of humanity. To remember this terrible experience is to become fully conscious of the salutary warning it entails: the spoiled seeds of anti-Judaism and anti-Semitism must never again be allowed to take root in any human heart."

It is also important for an objective understanding of the document to keep in mind that the CRRJ saw in this initiative the possibility of promoting among the Catholics in those countries that were far removed by geography and history from the scene of the *Shoah* an awareness of past injustices by Christians to the Jewish people and encourage their participation in the efforts of the Holy See to promote throughout the church "a new spirit in Jewish-Catholic relations: a spirit which emphasizes cooperation, mutual understanding and reconciliation, goodwill and common goals, to replace the past spirit of suspicion, resentment and distrust."[95]

Such a document had by its very nature to attract the attention of—and not alienate—those to whom it was addressed. It was seen by the CRRJ as "another step on the path marked out by the Second Vatican Council in our relations with the Jewish people" and Pope John Paul II expressed the hope that it would "help to heal the wounds of past misunderstandings and injustices."[96]

What the Document States[97]

The document is set in the context of the close of the second and the birth of a third Christian millennium. Pope John Paul II had called the church, in his apostolic letter *Tertio Millennio Adveniente*, "to become more fully conscious of the sinfulness of her children, recalling those times in history when they departed from the spirit of Christ and his Gospel and, instead of offering to the world the witness of a life inspired by the values of faith, indulged in ways of thinking and acting which were truly forms of counter-witness and scandal."[98]

We Remember: A Reflection on the Shoah refers to one of the main areas in which Catholics should seriously take to heart the pope's summons. While no one can remain indifferent to the "unspeakable tragedy" of the attempt of the Nazi regime to exterminate the Jewish people for the sole reason that they were Jews, the church has a special obligation to reflect on this "horrible genocide," "by reason of her very close bonds of spiritual kinship with the Jewish people and her remembrance of the injustices of the past" (I). Moreover, "the

Shoah took place in Europe, that is, in countries of long-standing Christian civilization" (II).

This raises the question of the relation between the Nazi persecution and the attitudes down through the centuries of Christians toward Jews. In such a short document, it was not possible to dwell at any length on the history of these relations, but the text admits clearly the prevalence over many centuries of anti-Judaism in the attitude of the church. It acknowledges the "erroneous and unjust interpretations of the New Testament regarding the Jewish people and their alleged culpability," a "generalized discrimination" in their regard "which ended at times in expulsions or attempts at forced conversions," and attitudes of suspicion and mistrust, while in times of crisis "such as famine, war, pestilence or social tensions, the Jewish minority was sometimes taken as the scapegoat and became the victim of violence, looting, even massacres" (III).

While lamenting this anti-Judaism, the document makes a distinction between this and the anti-Semitism of the nineteenth and twentieth centuries based on racism and extreme forms of nationalism, "theories contrary to the constant teaching of the Church on the unity of the human race and on the equal dignity of all races and peoples." The anti-Semitism of the Nazis was the fruit of a thoroughly neo-pagan regime, with its roots outside of Christianity and, in pursuing its aims, it did not hesitate to oppose the church and persecute its members also. The Nazi regime intended "to exterminate the Jewish people ... for the sole reason of their Jewish origin" (IV).

No attempt is made in the document to deny that "the Jewish people have suffered much at different times and in many places while bearing their unique witness to the Holy One of Israel and to the *Torah*" (II). But the *Shoah* was certainly the worst suffering of all. The inhumanity with which the Jews were persecuted and massacred during this century is beyond the capacity of words to convey. "All this was done to them for the sole reason that they were Jews" (II).

We Remember does not seek to deny that the Nazi persecution was made easier by anti-Jewish prejudices already imbedded in some Christian minds and hearts. This is clear in the document, which asks, however, that before making accusations against people as a whole or individuals, one should know what precisely motivated those people in their particular situation. There were members of the church who did everything in their power to save Jewish lives, even to the point of placing their own lives in danger. Many did not. Some were afraid for themselves and those near to them; some took advantage of the situation; and still others were moved by envy. The document makes this central point clear:

> As Pope John Paul II has recognized, alongside such courageous men and women (those who did their best to help), the spiritual resistance and concrete action of other Christians was not that which might have been expected from Christ's followers. We cannot know how many Christians in countries occupied or ruled by the Nazi powers or their allies were horrified at the disappearance of their Jewish neighbors and yet not strong enough to raise their voices in protest. For Christians, this heavy burden of conscience of their brothers and sisters during the Second World War must be a call to penitence. We deeply regret the errors and failures of those sons and daughters of the Church. (IV)

We Remember calls on Catholics to renew their awareness of the Hebrew roots of their faith, and of the fact that the Jews are their dearly beloved brothers, and in a certain sense their elder brothers. It then expresses regret by way of the following act of repentance:

> At the end of this Millennium the Catholic Church desires to express her deep sorrow for the failures of her sons and daughters in every age. This is an act of repentance *(teshuva)*, since, as members of the Church, we are linked to the sins as well as to the merits of all her children. (V)

While remembering the past, the Vatican document looks to a new future in relations between Jews and Christians. It closes with the prayer

> that our sorrow for the tragedy which the Jewish people has suffered in our century will lead to a new relationship with the Jewish people. We wish to turn awareness of past sins into a firm resolve to build a new future in which there will be no

more anti-Judaism among Christians or anti-Christian senti-ment among Jews, but rather a shared mutual respect, as befits those who adore the one Creator and Lord and have a common father in faith, Abraham. (V)

Reaction to the Document

The publication of the Vatican document received an enormous amount of publicity worldwide. The CRRJ was flooded with reac-tions from both Jewish and Catholic sources.

On the part of the Catholic Church—and it was to the members of this church that the document was primarily addressed—the reac-tions were in general very positive. The document was meant to teach, arouse interest, and cause reflection within the worldwide Catholic community.

Many of the early comments from the Jewish community were instead distinctly negative: "Vatican document dismays Jews" (*Aus-tralian Jewish News*); "It is too late, after 53 years, and it's not enough" (Chief Rabbi of Jerusalem, Yisreal Lau); "Document skirts the issue of Church's long silences—Jewish reaction is cool" (*The New York Times*); "An equivocal apology hurts more than it heals" (*Los Angeles Times*); apology "less-than-unreserved" (*Melbourne Age*); and so on. Rabbi Leon Klenicki expressed disappointment that this document was less forthright than the individual ones issued by various Euro-pean bishops' conferences.

Other Jewish reactions were more positive. While not denying that they would have wished for a more definitive statement, nor endorsing all the historical judgments contained in the document, these comments saw positive aspects of the Vatican's statement: "Mea culpa is a good start" (Rabbi Raymond Apple, Senior Rabbi of the Great Synagogue Sydney); "The Vatican's welcome first step" (Dr. Paul Bartrop of Bialik College, Melbourne); "Jews didn't get every-thing they wanted, but what they got was so significant and it doesn't prejudice other important steps. The old things that gave rise to anti-Semitism are no longer part of Catholic doctrine" (Michael Beren-baum, president of the Survivors of the Shoah Visual History Foundation, Los Angeles, California);[99] "It is my sense that the docu-ment, if read in the context of history, represents both a true act of

Christian repentance and an act of *teshuva* (David Gordis, president of Hebrew College in Brookline, Massachusetts);[100] "This is a dramatic statement" (Rabbi Kopnick of Fort Wayne, Indiana).

In an editorial, *The Philadelphia Inquirer* received the document with this comment:

> The document released Monday by the Vatican, "We Remember: A Reflection on the Shoah," is a remarkable, perplexing text, at once an acknowledgement, an apology and a repentance. The very title is a breakthrough. How crucial that the Roman Catholic Church would tell the world "We remember the Holocaust": That puts an end to three generations of official silence.[101]

Judith Banki, program director of the Marc Tanenbaum Center for Interreligious Understanding, in a letter to *The New York Times*, indicates another aspect of the document that had been generally overlooked. Banki states that the document *We Remember: A Reflection on the Shoah*

> stands as a clear rebuttal to an entire industry of Holocaust denial and revision. To some 800 million Catholic faithful and to the world at large, the Church has said "it happened." One cannot explain away as of no significance a document of the Catholic Church, inadequate or not in the opinion of the Jewish community, which expresses repentance for the actions or silence of its members in regard to a tragedy of 50 odd years ago. That tragedy must have happened.

An important point made in *We Remember* that raised questions with a number of people is the distinction between "the church" and "the members of the church," as found in the quote from an address of Pope John Paul II to the October 1997 Vatican symposium on "The Christian roots of Anti-Judaism": "In the Christian world—I do not say on the part of the church as such—erroneous and unjust interpretations of the New Testament regarding the Jewish people and their alleged culpability have circulated for too long, engendering feelings of hostility toward this people."[102]

This distinction—the church and the members of the church—runs through the Vatican document and is not readily understood by those who are not members of the Catholic Church. On various occasions the CRRJ has pointed out that when Catholics make this distinction, the term "members of the church" does not refer exclusively to any single particular category of church members, but according to the circumstances can include popes, cardinals, bishops, priests, or laity, since all are members of the church.

For Catholics the church is not synonymous, however, with the members that belong to it at any one time. It is looked upon as the bride of Christ, the heavenly Jerusalem, holy and sinless. Catholic doctrine does not speak of the church as sinful, but of the members of the church as sinful—a distinction others may find hard to understand, but one which is essential to the church's understanding of itself.[103] The above-mentioned editorial in *The Philadelphia Inquirer* on March 18, 1998, acknowledged that "in Catholic belief, it is impossible to conceive of the church, divinely ordained and inspired, itself falling into such evil error. But through free will, individual Catholics, even very prominent ones, could so sin."

Sixteenth Meeting of ILC

The publication of *We Remember*, the transfer of the Carmelite sisters to their new convent in Auschwitz, and the establishment of diplomatic relations between the Holy See and the State of Israel all created a favorable atmosphere for the ILC to resume its work. As already mentioned, no meeting had taken place as scheduled in 1996.

For the sixteenth meeting, the ILC met for the first time inside Vatican City, from March 23–26, 1998.[104] Again it was well attended, but some notable Jewish participants of earlier meetings were not present, among them Rabbi Israel Singer, Rabbi Jack Bemporad, and Seymour D. Reich. The discussions centered on four major themes:

- Education: What do we, how do we, and how ought we teach about each other?
- Approval of a joint statement on ecology
- Follow-up information on *We Remember*

- Possibilities and challenges of the coming celebration of the Jubilee Year 2000

In their opening addresses, the cochairs presented the differing but not incompatible concerns of the two world communities. As president of the CRRJ, I referred especially to the importance of each community knowing more about the other, and pointed out that there was a particular need within the Jewish community to have a better understanding of how the Catholic Church views itself. Christians must be allowed to be Christians and Jews to be Jews.

Dr. Gerhart Riegner for the Jewish delegation spoke mainly on the document *We Remember*, acknowledging the "very strong passages" in the statement, but also expressing serious disappointment that the document avoided "taking a clear position on the direct relationship between the teaching of contempt and the political and cultural climate that made the *Shoah* possible."

Various interventions indicated that progress was being made in the field of teaching about each other. The statement on ecology, originally proposed in Jerusalem in 1994, was approved with strong support. Discussion on the Jubilee Year centered on the theme of conversion and led to the hope that new insights in this regard might lay the foundation for further reconciliation between Jews and Catholics.

Although the sisters had moved to the new convent in Auschwitz, there remained behind on the former site of the convent a large cross that was proving to be an obstacle for the final resolution of this delicate question. The ILC expressed deep concern and made an appeal to all those involved "to work patiently in order to find an acceptable solution."

The participants were received in a special audience by Pope John Paul II, who praised the work of the committee for "the immense promise (it) held out by continuing dialogue between Jews and Catholics." The pope expressed the hope that "your present meeting discover ever more effective ways to make known and appreciated by Catholics and Jews alike the significant advances in mutual understanding and cooperation which have taken place between our two communities."[105]

Although this meeting did good work and was held in an atmosphere of goodwill on both sides, not all was well within the dialogue.

For one thing, the question of Pope Pius XII's wartime attitudes to the Nazi regime and to the Holocaust had been for some time impeding better Catholic-Jewish relations. But in 1998 tension in this regard began to manifest itself more openly. The World Jewish Congress, the most powerful member of IJCIC, was particularly involved in a bitter campaign of serious accusations against Pius XII.

In the years immediately following the end of the Second World War, a number of Jewish communities and Jewish leaders had expressed their gratitude for what Catholics had done for them during that terrible conflict, expressing gratitude at times to Pope Pius XII himself for his personal interventions in favor of the Jewish people and for those of his representatives who saved hundreds of thousands of Jewish lives.[106] This attitude changed radically with the stage presentation of Rolf Hockhuth's play *The Deputy* in 1961. Hockhuth accused the wartime pope of silence before clear evidence of Nazi atrocities against the Jewish community. He represented Pius XII as leaning favorably toward Hitler and his regime as a consequence of the years he had spent in Germany before becoming Vatican secretary of state and then pope, or at least as acting out of fear of possible Soviet domination of Europe in the event of a German defeat. In more recent years, a number of publications on Pope Pius XII and the Holocaust have appeared, especially in the United States, some attacking the pope's record, others defending it.

During the sixteenth meeting of the ILC in Rome, this problem was the subject of heated discussion, during which a strong demand was made by some Jewish participants for the Vatican Archives on the period of Pope Pius XII to be opened to accredited Jewish scholars. The CRRJ pointed out that the Holy See had already made available to the public some eleven volumes of documents from the archives and suggested that, as a first step, Jewish and Catholic scholars should together examine this vast source of information about the activities of the Holy See during the Second World War.

During the months following the Rome meeting no response was forthcoming to this offer. Attacks on the Vatican in the official publications of the World Jewish Congress continued to disturb the CRRJ, and there seemed to be serious internal divisions within IJCIC threatening its continuing existence. In a comment that I made on February 18, 1999, in Baltimore, I felt constrained to "sound a signal of alarm," explaining that "the reaction within the Catholic community to recent, aggressive attitudes manifested in our regard by certain Jewish agencies is the cause for concern. Catholics who for many years have been engaged in promoting Jewish-Christian relations have come to me to express their dismay at what is happening and their loss of interest in continuing along this chosen and, I believe, blessed path." I went on to point out that "our partner in dialogue for so many years, IJCIC, is no longer in existence," and regretted that the offer I had made at the Rome ILC meeting for Jewish and Catholic scholars to study together the already published material from the Vatican Archives had been completely ignored.[107]

The address received wide publicity, especially in the American press, and produced good results. IJCIC soon got its house in order again and that same month, under the auspices of the CRRJ and IJCIC, a group of experts, consisting of three Jewish scholars and the same number of Catholics, was appointed with the mandate to study the eleven volumes of the collection *Acts et Documents du Saint-Siège rélatifs à la Seconde Guerre Mondiale*. They were asked to report on their work and were given the assurance that, if at the end of their study there would be some questions that might need further elucidation from the archives, attempts would be made to have this done. The experts were never, at any time, led to expect that this meant they would have personal access to documents dated after 1922 in the Vatican Archives.[108] The experts began to meet regularly and the early signs promised that their study would prove of special value.

This was the situation at the beginning of the great Jubilee Year 2000. Before moving on to the special events of that celebration, however, it is necessary to look back at various developments that had taken place in the period between 1989 and 1999, including a number of important contributions to Catholic-Jewish relations made during that period by Pope John Paul II.

Special Events 1989–99

The pope during his many travels never missed an opportunity of meeting with Jewish representatives and encouraging dialogue. In the early nineties, some of the papal visits took His Holiness to countries that had been for many years under Soviet domination, and for this reason they remained mostly unaware of what had happened in the field of Catholic-Jewish relations during the previous twenty years. This was the case, for example, in Lithuania which John Paul II visited on July 11, 1992.[109] His Holiness also showed himself always ready to receive Jewish delegations that came on official business to Rome.[110]

An initiative of Pope John Paul II that perhaps spoke even louder than such regular encounters was the concert held in the Aula Paolo VI within Vatican City on April 7, 1994 to commemorate the *Shoah*.[111] The Royal Philharmonic Orchestra, conducted by Maestro Gilbert Levine, performed a moving program that included Max Bruch's *Kol Nidrei* and Leonard Bernstein's Kaddish *(Symphony No. 3)*, narrated by Richard Dreyfuss.

During the concert, Chief Rabbi Elio Toaff of Rome sat next to Pope John Paul II. Holocaust survivors attending the concert were received in a special and very moving audience the morning of that day, during which His Holiness spoke of the menorah candles that would be lit during the evening performance: "The candles, which will burn as we listen to the music, will keep before us the long history of anti-Semitism which culminated in the Shoah." While recalling "as a matter of historical fact" those Christians who, together with their pastors, strove to help their brothers and sisters of the Jewish community, "even at the cost of their own lives," the pope issued the following challenge: "In the face of the perils which threaten the sons and daughters of this generation, Christians and Jews together have a great deal to offer to a world struggling to distinguish good from evil, a world created by the Creator to defend and propagate life, but so vulnerable to voices which propagate values that only bring death and destruction."[112]

The pope spoke again at the end of the function, and with reference to those present "who physically underwent a horrendous experience, crossing the dark wilderness where the very source of love seemed dried up," made this appeal:

> Many wept at that time and we still hear echoes of their lament. We hear it here too, their plea did not die with them but rises powerful, agonizing, heartrending, saying: "Do not

forget us!" It is addressed to one and all.... We must therefore redouble our efforts to free man from the specter of
racism, exclusion, alienation, slavery, and xenophobia; to
uproot these evils that are creeping into society and under-
mining the foundations of peaceful human existence. Evil
always appears in new forms; it has many facets and its flat-
tery [is] multiple. It is our task to unmask its dangerous
power and neutralize it with God's help.[113]

Two years later, on April 15, 1996, the tenth anniversary of the
pope's visit to the Great Synagogue of Rome, Chief Rabbi Elio Toaff
made an official visit to the pope, accompanied by members of the
local Jewish community. His Holiness spoke on this occasion of the
"atmosphere of sincere friendship that has been established between
us" and of the meeting as "a sign of hope for a world that is anxiously
seeking authentic values of human brotherhood," a brotherhood
rooted in a common spiritual heritage that is extraordinarily rich and
profound. The pope suggested that "the new spirit of friendship and
mutual concern which marks Catholic-Jewish relations can be the
most important sign that Catholics and Jews have to offer a restless
world, which cannot decide to recognize the primacy of love over
hatred."[114]

A papal visit to Berlin, Germany, a few months later provided an
opportunity for Pope John Paul II to recall the heavy toll paid in blood
during the *Shoah* by the large Jewish community of that city. The
occasion was the ceremony of beatification of two priests, Bernhard
Lichtenberg and Karl Leisner. From the pulpit of St. Hedwig's Cathedral, Provost Bernhard Lichtenberg had denounced the November
1938 pogrom and each evening had publicly offered prayers "for persecuted non-Aryan Christians, for the Jews." For these prayers he was
arrested on October 23, 1941; he died two years later while being taken
to the concentration camp in Dachau. During his trial he included
among the "false principles" that he denounced before the Nazi judges
the "persecution of the Jews."[115]

In April 1997, the Pontifical Biblical Commission[116] began to
study the important but delicate relationship between the Old and
New Testaments, and the implication this has for Catholic-Jewish
relations. Pope John Paul II encouraged the commission in this task

"of enormous importance," pointing out how "centuries of reciprocal prejudice and opposition have created a deep divide between Christians and Jews, which the Church is now endeavoring to bridge." In the course of these polemics, the church has been tempted to separate completely the New Testament from the Old, but "it is impossible fully to express the mystery of Christ without reference to the Old Testament."[117]

The news of this promising study was followed a few months later by a symposium on "The Roots of Anti-Judaism, in the Christian Milieu," organized by the Historical Commission of the Central Committee for the Jubilee Year 2000.[118] It was held in Rome and attended by some sixty Catholic, Orthodox, and Protestant scholars. Pope John Paul II expressed gratitude to the participants in this colloquium "for the work you are doing on a very important theme that deeply concerns me," and took the occasion to stress the ongoing validity of the divine election of the Jewish people:

This people was gathered together and led by God, the Creator of heaven and earth. Thus its existence is not a mere fact of nature or culture, in the sense that through culture man displays the resources of his own nature. It is a supernatural fact. This people perseveres in spite of everything because they are the people of the Covenant, and despite human infidelity, the Lord is faithful to his Covenant.

Preparations for the celebration of the Jubilee Year 2000 were well on their way and Pope John Paul II considered this colloquium to be "in keeping with preparations for the Great Jubilee, for which I have invited sons and daughters of the Church to assess the past millennium, especially our century, in the spirit of a necessary examination of conscience, on the threshold of what should be a time of conversion and reconciliation."

The Jubilee Year 2000 and the Jewish People

At his general audience on April 28, 1999, Pope John Paul II spoke on Jewish-Christian dialogue in the context of preparations for the

Jubilee Year, and expressed the hope that "at the dawn of the third millennium sincere dialogue between Christians and Jews will help create a new civilization founded on the one, holy and merciful God and fostering a humanity reconciled in love."[119]

This theme of conversion and reconciliation, which permeated the celebration of the Jubilee Year 2000, brought forth two very special events that would radically change Catholic-Jewish relations.

On March 12, 2000, Pope John Paul II called for and presided over a special penitential service in St. Peter's Basilica, a "day of pardon" to ask forgiveness from the Lord "for the sins, past and present, of the sons and daughters of the Church."[120] One of the seven requests for pardon concerned "Sins against the People of Israel." Pope John Paul II had on several previous occasions expressed sorrow for sins committed by the sons and daughters of the church against the people of Israel, most notably in the document *We Remember.* But now, in the name of the Catholic Church throughout the world, the pope offered the following prayer to God:

> God of our Fathers, you chose Abraham and his descendants
> To bring your name to the nations:
> We are deeply saddened by the behavior of those who in the
>   course of history
> Have caused these children of yours to suffer,
> And asking your forgiveness
> We wish to commit ourselves to genuine brotherhood
> With the people of the covenant.

The introduction to this prayer recalled the sufferings endured by the people of Israel throughout history, and asked that Christians might purify their hearts by acknowledging the sins committed against the people of the covenant.[121]

Two weeks later, from March 21–26, Pope John Paul II was finally able to make a long-desired visit to Israel.[122] Several events of deep significance for Christians and Jews took place during those days. Indeed, the very visit itself was seen by the Jewish community as an important contribution to Catholic-Jewish relations.

Of the various events that merit special mention, the most memorable is undoubtedly that of March 26, 2000, when the pope and his entourage stood before the Western Wall of the Temple, also known as the Wailing Wall, a sacred place for the Jewish world. After silent prayer, John Paul II placed in the wall a personally signed copy of the above prayer that he had offered just two weeks earlier in St. Peter's Basilica, expressing sorrow for the suffering of the Jewish people at the hands of Christians down through the centuries and asking for-giveness from God.

Three days earlier, on March 23, His Holiness had visited the Yad Vashem Holocaust Memorial, rekindled the flame that recalls the six million victims of the *Shoah*, and laid a wreath of yellow and white daisies over the place where the ashes of many death camp victims are interred. During that moving ceremony in Jerusalem, the pope states, in continuation as it were of the prayer offered in St. Peter's:

> Here as at Auschwitz and many other places in Europe, we are overcome by the echo of the heartrending laments of so many. Men, women and children cry out to us from the depths of the horror that they knew. How can we fail to hear their cry? No one can forget or ignore what happened. No one can diminish its scale. We wish to remember. But we wish to remember for a purpose—namely, to ensure that never again will evil prevail, as it did for the millions of inno-cent victims of Nazism.[123]

On that same day, the pope paid a courtesy call on Ashkenazi Chief Rabbi Israel Meir Lau and Seraphic Chief Rabbi Eliyahu Baski-Doron at Hechel Shlomo, the headquarters in Jerusalem of the chief rabbinate. This very cordial meeting was destined to open the way to a new dialogue with the religious leaders of Israel, in response to the pope's short address, which concluded with the words: "There is much that we have in common. There is so much that we can do together for peace, for justice, for a more human and fraternal world. May the Lord of heaven and earth lead us to a new and fruitful era of mutual respect and cooperation, for the benefit of all!"[124]

At the close of the Holy Year 2000, Pope John Paul II looked back at the many outstanding events of those twelve months and did not hesitate to judge the visit to Jerusalem as one of the most signifi-cant. For those of us who were privileged to stand with him at the

Western Wall of the Temple, it seemed that all the efforts made over the previous thirty-five years to mend the broken and bloodstained fences between Jews and Christians had received the seal of God's blessing and could never be again undone.

The Seventeenth Meeting of the ILC

On March 3, 2001, my term as president of the Pontifical Council for Promoting Christian Unity came to a close. Cardinal Walter Kasper was appointed to take my place in the office and consequently became president of the CRRJ. He led the Catholic delegation to the sixteenth ILC meeting, which was held in New York from April 30 to May 4, 2001.[125] Mr. Seymour Reich had returned as chairman of IJCIC and as such led the Jewish representatives. The well-attended meeting was held in a relaxed atmosphere, and the participants considered at some depth the theme "Repentance and Reconciliation." This subject had been chosen to respond to the frustration on the Catholic side that even after many years of dialogue it had not been possible to enter into theological discussions with the Jewish partner, even though both CRRJ and IJCIC represented faith communities.

In fact, the New York gathering covered ground that previously had been "off limits" for many Jewish representatives. Two documents were discussed and approved. The first was a practical statement on a matter that had been a constant concern of ILC for a number of years: "A Recommendation on Education in Catholic and Jewish Seminaries and Schools of Theology." The other was the statement "Protecting Religious Freedom and Holy Sites," which concluded:

> We stand together as representatives of the Catholic and Jewish communities of faith in calling on men and women of all faiths to honor religious liberty and to treat the holy places of others with respect. We call on all people to reject attacks on religious liberty and violence against holy places as legitimate forms of political expression.
>
> We look forward, prayerfully, to the time when all people shall enjoy the right to lead their religious lives unmolested

and in peace. We long for the time when the holy places and all religious traditions will be secure and when all people treat one another's holy places with respect.[126]

As already mentioned, the main theme of the meeting was repentance and reconciliation. This was introduced by Rabbi Klenicki and developed in excellent papers by Rev. Lawrence Frizzell of Seton Hall University, Rabbi Dr. Michael Signer of the University of Notre Dame, Prof. David Novak of the University of Toronto, and Rev. James Loughran, SA. These papers provided ample material for reflection and discussion, offering each side of the dialogue new insights into the understanding of the other on such fundamental dimensions of religious faith.

The meeting did not, however, ignore the main tensions that still continued to disturb Jewish-Catholic relations. Jewish delegates expressed concern regarding the canonization of Edith Stein, the beatification of Pius IX, and the possible beatification of Pius XII. Particular reference was made by Prof. David Berger to the document *Dominus Jesus,*[127] published in August 2000 by the Vatican Congregation for the Doctrine of the Faith. He indicated that some in the Jewish community were worried by the assertion in the document that followers of other religions are in a gravely deficient situation in respect of salvation, that interreligious dialogue is part of the church's "mission" to the nations, and that equality in dialogue refers to the dignity of the participants and not to doctrinal content. While he himself found no legitimate grounds for Jewish objections to the passages about salvation and equality in *Dominus Jesus,* he suggested on the other hand that the passage about mission creates a major problem for dialogue, especially on doctrinal issues, and vindicates the concerns of Orthodox Jews who have largely avoided such discussions.

Cardinal Kasper replied that this document does not enter into Jewish-Catholic dialogue, nor call into the question the salvation of the Jews. The relation between the church and the Jewish people is unique and *Dominus Jesus* must be understood within the context of *Nostra Aetate* and the constant teaching of the post–Vatican II magisterium on Judaism.

In the agreed communiqué at the close of the meeting, the participants stated clearly that their partnership is secure and that the vital work of the ILC will continue to flourish in the years ahead. As official representatives of their organized religious communities, they expressed their determination "to engage our leadership and laity in dialogue and cooperation."

The joint historical study of the eleven volumes of documents from the wartime Vatican Archives that had followed the previous ILC meeting was also discussed by this meeting. Prof. Dr. Michael R. Marrus of the University of Toronto and Rev. Gerard P. Fogarty of the University of Virginia, two members of the panel of scholars, were present.

After several promising meetings, the panel of scholars had requested a meeting in Rome with the CRRJ. This had taken place in October 2000 during which the scholars presented a preliminary report, accompanied by a list of forty-seven questions. This was certainly not in strict accord with their mandate, which had not foreseen a preliminary report, but rather only a final report at the end of their study. The CRRJ had agreed to present at the time of the final report any of their remaining questions to the secretariat of state to see if further clarification might be possible. The situation became more difficult and complicated when the preliminary report itself was leaked to the press by one of the members and thus became the subject of controversial discussions and public rejection by other scholars.

At the New York meeting of the ILC, the two scholars expressed their conviction that the *preliminary report* made a valuable contribution to the historical record. The scholars reported that, while differing among themselves, as scholars regularly do, the members of the group were in agreement on the fact that the role of the papacy during the war remains unresolved. Opening the archives, in their opinion, will not definitely put this matter to rest, but it would help to remove the aura of suspicion and contribute to a more mature level of understanding. The ILC took note of the importance of this issue to both communities and encouraged a discourse on the subject that is characterized by mutual respect and appreciation for legitimately held points of view.

Unfortunately, in view of the different interpretations of the group's tasks and aim, coupled with a sentiment of distrust that had been engendered by indiscretions and polemical writings, continued joint study on the question was rendered practically impossible and in July 2001 the scholars suspended their work. In a special statement on the suspension, Cardinal Kasper admitted that the continuation of the study in the circumstances was no longer possible, but made an important statement for the future:

> Of course, understanding between Jews and Christians also requires an investigation of history. Access to all the relevant historical sources is therefore a natural prerequisite for this research. The desire of historians to have full access to all the archives concerning the Pontificates of Pius XI (1922–39) and of Pius XII (1939–58) is understandable and legitimate. Out of respect for the truth, the Holy See is prepared to allow access to the Vatican Archives as soon as the work of reorganizing and cataloguing them has been completed.[128]

Catholic-Jewish Relations at the National and Local Levels

On several occasions in previous pages, reference has been made to the implementation of the principles of *Nostra Aetate*, no. 4, at the national and local levels. Special commissions on Catholic-Jewish relations were set up as part of episcopal conferences in North America and Western Europe soon after the termination of the Second Vatican Council, but in 1972 Cardinal Willebrands, in a report to the plenary of the SPCU, expressed his astonishment at realizing "how poorly Christians and Jews know each other."[129] Documents like *Guidelines* and *Notes* proved helpful to groups of Christians and Jews seeking to enter into better relations at the local level, but *Guidelines* in its final section admitted that there was "still a long road ahead" and called on the bishops everywhere to do what they could to foster these relations.

In 1998 the report of the CRRJ to the PCPCU plenary indicated the need for "education" at the local level about developments in Catholic-Jewish relations at the international level. Particular mention was made to the formation of those destined to be leaders and teachers in the respective communities.[130] This was one of the four major themes of the ILC meeting in the Vatican City in 1998,[131] which was also featured prominently in the 2001 ILC meeting in New York.[132] Anyone who has been personally involved in speaking to Jewish or Catholic audiences will readily agree that the lack of education on what has been achieved continues to be an obstacle to improving relations at the local level.

At the same time, one must pay tribute to the efforts that have been made at the national and local level. The Catholic Church exists in and out of local churches, and these have a responsibility of their own. The declarations on Judaism that have already been issued by commissions of various bishops' conferences fill two quite substantial volumes.

In my opening address to the 1998 ILC meeting, I mentioned that in many places throughout the world Jews and Catholics were sharing in various forms of cooperation. "One finds parishes and synagogues working together, setting up together study groups, undertaking common initiatives for the good of the local community. Yet we must admit that relations at the grass roots level can be greatly expanded. All that is needed is a little thought and courage."[133]

The following information will, in the circumstances, be necessarily far from complete, but should offer encouraging examples of important responses to *Nostra Aetate*, no. 4 at these levels.

Undoubtedly the leaders in this regard are Catholic and Jewish organizations in the United States. This is, of course, the country that has the greatest number of Jewish residents outside of Israel. Under the leadership of outstanding and courageous leaders—such as Cardinals Bernardin, O'Connor, and Keeler—the Bishops' Committee for Ecumenical and Interreligious Affairs (BCEIA) of the United States Conference of Catholic Bishops has been particularly active in this field and has made valuable contributions to the task. The BCEIA has recently published a collection of key documents on the Catholic teaching regarding the church's relationship to the Jews and its opposition to anti-Semitism,[134] which includes its own documents as well as the more important international statements on the subject. Dr. Eugene Fisher, associate director of the Secretariat for Catholic-Jewish Relations of the National Conference of Catholic Bishops, has made a valuable personal contribution to these relations both at the national and international levels.

On the Jewish side, the American Jewish Committee has been responsible for a number of initiatives, including pioneer work in Eastern European countries, in particular the Catholic Church in Poland, in seeking to create a new Catholic-Jewish relationship in those countries after the fall of Communism. In 1998 I was able to pay tribute publicly to the contribution that the AJC was making to the process of reconciliation between Catholic and Jewish communities within the United States and far beyond its borders.[135]

A precious contribution to promoting Jewish-Christian relations has been made by North American universities. There are at least fifteen centers of Jewish-Christian learning at universities or theological schools in the United States. Special mention must be made of "The Institute of Judeo-Christian Studies" at Seton Hall University, New Jersey, founded and for many years directed by Monsignor John A. Oesterreicher, and of the Catholic Theological Union of Chicago, with the presence there of Rev. John T. Pawlikowski.

As another example of university involvement, in 1998 the AJC and the University of St. Leo jointly founded the Center for Catholic-Jewish Studies in Florida, which each year brings together clergy and laypeople to discuss matters of common interest. The 2003 meeting had as its theme "Adversity and Loss: Remaining Faithful in Difficult Times." Jewish and Catholic scholars delved into their religious traditions "to explore how Judaism and Catholicism, two ancient faiths, confront death and dying, physical suffering and the ultimate cry of the heart 'Why me?' when illnesses, accidents and other calamities assail us."[136]

On the occasion of the twentieth anniversary of *Nostra Aetate*, a very productive meeting took place between the Anti-Defamation League and Catholic institutions in the United States, which led to dialogues throughout the country in which Jews and Catholics came together, not simply to review the past, but more importantly to charter future courses of mutual activities toward deeper understanding.[137]

Over twenty institutes and centers in the United States dedicated to interreligious dialogue have come together to form the "Council of Centers on Jewish-Catholic Relations" in order to collaborate more effectively. Similar centers also exist in Europe and a number of these centers (Rome, Paris, Vienna, Cambridge, Brussels, Lucerne) came together from June 1–3, 2003, to foster mutual understanding and promote possible means of collaboration. As a result of this meeting, it is hoped that centers in Britain and other countries will likewise join to create a "Council of Centers in Europe."[138]

The CRRJ has maintained close relations with the International Council of Christians and Jews, with the president or secretary participating in many of its annual conferences. National member organizations of the ICCJ have fostered Christian-Jewish relations at that level. The British Council of Christians and Jews (BCCJ) has been particularly active in Britain in bringing Christians of all denominations and Jews to be a blessing for each other and in this way a blessing to their society.

In May 2000, leading members of Reform Judaism in England organized a millennium conference in London to discuss the theme "Catholics and Jews in Partnership." Invited participants discussed questions of profound religious significance for both faith communities in an open and cordial atmosphere.

The CRRJ and the Israeli Delegation for Relations with the Catholic Church, during a meeting in Jerusalem on December 1–3, 2003, signed a joint declaration titled *The Relevance of the Central Teachings of the Holy Scriptures which we share for Contemporary Society and the Education of Future Generations.*[139] Within Israel the Interreligious Coordinating Council in Israel (ICCI) has been dong fine work. The Israeli Jewish Council for Interreligious Relations (IJCIR) forms part of this organization. The ICCI sponsors regular conferences and seminars on interreligious subjects and conducts programs for Christian, Jewish, and Muslim reconciliation. One such program is Kedem—Voices for Religious Reconciliation. Kedem consists of fourteen local religious leaders—seven rabbis and seven Arabs (five sheikhs or imams and two Christian clergy)—who meet regularly and seek to bring together from throughout Israel local grassroots religious leaders of the three faiths for study, dialogue, and action in the field of reconciliation and peace-building. ICCI also fosters the program *Face to Face/Faith to Faith* for the youth of the three religions, promotes women's dialogue groups, and cosponsors lectures on interreligious themes.[140]

The Australia/Israel and Jewish Affairs Council is active in fostering better Christian-Jewish relations and responding to new manifestations of anti-Jewish sentiments in that country. The AIJAC publishes a monthly magazine, *The Review*. In some areas young people from Catholic, Jewish, and Muslim schools have been given the opportunity of coming together face to face, and an excellent textbook for Australian students, *Jewish-Christian Relations*, is available.[141]

Joint Jewish-Christian liaison committees have been at work in Hungary and the Czech Republic. The church in Poland, under the guidance of Archbishop Muszynski and then of Bishop Stanislaw Gadecki, has made available in Polish the official documents of the church concerning Catholic-Jewish relations. The church in Poland has also been involved with Jewish organizations in North America in offering future members of the Polish clergy education in this field.

As mentioned before, a first meeting on a continental scale of Catholics and Jews in Latin America took place in Bogotá, Colombia, August 20–21, 1968. This meeting recommended cooperation between the two communities at all levels—personal, family, and communal. It encouraged study and cultural exchanges; education to overcome continuing and mutual prejudices in textbooks, schools, seminaries, and families; and even sharing in worship. It was hoped that CELAM (the council of Latin American bishops) would help to promote these recommendations. Pope Paul VI, who was on a visit to Colombia at the time, met with the Jewish representatives and encouraged their efforts "for the good of all humanity."[142] In 1986, CELAM also met in Bogotá with the Anti-Defamation League of B'nai B'rith to map a joint program to improve the quality of teaching about Jews and Judaism in Catholic education in Latin America.[143]

In South America it is Brazil that leads the way in promoting Catholic-Jewish relations at a national and local level. When he visited Sao Paolo on July 3, 1980, Pope John Paul II met with Jewish representatives and was able to state: "I am very happy to know that this spirit of cooperation exists here in Brazil especially through the Jewish-Christian fraternity."[144] Rabbi Henry I. Sobel of Sao Paolo has been particularly active in promoting Jewish-Catholic relations in Brazil and in all Latin America, and has as well taken part in many international meetings. At his invitation and that of the National Council for Jewish-Christian Dialogue of the National Conference of Catholic Bishops of Brazil, I went to Sao Paolo in 1990 to celebrate the twenty-fifth anniversary of *Nostra Aetate* and was greatly encouraged by my experience. I was able to commend warmly the contribution made by the council "to the present happy state of relations between Catholics and Jews in the country."[145]

On January 28–29, 2002, in the city hall of Paris, a first meeting took place of European leaders of Judaism and Catholicism, organized by the European Jewish Congress, and with the participation of Cardinals Jean-Marie Lustiger, archbishop of Paris, and Walter Kasper of the CRRJ. The theme of the meeting was "After the Second Vatican Council and Nostra Aetate, Improving Relations between Jews and Catholics in Europe in the Pontificate of His Holiness Pope John Paul II." The pope noted that the meeting was a particularly timely "continuation of the recent Day of Prayer for Peace in the World, which was held in Assisi on January 24," and at which a Jewish delegation of prominent leaders had taken part.

From even such a brief summary, it is evident that serious efforts have indeed been made over the years, and continue to be made, in an effort to bring *Nostra Aetate*, no. 4, to the knowledge of Catholics and Jews throughout the world and to promote its teaching at the national and local levels, especially in those places that have significant numbers of Jewish and Christian residents.

PART IV
THE STATE OF THE QUESTION

RELATIONS WITH NON-CHRISTIAN RELIGIONS,
OTHER THAN JUDAISM

The initiatives promoted by the PCID and the responses they have received are a good indication of the present relationship between the Catholic Church and the other religious traditions. Beginning practically from scratch, the church has been able to establish relations with representatives of all the major world religions. Barriers have been broken down, misunderstandings corrected, and a new spirit of tolerance and trust created.

In this, the lead has been given by the PCID, but a great deal of the credit must also go to the local churches. In most places where Christians live side by side with members of other religions, commissions have been set up at the national and sometimes at the regional level to make contact with local religious leaders.

A particular difficulty often experienced in this process, at both the local and international levels, is the lack of recognized leaders able to speak with authority on behalf of the partner in dialogue. Hence, interreligious dialogue tends to center around members of other religions who have a particular personal interest in promoting a new relationship with the Christian communities, but who cannot necessarily be considered as representing officially their own community.

Within the Catholic Church in general, interreligious dialogue does not create the same emotional reactions as dialogue with other Christians and Jews. Nevertheless, the work done at the local level is essential to progress in the dialogue. Information about what is actually happening at that level is to be found in the PCID bulletin *Pro Dialogo*.

A dialogue that is of particular importance today is, of course, that with the Muslim world. While one will find members of Buddhist and Hindu religions in many countries in small numbers, the Muslim presence in traditionally Christian countries of Western Europe and North America is quite significant. Moreover, the Middle East is an area of particular concern to both Christians and Muslims. For these reasons, there is within the PCID a special commission for religious relations with Muslims, composed of a president, vice president, and secretary. A small group of eight consulters assists the commission in developing different aspects of Christian-Muslim relations.

In recent years the PCID has dedicated a great deal of time and taken various important initiatives in order to promote Catholic-Muslim relations. In 1985, twelve Muslim experts from Pakistan, India, Bangladesh, and Lebanon were in Rome for discussions on the topic "Holiness in Islam and Christianity." In 1988, the PCID invited Muslims from six North African countries to Assisi for discussions on the topic "Co-existence in Diversity."[146] On June 8, 1994, the PCID met with representatives of three Muslim organizations—the World Muslim League, the Organization of the Islamic Conference, and the World Muslim Congress—to discuss a draft document on population and development in preparation for the UN conference on this important international question, to be held in Cairo in September 1997. Also in 1994, from August 1–5, the council organized at Pattaya, Thailand, an Islamic-Christian gathering of South East Asian nations on the theme "Harmony among Believers of the Living Faiths: Christians and Muslims in South East Asia." A meeting in Vienna in October 1997 with the World Islamic Society discussed the theme "Mass Media and Religion."[147]

Cardinal Arinze was in Egypt in May 1995, at the invitation of His Excellency Dr. Muhammad Sayed Tantawi, the Egyptian Gran Mufti and a firm supporter of relations between Islam and Christianity. Then on June 22, 1995, the PCID met in Rome with the Islamic World League, the Islamic World Congress, the Organization of the Islamic Conference, the Islamic International Council for Da'wah and Humanitarian Aid, as well as with representatives of the Al-Azhar University in Cairo. A decision was made to set up a permanent joint committee for an exchange of questions of common interest to Muslims and Christians. This is known as the Islamic-Catholic Liaison Committee.

The Islamic-Catholic Liaison Committee met for the first time in Cairo, May 29–June 1, 1996, to consider three topics: the relation between justice and human dignity; preserving the environment and human security; and poverty and the means of aid. The committee met a second time in 1997 in Rabat, Morocco, to reflect on how Christians and Muslims speak about each other, and to consider the position of minority groups. In 1998 the theme in Cairo involved discussions on the duties of men and women, on human rights and duties, and on children's rights in the family and in society. The 1999 meeting in Paris (June 17–23) considered the theme "The Building Up of a Culture of Dialogue in the Present Generation and the Third Way."

An extraordinary meeting of the Islamic-Catholic Liaison Committee was held in Rome February 21–22, 2001, to reflect on the tragic situation in the Holy Land. The general meeting in July discussed the theme of the role of religions in the dialogue between civilizations in the era of globalization. After September 11, 2001, the committee made a joint declaration condemning terrorism, and held an extraordinary meeting in Cairo October 27–30, 2001, organized by the Muslim partner, but with PCID participation. The 2002 meeting was held in Markfield, Great Britain, on July 12–13. Discussions centered on the theme "Religion and Racism, and Toward a Culture of Dialogue." A ninth meeting took place in the offices of the PCID on January 19–20, 2004. The topic was "Human Dignity and Humanitarian Rights in Armed Conflicts." The subject, according to the press release, "was treated from a religious point of view according to the teaching of our two religious traditions." The closing statement affirmed that "justice and peace are the basis of relations and of interaction among human persons" and called for "an immediate end to all conflicts, as well as forms of aggression against the security and stability of peoples." On this occasion, as in the earlier meeting, an appeal was made for continuous prayer for peace.[148]

In March 2004, the Islamic-Catholic Committee published a declaration on the current situation in the Holy Land, and in August of the same year issued a joint statement on the situation in Iraq,[149] both signed by Archbishop Fitzgerald and the leader of the Islamic delegation, Prof. Dr. Hamid Bin Ahmad Al-Rifaie, president of the Islamic Forum for Dialogue in Jeddah, Saudi Arabia. In the statement on Iraq, the two presidents of the committee condemned the terrorist acts that continue to be perpetrated in Iraq, and "in particular the suicide attacks in areas in which are located places of worship, both against Muslims and Christians gathered for worship." The statement declared that "such acts of blind violence offend the sacred name of God and true religion," and expressed the hope that "with the help of the Almighty and Merciful God the Iraqi people may finally enjoy the gift of peace."

Regular meetings have also been conducted with the Al Albait Foundation of Amman, Jordan: the first in Amman in 1990 considered religious education and modern society;[150] a second in 1991 the rights and education of children in Islam and Christianity;[151] a third in the series discussed women in society according to Islam and Christianity; a fourth, religion and nationalism; a fifth in 1996, religion and the use of the Earth's resources; a sixth in 1997 discussed human dignity.

In 1996 a permanent committee was set up with the Al-Azhar University, Cairo, the oldest and most prestigious of the Islamic world. In 1999 this committee discussed dialogue with monotheistic religions. Then in the year 2000, Pope John Paul II during his pilgrimage to Mount Sinai in Egypt, met with Muslim leaders at the Al-Azhar University. Later in the year, in July, the committee discussed the theme "Rights and Duties of Citizens" and agreed to future yearly meetings to take place on the anniversary of the day on which the pope had visited Al-Azhar, February 24. The meeting in 2001 issued a joint declaration on the situation in the Balkans and in particular in Kosovo. A second declaration dealt with the grave situation in the Holy Land, while there was also an exchange of views on the proposed new mosque in Nazareth. After September 11th, the committee issued a declaration condemning terrorism and the 2002 meeting had as its theme "Extremism and Its Influence on Humanity." In 2004 the Joint Committee of the Permanent Committee of Al-Azhar for Dialogue with Monotheistic Religions and the PCID, after meeting in Rome, issued a common declaration appealing "to all to avoid generalizations in judging people and to allocate responsibility only to those who have committed transgressions and not to blame innocent people for the misdeeds of others." It also appealed to all to practice examination of conscience and to admit guilt wherever applicable as a way of returning to right conduct. The declaration stated that the aim of the joint committee, in addressing this appeal, "is to universalize justice, peace and love among all."[152]

An important initiative in view of the difficult Christian-Islam relationship in the Middle East as a consequence of the Iraqi invasion was the 2004 Qatar Conference on Muslim-Christian Dialogue. Leaders of the two religions from around the world attended this conference, organized by the Commission for Religious Relations with Muslims within the PCID, and the Gulf States Center at the University of Qatar. The Commission for Religious Relations with Muslims within the PCID was set up already in 1974 and had been meeting regularly on a yearly basis. The members were all Catholic and they alone took part in these annual gatherings. Qatar was the first time that Catholics and Muslims had met within the commission.

Public sessions on May 27, 2004, were addressed by Cardinal Jean-Louis Tauran, librarian and archivist of the Vatican;[153] Archbishop Michael Fitzgerald, president of the PCID; Shayk Hamad Bin Khalifa Al-Thani, the Emir of Qatar; His Holiness Shenouda III, pope of Alexandria and of the Coptic Orthodox Church; Youssef al-Qaradawi of the University of Qatar; Muhammad Sayyed Tantawi, Grand Imam of al-Azhar; and Prof. Dr. Hamid Bin Ahmad Al-Rifaie, president of the international Islamic Forum for Dialogue.

In his address, Cardinal Tauran called the Qatar meeting "an eloquent witness to fraternity" by believers belonging to two different religions, both rich in their own spiritual traditions. While stressing the many things that Muslims and Christians have in common, the cardinal stated that in order to avoid any syncretism or caricature of others, "it is important that each person remain loyal to his or her own faith." He said:

> Political leaders have nothing to fear from true believers. Authentic believers are also the best antidote to all forms of fanaticism, because they know that preventing their brothers and sisters from practicing their religion, discriminating against a follower of a religion other than one's own, or worse still, killing in the name of religion, are abominations that

offend God and which no cause or authority, be it political or religious, can ever justify.[154]

On May 28 and 29 the commission met in closed sessions. The ten Catholic commission members were joined by ten invited Muslim guests, including several professors of Islamic law, theology, and philosophy, and directors of Islamic religious studies and comparative religions from Tunisia, Qatar, Egypt, the United States, Pakistan, Turkey, the United Kingdom, and Iran.[155]

The meeting did not issue a formal statement, but at a press conference on the final afternoon, participants stated that the meeting was very positive and that both religions hoped to continue and to deepen the dialogue established between them. Dr. El-Hage reported that the sessions were marked by transparency and cordiality, and Archbishop Fitzgerald indicated that the theoretical part of the meeting looked at the declaration of human rights, the magisterium of the church in the matter of religious freedom, and the views of modern religious authors and thinkers on this topic in Islamic law. While noting the differences between the Catholic and Islamic teaching on religious freedom, the archbishop was nonetheless able to report: "We agreed that religious freedom is part of human dignity that comes from God." He noted the difference between freedom *of* religion (freedom to believe and practice one's faith, or freedom not to believe) and freedom *within* religion. The former is a full right; the latter is not, because being a believer implies living a specific set of rules and behavior, and not being free to change them.

In conclusion, Archbishop Fitzgerald pointed out the difficulties that exist where there is no central authority or hierarchical structure such as the Catholic Church has. "Often," he said, "in the Muslim world people represent themselves, not a Church or a group."[156] This is something already mentioned in my text above.

The presence of several Muslim observers at the Special Synod for Lebanon in 1995 was a very significant sign of this new Catholic-Muslim relationship. Over the years, it had become usual for Christian observers or fraternal delegates to be invited to regional synods. This was the first occasion, however, when members of a non-Christian religion were asked to be present in this capacity.

In recent years, there has been a development that takes us back to *Nostra Aetate*, where Jewish-Christian relations are considered together with the relations between the church and other religious traditions. At the various Assisi Days of Prayer for Peace, Jewish representatives were present together with Christians and members of other religions. This joint approach is being encouraged by the Vatican, and on January 17, 2004, a concert took place in the Paul VI Hall in the Vatican, in the presence of Pope John Paul II, dedicated to reconciliation among Jews, Christians, and Muslims and with the musical themes of the veneration of the patriarch Abraham and the resurrection of the dead.[157] Among those at the concert were representatives from various international Jewish organizations, Islamic groups, and Christian churches and ecclesial communions. At the end of the concert Pope John Paul II made the following comments on Christian-Jewish-Muslim relations:

> The history of relations among Jews, Christians and Muslims is marked by lights and shadows, and, unfortunately, has known painful moments. Today the pressing need is felt for a sincere reconciliation among all believers in one God. This evening, we are gathered here to give concrete expression to this commitment to reconciliation entrusting ourselves to the universal message of music. Our common desire is that all human beings be purified from the hatred and evil that continually threaten peace, and that they may know how to extend hands that have never known violence but which are ready to offer help and comfort to those in need.

The pope emphasized that the followers of the three world religions must find within themselves the courage of peace.

Cardinal Arinze participated in a meeting of Christians, Muslims, and Jews in Brussels on December 19–20, 2001, organized by His Holiness, Patriarch Bartholomew I of Constantinople. In England, a council of Christians, Jews, and Muslims has been in existence for some ten or more years. It has attracted particular attention and praise for its efforts to bring these communities closer together and has received support from the leaders of all three communities.

In reflecting on Muslim-Catholic relations, it is also necessary to mention the visit that Pope John Paul II made to Morocco on August 19, 1985, the pope's first visit to a Muslim country. He was received by King Hassan II ben Mohammed, who was not only head of state, but also the spiritual head of his country, as Amir al-Muminime (Prince of Believers). On this occasion, the pope met with some fifty thousand young Muslims from twenty-three countries in the Casablanca Stadium, who had come together in Morocco for the Pan-Arabic Games. King Hassan II presented Pope John Paul II to the gathering as "Teacher and Defender of values common to the Islamic faith and the Christian faith." The pope in his reply proclaimed his own faith in God, the merciful creator, who enlightens, guides, assists, and pardons, and he asked, "In a world that deserves peace and unity, but nevertheless knows a thousand tensions and conflicts, should not those who believe promote friendship and unity among the peoples who make up a single community on earth?"[158]

Today, there are also regular opportunities for dialogue with Shinto and Buddhist communities. Already in 1985 we read of visits to the secretariat of a group of Shinto priests, accompanied by thirty representatives from the Federation of Buddhist Women, representatives of the Buddhist movement Agon-shu, and young members of Rissho Kosei-kai, a Buddhist lay movement.

A very significant dialogue event took place that same year on the occasion of the eightieth birthday of Dr. Nikkyo Niwano, founder and president of the Rissho Kosei-kai movement, and an observer at the Second Vatican Council. The under-secretary of the PCID was present at the birthday celebration, together with the apostolic pro-nuncio and Chiara Lubich, founder and president of the Focolare Movement. It is worthwhile to quote briefly for our purpose from the official speech of Dr. Niwano on this occasion:

> After my participation as an observer at the last session of Vatican II, and after the meeting with Paul VI, my idea of the Catholic Church changed. The Church of the Council also changed my attitude toward the followers of other religions. The pope confirmed for me his respect for Buddhism and showed me the way of dialogue and collaboration. I have become a "Buddhist child of the Council." For

this I have been involved in interreligious dialogue and collaboration during the past twenty years, and among other initiatives I founded the World Conference of Religions for Peace.[159]

Dr. Niwano received an honorary doctorate from the Pontifical Salesian University in Rome on March 20, 1986.[160]

Following the Assisi meeting of 1986, a Day of Prayer for Peace was held at Mount Hiei in Japan, organized by a special conference of religious representatives of that country, which included most of the religions of Japan: Shinto, Buddhist, Christian, and new religions. The meeting was attended by twenty-four representatives from other countries and religions: Jews, Sikhs, Confucians, and Muslims. Cardinal Arinze was present with members of the PCID and some Japanese bishops. Each group presented their "way to peace." The Mount Hiei Day of Prayer has since become an annual event.

In 1989, the Dalai Lama visited the PCID.[161] The first Buddhist-Christian Colloquium was held in Kaohsiung, Taiwan, July 29–August 4, 1995. This was organized in response to the tension in Catholic-Buddhist relations following comments on Buddhism made by Pope John Paul II in his book *Crossing the Threshold of Hope* that had not been well received in Buddhist circles. In Kaohsiung, Christians and Buddhists of various schools from a number of countries (Italy, Japan, Sri Lanka, Taiwan, Thailand, and the United States) discussed the topic "Salvation in Buddhism and in Christianity," and the meeting concluded with a declaration on points of agreement and disagreement between Buddhism and Christianity.[162]

The second Buddhist-Christian Colloquium took place in Bangalore, India, in 1988 with the theme "Word and Science in Buddhist and Christian Traditions"; and the third colloquium in Tokyo, Japan, September 30–October 3, 2002, dedicated to the topic "Sangha in Buddhism and Church in Christianity." The discussion covered questions such as Buddha and Sangha, or community, and Jesus Christ and his church; Buddhas, bodhisattvas, arhats, and lamas in Buddhism, and apostles, martyrs, saints, and doctors of the church in Christianity; — bhiku, bhikuni, and monasteries in Buddhism and their place in society, and monks, nuns, religious, and consecrated persons in Christianity and their role of service to society.[163]

Unfortunately, it has not so far been possible to establish a similar forum for dialogue with Hindus. In his message to Hindus for the feast of Diwali in 2003, Archbishop Michael Fitzgerald, president of PCID, asked for suggestions on how to promote together and protect the dignity of every human person. "Let us come together," he writes, "and share our common concerns, making an effort to listen to one another attentively. Let us speak honestly, aware of our own responsibility with regard to the choices that have to be made to resolve current problems in the world today."[164]

There have been, however, good contacts between the PCID and individual Hindu spiritual leaders. Some of these have been present at the important gatherings organized by the PCID like those of Assisi mentioned above. A Christian-Hindu meeting took place in Varanasi, India, in 1992 on the theme "Our Common Spiritual Heritage and Our Contribution to Harmony and Integration—Human Solidarity." Then in Madurai, India, from October 9–11, 1995, representatives of the Catholic Bishops' Conference of India, the National Council of Churches India, the WCC, and Madurai Kamaraj University considered guidelines for dialogue between Christians and Hindus. From October 24–28 the same year, the Office of the Federation of Asian Bishops Conferences (FABC–BIRA/3) invited Christians and Hindus to discuss together the topic "Working for Harmony in the Contemporary World."[165] In February 2001 a Hindu-Christian dialogue was held in Mumbai, India, on the theme "The Mahavakya (Great Sayings) in Hinduism and Christianity." Delicate political situations and the special Hindu approach to other religions makes Hindu-Christian dialogue difficult, but these meetings have helped to create a better climate of trust.[166]

A particular friend of the council was the late Hindu leader Pandurangshastri Athavale, who passed away in October 2003. He dedicated his life to the good of others and to peace and harmony in society. He was the founder of the Swadhyaia Family, a popular movement in India of millions of followers dedicated to dialogue among the religions and to concrete help for the most needy. He worked closely with the Focolare Movement of Chiara Lubich and showed great respect for Christianity.

Cardinal Arinze, during his period as president of the PCID, made good use of his African knowledge and contacts to call for greater interest on the part of the Catholic Church in African Traditional Religion. In 1988 he wrote a letter on the topic "Pastoral Attention to African Traditional Religion."[167] In 1992, His Eminence was in Senegal, Gambia, and Guinea to meet with and encourage those involved in interreligious dialogue to do more to create a climate of collaboration with believers of different religions.[168] In 1995 he met with the Association of Episcopal Conferences of Anglophone West Africa (AECAWA) in Africa to remind the participants of the importance of pastoral attention to African Traditional Religion. In the following year discussions took place in Abidjan, Ivory Coast, on the topic of the meeting of the Gospel and traditional religions, with twenty-four participants from five continents.[169] Toward the end of 2001, the PCID published the reflection "Christianity in Dialogue with African Traditional Religion and Culture."

From time to time the PCID has had contacts with other religions, though on a far less regular basis than those to which reference has already been made. Delegations have been received by the PCID from Jainism (February 14–15, 1995); and on November 27, 1997 a delegation of four Taoists from Central China visited the offices of the PCID. This was the first group from mainland China to be received there.[170] The first meeting of the PCID with representatives of Tenrikyo, a Japanese religion born in the twentieth century, took place in 1998.[171] During the Jubilee Year 2000, there were visits to Rome of members of Shinto and of a group of Sikhs from England.

On the thirtieth anniversary of *Nostra Aetate* September 21–26, 1994, the PCID in collaboration with the Pontifical Council for the Family organized a seminar on marriage and family in today's world. Thirty representatives of other religions took part, and the encounter closed with a declaration of common commitment and cooperation to promote family values and dignity.[172] Cardinal Arinze played an important role in the Millennium World Peace Summit of Religious and Spiritual Leaders held at UN Headquarters in New York from August 28–31, 2000. In 2001, on the 2600th anniversary of the birth of Mahavir, Cardinal Angelo Sodano, in the name of Pope John Paul II, sent a message of good wishes to the worldwide Jain community.

Catholic bishops' regional conferences continue to contribute notably to interreligious relations in Africa (AECAWA) and Asia (FABC). The FABC has held several regional meetings with Hindus, Taoists, and Confucians (BIRA meetings). In September 2001, Cardinal

Arinze, Bishop Fitzgerald, and members of the PCID, together with six consulters of the Pontifical Council met in Suwon, Korea, with twelve secretaries of the ecumenical and interreligious commissions of Asian bishops' conferences to discuss "Interreligious Dialogue as a way to face together the various problems in Asia." The cardinal went on to visit various Catholic institutions and meet with representatives of other religions in Korea.

At both the international and local levels, lay members of the Catholic Church have a decisive role. This fact is well illustrated in the *Interreligious Dialogue Directory* that the PCID published in 2001. Particularly active at the local level are the Center for the Study of Islam and Christian-Muslim Relations at the University of Birmingham, in Selly Oak, Birmingham, England; the Center for Muslim-Christian Understanding at Georgetown University, Washington, DC; and the Columban Center for Christian-Muslim Relations, North Turramurra, New South Wales, Australia.

Special mention should also be made here of two international lay organizations within the Catholic Church that are making a particular contribution to the ongoing interreligious dialogue throughout the world.

At the first World Day of Prayer at Assisi in 1986, Pope John Paul II invited those present to continue spreading the message of peace and living the spirit of Assisi. In response to this call, the Sant'Egidio Community, a relatively young lay organization based in Rome, with the encouragement of Pope John Paul II, has since arranged a yearly meeting of religious leaders on the subject of religions and peace. Beginning already in 1987, the community invited leaders of the Christian churches, together with Jewish representatives and prominent members of other world religions, to come together in various European cities for dialogue, prayer, and common witness to peace. These meetings have been well attended and undoubtedly are helping to break down barriers of misunderstanding between men and women of different religious traditions.[173]

The Sant'Egidio Community also took the initiative to organize a Christian-Muslim Summit on October 3–4, 2001, immediately after the tragic events of September 11, 2001. At such a delicate time for Christian-Muslim relations, the community recognized the urgent need of bringing Muslim and Christian representatives together in dialogue and shared witness, so as to avoid the temptation of creating a clash of cultures and the subsequent danger of conflict. The climate of peace among Christians and Muslims had to be strengthened. Leaders of the Catholic Church, the Orthodox Churches, the Lutheran World Federation, the World Methodist Council, and the Episcopal Church USA were joined by Islamic religious and cultural leaders from Egypt, Saudi Arabia, the United Arab Emirates, the United States, Algeria, Qatar, and Iran. The Sant'Egidio Community has also organized other gatherings at both the international and the local level to promote dialogue and cooperation among the world religions.[174]

Another lay movement within the Catholic Church, briefly mentioned before, is the Focolare Movement (Work of Mary); it, too, is making a similar valuable contribution to ecumenical and interreligious relations. The Focolare Movement began reflecting on the inherent role of interreligious dialogue in its charism when, in 1977, lay founder Chiara Lubich received the Templeton Prize for Progress in Religion. Her encounter with representatives of some of the world religions at the ceremony held in this connection suggested to her "a new opening." She realized that "from then on we would have to try to take our spirit, our life, not only to other Churches or Christian Communities, but also to our brothers and sisters of other faiths."[175]

In the course of the years since 1977, members of the Focolare Movement have dialogued with Shintoists, Taoists, Sikhs, Hindus, Zoroastrians, Baha'i, and followers of Traditional Religions. But perhaps the most developed relationship has been with Buddhists and Muslims. Chiara Lubich herself has spoken of her spiritual experience to thousands of Buddhists in Japan, and in 1997 she became the first Christian laywoman to address a group of Buddhist monks and laity at both the Buddhist University and the monastery in Chiang Mai, Thailand. She has also spoken to three thousand African-American Muslims at the Malcolm Shabazz Mosque in Harlem, New York.

Around thirty thousand members of other religions share the spirituality of the Focolare Movement in ways appropriate to the circumstances. Some are involved in common humanitarian projects, while others engage in an intense exchange of religious experience. At the school for interreligious dialogue at Tagatay, Manila, in the Philippines, people of different religions come together to share the spirituality of the Focolare Movement.

When asked why this involvement in interreligious dialogue has been so rapid and fruitful, Chiara Lubich responds by pointing out a principle that is fundamental also in ecumenism and Christian-Jewish relations:

> The decisive element and characteristic is love, loved poured in our hearts by the Holy Spirit. Love finds a spontaneous and immediate echo in other religions and cultures. And that is why in all there is present the so-called "Golden Rule" that for us is expressed "Do unto others as you would have them do unto you" (Luke 6:31).... This love consists "in loving without distinction, in loving first without expecting that the other loves us (like the love of God for us)" and "in being one," that "is to be all things to all people (1 Cor 9,22)."[176]

It is interesting that, at the beginning of this new Christian millennium, both the PCID and the PCPCU are placing new emphasis on the place of spirituality in religious dialogue. Reference has already been made to the role that is being given now to spiritual ecumenism. On March 3, 1999, His Eminence Cardinal Francis Arinze, PCID president, sent a letter to presidents of bishops' conferences throughout the world on the spirituality of dialogue. This was a follow up to the plenary session of the PCID in 1995, which discussed at length the topic "Spirituality of Dialogue; Dialogue of Spirituality."[177]

In his letter, Cardinal Arinze explained that Catholics and other Christians engaged in interreligious dialogue are becoming more and more convinced of the need of a sound Christian spirituality to uphold their efforts. In words that recall the teaching in *Dialogue and Proclamation*, the letter points out that the Christian who meets other believers is not involved in an activity that is marginal to his or her faith, but is something that arises from the demands of that faith. "It flows from faith and should be nourished by faith."

In dialogue the Christian is called to be a witness to Christ, imitating the Lord in his proclamation of the kingdom, his concern and compassion for each individual person, and his respect for that person's freedom. It is part of the Christian faith understanding that God wants all persons to be saved. The Christian who engages in interreligious dialogue needs to understand other religions in order precisely to understand the followers of these religions and acknowledge the many points of contact that exist. The differences, however, should not be overlooked. "A Christian spirituality of dialogue will grow," wrote Cardinal Arinze, "if both these dimensions are maintained. While appreciating the workings of the spirit of God among people of other religions, not only in the hearts of individuals but also in some of their religious rites, the uniqueness of the Christian faith will be respected."[178] The spirituality that is to animate interreligious dialogue, according to this letter, is one that is lived out in faith, hope, and charity, and nourished by prayer and sacrifice.

In conclusion, the president of PCID asks the bishops' conferences for their reflections and suggestions, based on the experience gained in their own areas. It is expected that the PCID will publish in due course a document on the spirituality of dialogue.

Already on the twentieth anniversary of its existence, the Secretariat for Non-Christians was able to claim that the initiatives it had undertaken, together with the encyclical *Ecclesiam Suam*, could rightly be considered a promising reply to the expectations and needs of the church and the world. They had contributed to greater understanding among peoples, thus diminishing tension and promoting a climate and a mentality of openness and reciprocal trust, and marking a new stage in the story of humanity. The secretariat noted that their influence had been especially notable in countries with a non-Christian majority, helping to create ecclesial sensibility in places and with people that otherwise would have been impenetrable. It concluded that the experience of those first twenty years had shown how opportune an institution like the secretariat had been for the life of the church and for relations between religions and peoples.[179]

Then in his letter to the episcopal conferences of March 3, 1999, the president of the PCID was able to write:

> In the intervening years, guided by the teaching of the Pontifical Magisterium, and by such documents as *The Attitude of the Churches toward the Followers of Other Religions (1984)* and *Dialogue and Proclamation* (1991), Catholics have been making considerable efforts to meet the followers of other religions. They have undertaken various initiatives and, with time, these have increased in number and become more widespread.

> Encounters with peoples of other religions occur at the level
> of daily life, in the joint promotion of social projects, in the
> exchange of religious experience, and in formal exchanges
> where Christians and other believers discuss elements of
> belief or practice.[180]

It would seem then that the hopes and expectations of the council fathers, as expressed in the declaration *Nostra Aetate*, have indeed brought forth a response that has radically changed the approach of the Catholic Church to other world religions. Of particular importance, I believe, is the development in *Dialogue and Proclamation* and other official church documents of the theological understanding of the church's mission in fostering interreligious dialogue. The delicate balance achieved in this teaching between interreligious dialogue and proclamation, as "both legitimate and necessary," has thrown new light on interreligious dialogue as an essential element of the church's mission of proclaiming the good news of God's universal salvific will. This has given interreligious dialogue a new place in the church's mission in which all Christians are called to be personally involved.

The various interreligious initiatives promoted by Pope John Paul II in favor of world peace have made a valuable contribution to this dialogue. The experience of Assisi in 1986 and 2002, the 1999 interreligious assembly in Rome, and the interreligious encounters of the pope during his visits outside of Italy have certainly changed the attitude of many non-Christian leaders to Christianity and to the Catholic Church. The activities undertaken by the PCID have also made a deep impression on those of other religions who have been involved. The example given by the Holy See has stirred the bishops' conferences throughout the world to become more active in promoting these relations at their regional, national, and diocesan levels.

This is not an easy dialogue. As already mentioned, most of the members of other religions who take part in it do so as private individuals, and not as official representatives of their communities. At the same time, it is true that some of these are scholars and persons of importance in their societies, and it may well be that their influence on interreligious relations is much greater than may appear at first sight.

From what has been stated above, the Christian-Muslim dialogue has become in recent years more organized through special commissions both within the PCID and the Muslim world. More and more Muslims are living today in countries that have been in the past almost exclusively Christian. The Christian churches in countries with a large Muslim majority often find their mission extremely difficult. The danger of conflict and even war between countries of the West and the Middle East cannot be ruled out. All of this makes the Christian-Muslim dialogue vital for the future of world peace.

When Pope John Paul II met with the members of the PCID on the fortieth anniversary of their dicastery, on May 15, 2004, he praised the council for its "zealous ecclesial service... finding positive collaboration and reciprocal advantages in many dioceses and in church and Christian communities of different denominations." He noted that many organizations of other religions have come to recognize the importance of the work done by the council and the importance of interreligious dialogue for "establishing a sure basis for peace."[181]

Given the difficulties involved and the frustration often experienced in interreligious dialogue, it may be good to keep in mind those words of Pope Paul VI to the Secretariat for Non-Christians almost at the beginning of its work in 1967. As he encouraged the officials not to lose heart in the face of difficulties, he urged them to be patient and docile to the Spirit, even should they find themselves working as if in the dark, and concluded: "Our trust is in Christ. He will know how to make the fruit ripen."[182]

CATHOLIC-JEWISH RELATIONS

In the forty years since the publication of *Nostra Aetate*, there has been a radical change also in the attitude of the Catholic Church to the Jewish people, and as a consequence a new relationship has been built up worldwide between the people of the two covenants. The change in Catholic attitudes has not simply affected the practical fellowship of these communities. It has penetrated deeply into the theological and doctrinal teaching of the Catholic Church, which over these forty years has come to see God's action in regard to the Jewish people as part of its own mystery, and the first covenant as never having been revoked. It has realized, moreover, that one cannot fully understand the New Testament without seeing it as part of the total revelation of God that includes the Old Testament.

Much indeed has been accomplished. Still much has to be done to consolidate and further develop these new understandings. As the two communities move forward in consolidating their relationship, they have to remember the *caveat* pronounced on several occasions by both Pope John Paul II and Cardinal Willebrands. There is a fundamental difference between ecumenical dialogue and Christian-Jewish dialogue. The aim of the first is to seek within the Christian communities a profound unity of faith, while that is simply impossible in the second. While Jewish and Catholic faith traditions have much in common, they also differ fundamentally on many questions, beginning, of course, with the place of Jesus Christ in God's saving plan for mankind. Care must be taken also in not presuming that the use of similar expressions and fairly common terms in both traditions automatically indicates agreement on the realities behind those expressions. The word *salvation* is just one of these expressions, as already mentioned in relation to the theological colloquium held in Rome in 1986.[183] For this reason it is important that the theological dialogue which was tentatively begun at that time be more urgently pursued in the coming decades.

The Eighteenth Meeting of the ILC

As indicated already, the 2001 New York meeting of the ILC finally moved in that direction with its discussion on repentance and reconciliation. For most of the first forty years of Catholic-Jewish dialogue, IJCIC was considered to be the almost exclusive Jewish dialogue partner by the CRRJ. In fact, Cardinal Willebrands affirmed during an address to IJCIC in New York on May 16, 1989, that the ILC "remains the most important instrument for the building up of this relationship, and its activity must continue without interruption."[184] In the period since then, the CRRJ has moved away somewhat from this understanding by entering into valuable relationships with other

Jewish organizations, especially those involving Jewish faith organizations. This would seem quite logical, given that the Catholic-Jewish dialogue is a dialogue between two faith communities.

At the same time, IJCIC remains a valuable dialogue partner for the CRRJ. There are still many practical aspects of the Jewish-Christian relationship, and for these IJCIC remains the natural partner. In fact, the ILC met for the eighteenth time, and for the first time in Latin America, in Buenos Aires, from July 5 to 8, 2004, with the theme *"Tzedeq and Tzedaqah (Justice and Charity)*: Facing the Challenges of the Future; Jewish and Catholic Relations in the 21st Century."

A *Joint Declaration*[185] published by this meeting must bring renewed hope for further developments in Catholic-Jewish relations. The document begins by acknowledging the "far-reaching change since the declaration of the Second Vatican Council, *Nostra Aetate*," and the special contribution made by Pope John Paul II over the last quarter century to promoting dialogue between the two faith communities; it also acknowledges Pope John XXIII "for initiating the fundamental change in Catholic-Jewish relationship."

Deliberations on the theme of justice and charity were inspired by God's command to "love one's neighbor as oneself" (Lev 19:18; Matt 22:39). "Drawing from our different perspectives, we have renewed our joint commitment to defend and promote human dignity, as deriving from the biblical affirmation that every human being is created in the likeness and image of God (Gen 1:26)."

The committee sees this joint commitment to justice as being "deeply rooted in both our faiths," which call on their followers to come to the aid of the needy neighbor. While created in diversity, human beings have the same dignity, and every person "the right to be treated with justice and equality." The declaration states that "Jews and Christians have an equal obligation to work for justice with charity (*Tzedaqah*) which ultimately will lead to Shalom for all humanity. In fidelity to our distinct religious traditions, we see this common commitment to justice and charity as man's cooperation in the Divine plan to bring about a better world."

The document recognizes the following as "immediate challenges": the growing economic disparity among people, increasing ecological devastation, the negative aspects of globalization, and the urgent need for international peace-making and reconciliation.

There is a strong commitment by both parties to "prevent the reemergence of anti-Semitism" and to struggle against terrorism. The document concludes by saying, "Terror, in all its forms, and killing 'in the name of God' can never be justified. Terror is a sin against man and God. We call on men and women of all faiths to support international efforts to eradicate this threat to life, so that all nations can live together in peace and security on the basis of *Tzedeq* and *Tzedaqah*."

The importance of this statement is in the fact that a question of common concern—justice and charity—is reflected upon in the light of the two faith traditions. The declaration is also important at this time for the special reference to the fortieth anniversary of *Nostra Aetate*. The relative paragraphs merit quotation in full:

> As we approach the 40th anniversary of *Nostra Aetate*—the groundbreaking declaration of the Second Vatican Council which repudiated the deicide charge against Jews, reaffirmed the Jewish roots of Christianity and rejected anti-Semitism— we take note of the many positive changes within the Catholic Church with respect to her relationship with the Jewish People. The past forty years of our fraternal dialogue stand in stark contrast to the almost two millennia of a "teaching of contempt" and all its painful consequences. We draw encouragement from the fruits of our collective strivings which include the recognition of the unique and unbroken relationship between God and the Jewish People and the total rejection of anti-Semitism in all its forms, including anti-Zionism as a more recent manifestation of anti-Semitism.
>
> For its part, the Jewish community has evinced a growing willingness to engage in interreligious dialogue and joint action regarding religious, social and communal issues on the local, national and international levels, as exemplified in the new direct dialogue between the Chief Rabbinate in Israel and the Holy See. Further, the Jewish community has made strides in educational programming about Christianity, the elimination of prejudice and the importance of Jewish-Christian dialogue. Additionally, the Jewish community has become more aware of, and deplores, the phenomenon of anti-Catholicism in all its forms, manifesting itself in society at large.

The positive reference by the ILC to the new dialogue between the Holy See and the chief rabbinate of Israel is also most encouraging. It would seem that theological dialogue between the two faith communities can finally hope to have a future destined to deepen further Jewish-Catholic understanding and cooperation.

This expectation has been strengthened also by other important developments within the Jewish community. Rabbi Eric H. Yoffie, the president of the Union of American Hebrew Congregations, which unites 1.5 million Reform Jews in 895 synagogues in North America, in the wake of the papal Jubilee apology, on March 23, 2000, called for Catholics and Jews to reflect together on faith questions and urged the Catholic Church and his organization to undertake a joint campaign about the two religions. "This means," he said, "that the Catholics need to educate Catholics about Jews, and the Jews to educate Jews about Catholics." While the Holocaust remains for him, as for Catholics, a deep concern, he believes that *"a dialogue of grievance can no longer dominate our relations"* (emphasis mine).[186]

Dabru Emet (Proclaim the Truth)

Rabbi Yoffie's challenge was followed within a few months by an initiative on the part of a group of prominent Jewish scholars who published in September 2000 the document *Dabru Emet: A Jewish Statement on Christians and Christianity. Dabru Emet* means "Proclaim the Truth." The document opens with the statement: "In recent years, there has been a dramatic and unprecedented shift in Jewish and Christian relations," and considers that the changes made by Christians in this period "merit a thoughtful Jewish response....We believe that it is time for Jews to learn about the efforts of Christians to honor Judaism. We believe it is time for Jews to reflect on what Judaism may now say about Christianity." It then offers, as a first step, eight brief Jewish statements aimed at promoting a better relationship with Christians, quoted here: [187]

- *Jews and Christians worship the same God.* Christians also worship the God of Abraham, Isaac, and Jacob, creator of heaven and earth. While Christian worship is not a viable religious choice for Jews, as Jewish theologians we rejoice that, through Christianity, hundreds of millions of people have entered into relationship with the God of Israel.

- *Jews and Christians seek authority from the same book—the Bible (what Jews call "Tanakh" and Christians call the "Old Testament").* Turning to it for religious orientation, spiritual enrichment, and communal education, we each take away similar lessons: God created and sustains the universe; God established a covenant with the people Israel; God's revealed word guides Israel to a life of righteousness; and God will ultimately redeem Israel and the whole world. Yet Jews and Christians interpret the Bible differently on many points. Such differences must always be respected.

- *Christians can respect the claim of the Jewish people upon the land of Israel.* The most important event for Jews since the Holocaust has been the reestablishment of a Jewish state in the Promised Land.... Many Christians support the State of Israel for reasons far more profound than mere politics. As Jews we applaud this support. We also recognize that Jewish tradition mandates justice for all non-Jews who reside in a Jewish state.

- *Jews and Christians respect the moral principles of Torah.* Central to the moral principles of Torah is the inalienable sanctity and dignity of every human being. All of us were created in the image of God. This shared moral emphasis can be the basis of an improved relationship between our two communities. It can also be the basis of a powerful witness to all humanity for improving the lives of our fellow human beings and for standing up against the immoralities and idolatries that harm and degrade us....

- *Nazism was not a Christian phenomenon.* Without the long history of Christian anti-Judaism and Christian violence against Jews, Nazi ideology could not have taken hold nor could it have been carried out. Too many Christians participated in, or were sympathetic to, Nazi atrocities against Jews. Other Christians did not protest sufficiently against these atrocities. But Nazism itself was not an inevitable consequence of Christianity. If the Nazi extermination of the Jews had been fully successful, it would have turned its murderous rage more directly to Christians. We recognize with gratitude those Christians who risked or sacrificed their lives to save Jews during the Nazi regime. With that in mind, we encourage the continuation of recent efforts in Christian theology to repudiate unequivocally contempt of Judaism and the Jewish people....

- *The humanly irreconcilable difference between Jews and Christians will not be settled until God redeems the entire world as promised in the Scripture.* [Each community knows and serves God through their own tradition.] Jews can respect Christians' faithfulness to their revelation just as we expect Christians to respect our faithfulness to our tradition....

- *A new relationship between Jews and Christians will not weaken Jewish practice....* It will not change traditional Jewish forms of worship, nor increase intermarriage between Jews and non-Jews, nor persuade more Jews to convert to Christianity, nor create a false blending of Judaism and Christianity.... Only if we cherish our own traditions can we pursue this relationship with integrity.

- *Jews and Christians must work together for justice and peace.* Jews and Christians, each in their own way, recognize the unredeemed state of the world.... Although justice and peace are finally God's, our joint efforts, together with those of other faith communities, will help bring the kingdom of God for which we hope and long.

Dabru Emet goes further than any other Jewish document in acknowledging the close links that bind Jews and Christians together and in calling for closer collaboration in favor of justice, peace, and the preservation of the moral order. The statement on Christianity and Nazism is particularly welcome in Catholic circles, especially in view of some of the criticism leveled at *We Remember*, while the acknowledgment that "the humanly irreconcilable difference between the Jews and Christians will not be settled until God redeems the whole world as promised in Scripture" is a timely reminder that, as Catholics and Jews look to the future, they must not dialogue with the expectation that they will agree on everything.

At the Hebrew Union College Cincinnati Commencement Address, May 30, 2001, Rev. John T. Pawlikowski of Catholic Theological Union in Chicago praised *Dabru Emet* as a remarkable document, and from the Christian perspective in the dialogue, as a genuine advance in Christian relations with the Jews. He explained its importance in these words:

> While I have always insisted that it is incumbent upon the churches to cleanse their teachings of anti-Semitism for their own moral integrity whether any Jew noticed or not, clearly the dialogue will be stymied if Christians affirm a theological bonding with Jews...without an acknowledgement of such bonding from the Jewish side.[188]

Abraham's Heritage—A Christmas Gift

Within a few months of the publication of *Dabru Emet*, an article by Cardinal Joseph Ratzinger published in *L'Osservatore Romano* contributed further to this new trend in dialogue. Many members of the Jewish community worldwide had read with concern the August 2000 statement of the Vatican Congregation for the Doctrine of the Faith *Dominus Jesus*.[189] They were worried by the assertion in *Dominus Jesus* that followers of religions other than Christianity were in a gravely deficient situation in respect of salvation. The short article by Cardinal Ratzinger—which appeared on the front page of *L'Osservatore Romano* on December 29, 2000, and was entitled "Abraham's Heritage—A Christmas Gift"—seemed to be an attempt to dispel that concern. The article proved, however, to be a much more significant document, providing further encouragement for Catholic-Jewish theological dialogue.

Referring to the very negative Jewish reaction to the document *Dominus Jesus,* "Abraham's Heritage—A Christmas Gift" affirms: "It is evident that, as Christians, our dialogue with the Jews is situated on a different level than that in which we engage with other religions. The faith witnessed to by the Jewish Bible is not merely another religion to us, but is the foundation of our own faith."

Cardinal Ratzinger then gives what has been called "a new vision of the relationship with the Jews."[190] After tracing briefly the history of God's dealings with the Jewish people, the cardinal expresses "our gratitude to our Jewish brothers and sisters who, despite the hardness of their own history, have held on to faith in this God right up to the present and who witness to it in the sight of those peoples who, lacking knowledge of the one God, *dwell in darkness and the shadow of death* (Luke 1:79)."

The article includes the following interesting comment on relations between Christians and Jews down through the centuries:

> Certainly from the beginning relations between the infant church and Israel were often marked by conflict. The church was considered to be a degenerate daughter, while Christians considered their mother to be blind and obstinate. Down through the history of Christianity, already-strained relations deteriorated further, even giving birth to anti-Jewish attitudes that throughout history have led to deplorable acts of violence. Even if the most recent, loathsome experience of the *Shoah* was prepared in the name of an anti-Christian ideology that tried to strike the Christian faith at its Abrahamic roots in the people of Israel, it cannot be denied that a certain insufficient resistance to this atrocity on the part of Christians can be explained by the inherited anti-Judaism in the hearts of not a few Christians.

For the cardinal, it is perhaps this latest tragedy that has resulted in a new relationship between the church and the people of Israel, which he defines as "a sincere willingness to overcome every kind of

anti-Judaism and to initiate a constructive dialogue based on knowledge of each other and reconciliation." If such a dialogue is to be
fruitful, the cardinal suggests that

> it must begin with a prayer to our God first of all that he
> might grant to us Christians a greater esteem and love for
> that people, the people of Israel, to whom belong "the adop-
> tions as sons, the glory, the covenants, the giving of the law,
> the worship and the promises; theirs the patriarchs, and from
> them, according to the flesh, is the Messiah" (Rom. 9:4–5),
> and this not only in the past, but still today, "for the gifts and
> the call of God are irrevocable" (Rom. 11:29).

Cardinal Ratzinger goes on to propose to Christians that they in
their turn might pray to God "that he grant also to the children of
Israel a deeper knowledge of Jesus of Nazareth, who is their son and
the gift they have made to us." His final conclusion reminds us of the
sixth statement in *Dabru Emet:* "Since we are both waiting the final
redemption, let us pray that the paths we follow may converge."

Dialogue with the Chief Rabbinate of Israel

Perhaps the most significant event in relation to possible theological
discussions between Catholics and Jews has been the beginning of a
dialogue between the CRRJ and the chief rabbinate of Israel. This
was certainly made possible by the visit of Pope John Paul II to Israel
in 2000, who on that occasion spent quite some time at the chief rabbinate in discussion with the two chief rabbis of Israel. This event
also offered members of the pope's entourage and a number of rabbis
the possibility of coming to know one another. Cardinal Walter
Kasper followed up these promising contacts with a personal visit to
Israel in November 2001.

After a preliminary meeting in Jerusalem on June 5, 2002, high-
ranking delegations of the CRRJ and the chief rabbinate of Israel met
in Villa Cavalletti, Grottaferrata, in the vicinity of Rome from February 23–27, 2003. The Jewish delegation was led by the chief rabbi of
Haifa, Shar Yishuv Cohen, and the Catholic delegation by Cardinal

Jorge Mejia, a former secretary of the CRRJ. The meeting was held in a warm and friendly atmosphere of mutual goodwill, and was characterized by the effort to highlight common aspects of both traditions. Two main issues were raised, namely, the sanctity of life, and the value of the family.

A common declaration was signed at the end of the meeting, in which the two delegations rejected any attempt to destroy human life, based on their common religious understanding that the human being is created in the image of God. Every human life is "holy, sacrosanct and inviolable." They stated clearly that it is a profanation of religion to declare oneself a terrorist in the name of God or to do violence to others in his name. They emphasized the need of both communities, particularly the younger generation, for education in respect of the holiness of human life, and agreed that "against the present trend of violence and death in our societies, we should foster our cooperation with believers of all religions and all people of goodwill in promoting a *culture of life*." The participants at this gathering also insisted on the institution of the family as stemming from the will of the Almighty. "Marriage," they declared, "in a religious perspective has a great value, because God blessed this union and sanctified it.... The family unit is the basis for a wholesome society."[191]

This meeting was a historical breakthrough, as until then it had not been possible to organize an official dialogue between the CRRJ and institutes in Israel. Moreover, for the first time the church was able to enter into dialogue with all the different forms of Judaism: Orthodox, Conservative, and Reformed.

A second meeting between the chief rabbinate of Israel and the CRRJ took place in Jerusalem December 1–3, 2003, to discuss the theme "The Relevance of Central Teachings in the Holy Scriptures Which We Share for Contemporary Society and the Education of Future Generations." The joint declaration issued on this occasion noted that once again the deliberations had taken place in an atmosphere of mutual respect and amity, and that satisfaction was expressed "regarding the firm foundations that have already been established between the two delegations with great promise for continuity and effective collaboration."

The participants in this second formal meeting continued their reflections on the relation of the family to the Scriptures and declared that "humankind is one family with moral responsibility for one another." They saw that "awareness of this reality leads to the religious and moral duty that may serve as a true charter for human rights and dignity in our modern world and provide a genuine vision for a just society, universal peace and well-being." It was emphasized that "the response to the challenge of promoting religious faith in contemporary society requires us to provide living examples of justice, loving kindness, tolerance and humility," as set forth in the Scriptures.

The meeting stressed the need for religious education to provide hope and direction for positive living in human solidarity and harmony in our complex modern society. The participants called on religious leaders and educators to instruct their communities to pursue the paths of peace and well-being of society at large. A special appeal was addressed to the family of Abraham and a call made to all believers "to put aside weapons of war and destruction—'to seek peace and pursue it' (Ps 34:15)."[192]

Reflections on Covenant and Mission

The year 2002 saw the publication of a statement in the United States that created great interest among Jews and Catholics involved in dialogue. On August 12, 2002, the Ecumenical and Interreligious Affairs Committee of the United States Conference of Catholic Bishops and the National Council of Synagogues USA issued a truly remarkable document entitled *Reflections on Covenant and Mission*.[193] This was the result of discussions between leaders of Jewish and Roman Catholic communities in the United States, who had been meeting twice a year over a period of two decades.

For some time it had seemed to many that the time was ripe for a study on the relationship between the two covenants that basically describe the nature of the two religious communities, and on the consequences of that for Christian mission. The document *Reflections on Covenant and Mission* is an encouraging response that marks a significant step forward in the dialogue, especially in the United States.

The Jewish and Catholic reflections are presented separately in the document, but affirm together important conclusions. The Catholic reflections describe the growing respect for the Jewish tradition that has unfolded since the Second Vatican Council, and state that "a deepening Catholic appreciation of the eternal covenant between God and the Jewish people, together with the divinely-given mission to Jews to witness to God's faithful love, lead to the conclusion that campaigns that target Jews for conversion to Christianity are no longer theologically acceptable in the Catholic Church."

The document stresses that evangelization, or mission, in the church's work cannot be separated from its faith in Jesus Christ in whom Christians find the kingdom present and fulfilled. But it points out that this evangelizing mission goes far beyond "the invitation to a commitment to faith in Jesus Christ and to entry through baptism into the community of believers that is the church. It includes the church's activities of presence and witness; commitment to social development and human liberation; Christian worship, prayer, and contemplation; interreligious dialogue; and proclamation and catechesis."

But given the "utterly unique relationship of Christianity with Judaism" and the many aspects of this spiritual linkage, "the Catholic Church has come to recognize that its mission of preparing for the coming of the kingdom is one that is shared with the Jewish people, even if Jews do not conceive of this task christologically as the Church does." In view of this, the document quotes Prof. Tommaso Federici and Cardinal Walter Kasper to state that there should not be in the church any organization dedicated to the conversion of the Jews. From the Catholic point of view, Judaism is a religion that springs from divine revelation. The quotation from Cardinal Kasper states: "God's grace, which is the grace of Jesus Christ according to our faith, is available to all. Therefore, the church believes that Judaism, i.e., the faithful response of the Jewish people to God's irrevocable covenant, is salvific for them, because God is faithful to his promises."

Since, in Catholic teaching, both the church and the Jewish people abide in covenant with God, they both therefore have missions before God to undertake in the world. The church believes that the mission of the Jewish people is not restricted to their historical role as the people of whom Jesus was born "according to the flesh" (Rom 9:5) and from whom the church's apostles came. It quotes the following statement from Cardinal Ratzinger: "God's providence . . . has obviously given Israel a particular mission in this *time of the Gentiles*." Only the Jewish people themselves can articulate their mission, "in the light of their own religious experience."

The Catholic section of the document concludes with this profound statement: "With the Jewish people, the Catholic Church, in the words of *Nostra Aetate*, "awaits the day, known to God alone, when all peoples will call on God with one voice and serve him shoulder to shoulder."

The Jewish reflections are given the title: *The Mission of the Jews and the Perfection of the World*. This mission is described as threefold, rooted in Scripture and developed in later Jewish sources:

> There is, first, the mission of covenant—the ever-formative impetus to Jewish life that results from the covenant between God and the Jews. Second, the mission of witness, whereby the Jews see themselves "and are frequently seen by others" as God's eternal witnesses to His existence and to his redeeming power in the world. And third, the mission of humanity, a mission that understands the Biblical history of the Jews as containing a message to more than the Jews alone. It presupposes a message and a mission addressed to all human beings.

The document describes the mission of covenant and witness, before dealing at greater length with the mission of humanity, stating that the message of the Bible is a message and a vision not only to Israel but to all of humanity. It then reminds the reader that Isaiah speaks twice of the Jews as a light to peoples, and quotes the experience of Jonah to illustrate that it is a mistake to think that God is concerned only with the Jews:

> The God of the Bible is the God of the world. His visions are visions for all of humanity. His love is a love that extends to every creature.... Adam and Eve were His first creations and they are created long before the first Jews. They are created in *the image of God*, as are all of their children to eternity. Only the human creation is in the divine image. *Tikun ha-olam*, perfection or repairing of the world, is a joint task of the Jews and all humanity. Though Jews see themselves as liv-

ing in a world that is as yet unredeemed, God wills His crea-
tures to participate in the world's repair.

Finally, the Jewish reflections point out certain practical conclusions that follow from the threefold "mission" in classical Judaism,
and which suggest a joint agenda for Christians and Jews. The reflection begins with the following statement: "Although Christians and
Jews understand the messianic hope involved in that perfection quite
differently, still, whether we are waiting for the Messiah—as Jews
believe—or for the Messiah's second coming—as Christians believe—
we share the belief that we live in an unredeemed world that longs for
repair."

Then the reflection asks: "Why not articulate a common agenda?
Why not join together our spiritual forces to state and to act upon the
values we share in common and that lead to the repair of the unredeemed world?" Looking then to the Talmud, the document draws
from that source thoughts about repairing the world, giving details of
charity directed to the poor and deeds of kindness to all, the poor and
the rich, the living and the dead; creating an economy where people
are encouraged to help one another financially as an expression of
their common fellowship; fulfilling obligations to the sick and mourn-
ers; and preserving the dignity of the aged. While Jewish law is, of
course, directed at Jews, and its primary concern is to encourage the
expression of love to the members of the community, it points out
that many of these actions are mandatory toward all people, and
quotes the Talmud: "One must provide for the needs of the gentile
poor with the Jewish poor. One must visit the gentile sick with the
Jewish sick. One must care for the burial of a gentile, just as one must
care for the burial of a Jew. [These obligations are universal] because
these are the ways of peace."

Not everyone in the two communities will agree with all that is
stated in this document. In fact, when these reflections were published, they created a wide-ranging dispute within the Catholic
Church in the United States, but also in wider ecumenical and interfaith circles. Most of the argument centered on the question of
whether or not Christians should desire and pray for the conversion
of Jews. There was no question in this discussion of church organizations aiming to convert Jews, but leading church officials expressed

the view that it would be absurd to think that the mission given to the church by Christ is for pagans and not also for Jews, when all of Christ's preaching and his call to conversion was addressed precisely to the Jews. At the same time, Pope John Paul II has on a number of occasions made it clear that the first covenant has not been revoked and that therefore the church is called to concentrate on its mission "with" the Jews, rather than "to" the Jews.[194] The national Jewish-Catholic dialogue in the United States has certainly posed a challenge that can and should be fully shared by Christians and Jews.

Other Promising Initiatives

On February 13, 2003, Dr. Riccardo Di Segni, who had succeeded Rabbi Toaff as chief rabbi of Rome, visited Pope John Paul II in the Vatican. On this occasion he invited the pope to return to the Rome synagogue in 2004 on the occasion of the one hundredth anniversary of the synagogue, assuring the pope that "the doors of this sacred building (the synagogue) are always open."[195] While Pope John Paul II was not able to accept this invitation personally, he was represented at the ceremony on May 23, 2004, by two cardinals: his vicar for Rome, Cardinal Camillo Ruini, and the president of the CRRJ, Cardinal Walter Kasper. Cardinal Ruini delivered a message from Pope John Paul II in which he recalled with deep emotion his 1986 visit to the synagogue. With special reference to the members of the Rome Jewish community who, in October of 1943, were taken to Auschwitz, he stated that "it is not enough to deplore and condemn hostility against the Jewish people; . . . it is necessary to also foster friendship, esteem, and fraternal relations with them." The pope called for greater collaboration between Catholics and Jews in the face of the violence, conflict, and hostility that continue to scar the modern world. "If we know how to unite our hearts and hands in order to respond to the divine call, the light of the Eternal One will draw close to illuminate all peoples, showing us the ways of peace, of Shalom."[196]

In January 2003, the Pontifical Gregorian University announced the establishment of a program of Jewish studies. Over the years this university and other pontifical universities in Rome had provided students with the opportunity of short courses in Jewish studies offered by visiting Jewish scholars. Under the auspices of the Holy See, a more complete and ongoing program of Jewish studies had been offered to students over a number of years at the Pontifical Ratisbonne Institute in Jerusalem. As a consequence of the troubled political situation and conflict in the Holy Land, the Holy See eventually found it impossible to maintain this program, and after much discussion and consultation the CRRJ "had decided to continue the original purpose of the Ratisbonne project and to strengthen the program by transferring it to the newly reorganized Cardinal Bea Institute for Jewish Studies of the Pontifical Gregorian University."[197]

There have been other positive events that merit a brief reference. Already mentioned before was the concert on January 17, 2004, arranged in the Vatican by the CRRJ to foster harmony between the world's three major monotheistic religions: Christianity, Judaism, and Islam. The two chief rabbis of Israel were present, with Pope John Paul II, at this special event. On the morning of the concert, the two chief rabbis were received in private audience by the pope. During a meeting that lasted about ninety minutes, the pope was reported as having responded "positively" to a request from the chief rabbis to endorse a world "anti-Semitism day."[198]

Reference has also already been made to the work of the group of Jewish and Catholic experts appointed in 1999 by the members of the ILC to study the eleven volumes of Vatican Archive documents that had been made public some years earlier. The study was suspended after the group had unexpectedly presented a preliminary report that included a list of questions requiring direct access to the archives. An important move forward in this connection was the announcement in February 2002 that, even though the cataloguing of all the material between 1922 and 1939 would take about three more years, Pope John Paul II had decided to open to researchers, from the beginning of 2003, the documents in the archives of the section of the Secretariat of State for Relations with the States and in the Vatican "Secret Archives" concerning Germany for the period 1922–39.

The announcement went even further with the promise that once the Vatican Archives for the pontificate of Pius XI are fully opened, the Holy See will give top priority to making accessible the Vatican-German documentary sources for the pontificate of Pius XII (1939–58). The statement confirms what must at once be perfectly clear, namely, that "the Holy Father has very much at heart this further opening of the Vatican Archives because it was during the Pontificate of Pius XII that the Second World War broke out and with it came the deportation of the Jews and the tragedy of the *Shoah*." While expressing understanding of the fact that historians may well feel frustrated in their research by having access for the present to only one set of documents, the statement expressed the hope that this announcement will be "a sound premise for future study and research." The Holy See announced at the same time that it is publishing in two volumes, with the title *Inter Arma Caritas: The Information Office in the Vatican for Prisoners of War Instituted by Pius XII (1939–47)*, the data "concerning prisoners of the last war (1939–1945)" that are preserved in the collection of the Vatican Secret Archives. The dossier containing these documents is complete, homogeneous, and catalogued.[199]

A further very encouraging event took place in New York at the beginning of 2004. A Catholic delegation including eight cardinals and two presidents of bishops' conferences met with six chief rabbis and a contingent of European, American, and Israeli Jews to discuss how to promote peace and to stand together against growing anti-Semitism. The function was hosted at the Museum of Jewish Heritage by Cardinal Jean-Marie Lustiger, archbishop of Paris, and sponsored by the World Jewish Congress. Participants described the meeting as the highest-level talks yet in the troubled history of Catholics and Jews. In a statement issued at the end of the two-day meeting, the participants "expressed consternation at continuing expressions of hatred in the world and noted with concern the recent rise of anti-Semitic manifestations."[200]

Almost at the same time, church leaders in Britain together with Chief Rabbi Dr. Jonathan Sacks pledged to combat "the evil of anti-Semitism" in a hard-hitting statement to coincide with Holocaust Memorial Day. All the CCJ presidents are signatories to the statement, which noted that anti-Semitism was resurfacing as a phenomenon in many parts of the world. They described anti-Semitism as abhorrent and stated: "Our total rejection of anti-Semitism, amid evidence of its resurgency, is a signal that we will not permit it to stain our Continent's future as it has in the past. This is our common pledge and one we call on others to join."[201]

Conclusion

In an article published by *The Tablet* on July 7, 2001, Edward Kessler, executive director of the Center for Jewish-Christian Relations in Cambridge, Great Britain, states that "many of the main divisive issues that have afflicted relations between Christians and Jews have either been eliminated or taken to the furthest point at which agreement is possible." He sees the aim now as getting "these changes into the everyday understanding of all the faithful—in the pew and in the *shul*. Critically important are educational guidelines designed for each region."[202] He stresses, moreover, the need of a Jewish theology of Christianity, and I would add that we similarly need further reflection on a Catholic theology of Judaism.

While satisfaction is the predominant feeling as the Catholic Church looks back over forty years at *Nostra Aetate*, no. 4, the work is certainly not yet complete. Indeed, as is obvious from the preceding reflections, under some aspects it can be said to have only just begun. The need for education to continue and have a much greater place in the life of the two communities has been stressed over and over again even in the past few years. The reader will recall that Cardinal Johannes Willebrands was astounded at the beginning of his work "to realize how poorly Christians and Jews know each other."[203] In 1992, Dr. Geoffrey Wigoder of the Institute of Contemporary Jewry of the Hebrew University, Jerusalem, reminded the ILC at its meeting in Jerusalem in 1994 "of the abyss of ignorance in both our communities concerning the other, which includes dangerous myths and prejudices."[204]

Such education seems all the more necessary in view of the number of new manifestations of anti-Semitism that are reported. The ongoing violence in the Holy Land between Israel and the Palestinian population has hardened some hearts once again against the Jewish people, who see such an intimate connection between the land of Israel and their religion. Also, on the tenth anniversary of diplomatic relations between the Vatican and the State of Israel, Rev. Fr. David-Maria A. Jaeger, OFM, a legal expert with special interest in the document *Fundamental Agreement of the Holy See and the State of Israel*, expressed disappointment that the government of Israel has still not transformed the agreement into law.[205]

The world today urgently needs common witness to the truths that God has entrusted to Jews and Christians. At this time it would seem that Jews and Christians are moving further away from the old mistrust and suspicion to a partnership in the cause of "peace, justice and a more human, fraternal world." While preserving past gains, they are entering on a dialogue as two equal partners seeking together to build a better world. They began their discussions in order to solve problems and promote a new relationship, and now they are being challenged to move their gaze from their bilateral relations to become a common blessing to a wider world.

The Jewish section of the document *Reflections on Covenant and Mission* expressed this challenge well:

> Does not humanity need a common vision of the sacred nature of our human existence that we can teach our children and that we can foster in our communities in order to further the ways of peace? Does not humanity need a commitment of its religious leadership, within each faith and beyond each faith, to join hands and create bonds that will inspire and guide humanity to reach toward its sacred promise? For Jews and Christians who have heard the call of God to be a blessing and a light to the world, the challenge and mission are clear. Nothing less should be our challenge—and that is the true meaning of mission that we all need to share.[206]

In a letter to Cardinal Kasper for the 2002 meeting of European leaders of Judaism and Catholicism, Pope John Paul II stated that "since the Conciliar Declaration *Nostra Aetate*, great progress has been made—and I am very glad of it—toward better mutual understanding and reconciliation between our two communities. A text of this kind constitutes a starting point, an anchor and a compass for future relations."[207]

Cardinal Kasper developed this brief statement in an address on November 7, 2002, at Boston College,[208] with which I will bring to a close this attempt to "rediscover" *Nostra Aetate* forty years after it was promulgated. With reference to *Reflections on Covenant and Mission*, what he calls "the strongly contested document of the National Council of Synagogues and Delegates of the Bishops' Committee on

Ecumenical and Interreligious Affairs," the cardinal sees it as touching "on the fundamental question that stands between us," namely Christian missionary activity.

For Cardinal Kasper *Covenant and Mission* is to be considered as an "invitation and challenge for further discussion," and it is in that light that he then presents a significant and thought-provoking reflection on this fundamental present challenge. There is certainly great sensitivity with regard to Christian mission on the part of both Jews and Christians. For the Jews, the word "mission" raises still today insurmountable misunderstandings, suspicion, and resistance; while Christians, even when rejecting all means of coercion in matters of faith, see mission as central to the New Testament. For the cardinal, "the problem of mission touches the substance of what we have in common and of what divides us as well, and both our rich common heritage and our incontestable differences are constitutive for our respective identities."

In Part III of his address, Cardinal Kasper concludes that, because of what we have in common and because as Christians

> we know that God's covenant with Israel by God's faithfulness is not broken (Rom 11:29; cf. 3:4), mission understood as call to conversion from idolatry to the living and true God (1 Thess 1:9) does not apply and cannot apply to Jews. They confess the living true God, who gave and gives them support, hope, confidence and strength in many difficult situations of their history. There cannot be the same kind of behavior toward Jews as there exists toward Gentiles. This is not a merely abstract theological affirmation, but an affirmation that has concrete and tangible consequences.

The cardinal points out, for example, that there is no organized Catholic missionary activity toward Jews as there is for all other non-Christian religions. Rome has a special dicastery for evangelization "ad gentes," the congregation known for many years as *Propaganda Fide*.

Paradoxically, the cardinal says, we differ from the Jews in what we have in common. We have different readings for the Sacred Scriptures that we have in common.[209] The sacred text "is an open text pointing to the future which will be determined by God at the end of time." But while Jews expect the coming of the Messiah, who is still unknown, Christians believe that he has already shown his face in Jesus of Nazareth,

> whom we as Christians therefore confess as the Christ, he who at the end of time will be revealed as the Messiah for Jews and for all nations. The universality of Christ's redemption for Jews and for Gentiles is so fundamental throughout the entire New Testament (Eph 2:13–18; Col 1:15–18; 1 Tim 2:5 and many others) and even in the same Letter to the Romans (3:24; 8:32) that it cannot be ignored or passed over in silence....
>
> This does not mean that Jews in order to be saved have to become Christians; if they follow their own conscience and believe in God's promises as they understand them in their religious tradition they are in line with God's plan, which for us comes to completion in Jesus Christ.

The president of the CRRJ acknowledges that this exposition of Christian theology might well prove painful to Jewish listeners but insists that Christians can only look at Jews with Christian eyes, and of course that Jews in their turn can only look at Christians through Jewish eyes. "We must," he says, "endure and withstand this difference, because it constitutes our respective identities. We must respect each other in our respective otherness." The question of "mission" belongs in this larger context and cannot be dealt with in isolation from it.

These words indicate once again the importance of developing a much more profound overall Christian theology of Judaism, and consequently a similar Jewish theology of Christianity. Cardinal Kasper calls for a dialogue that goes beyond polite expressions of friendship and beyond just tolerating the other. He warns against approaching this task "with naive expectations of a harmonious understanding," since much still has to be done.

As he looks to the future, he reminds us that the dialogue should not only deal with religious questions of principle, nor simply seek to clarify the past. "Our common heritage should be profitably made available in response to contemporary challenges: to issues involving the sanctity of life, the protection of the family, justice and peace in the world, the hostages of terrorism, and the integrity of creation, among others."

Cardinal Walter Kasper, as president of the CRRJ, concludes with words that I readily make my own:

> Only at the end of time shall the historically indissoluble relation between Israel and the church find a solution. Until then though they may not be united in one another's arms, neither should they turn their backs to each other. They should stand shoulder to shoulder as partners, and—in a world where the glimmer of hope has grown faint—together they must strive to radiate the light of hope without which no human being and no people can live. Young people especially need this common witness to the hope of peace in justice and solidarity. Never again contempt, hatred, oppression and persecution between races, cultures and religions!
>
> Jews and Christians together can maintain this hope. For they can testify from the bitter and painful lessons of history that—despite otherness and foreignness and despite historical guilt—conversion, reconciliation, peace and friendship are possible.[210]

That the president of the CRRJ could in 2002 make such a public reflection on such profound aspects of Jewish-Christian dialogue is an eloquent sign of just how far the two communities have come in the forty years since the promulgation of *Nostra Aetate*. Christian-Jewish relations can surely look forward to an exciting future.

NOTES

THE DECREE ON ECUMENISM: *UNITATIS REDINTEGRATIO*

1. Walter M. Abbott, SJ, *The Documents of Vatican II* (London and Dublin: Chapman, 1966, 336.

2. The text of the declaration may be found in English in Abbott, *The Documents of Vatican II*, 725–27. The translation used here is that of the Holy See as found on the Vatican Internet Web site, www.vatican.va.

3. Thomas Stransky, CSP, "The Observers at Vatican Two: A Unique Experience of Dialogue," *Centro pro Unione Bulletin* 63 (Spring 2003), 8–14.

4. Ibid.

5. Abbott, 340.

6. Ibid., 387–88.

7. *Europaica*, Bulletin of the Representation of the Russian Orthodox Church to the European Institutions, No. 19, 26 June 2003.

8. The text of this document is to be found in the SPCU journal *Information Service*, No. 2, 5–12 (also the journal *Acta Apostolicae Sedis*, 1967, 574–92). The *Information Service* of the SPCU (PCPCU) is referred to in these Notes as *IS;* the *Acta Apostolicae Sedis* as *AAS*.

9. *IS*, No. 10 (1970/II), 3–10 (*AAS* 1970, 705–24).

10. *IS*, No. 9 (1970/I), 21–23.

11. *IS*, No.12 (1970/IV), 5–11.

12. *IS*, No. 18 (1972/III), 3–6.

13. *IS*, No. 23 (1974/I), 25.

14. PCPCU, *Directory for the Application of Principles and Norms on Ecumenism* (*ED*) (Vatican City: Libreria Editrice Vaticana, 1993).

15. Pope John Paul II, apostolic letter *Tertio Millennio Adveniente*, 34.

16. Cf. Richard John Neuhaus, *Crisis*, September 1995, 25–27.

17. The quote is from the homily preached by John Paul II in St. Peter's Basilica in the presence of Patriarch Dimitrios I on December 6, 1987—*AAS* 80, 1988, 714.

18. Neuhaus, 25.

19. Letter of Mary Tanner to Cardinal Edward Cassidy, 29 January 1998.

20. House of Bishops Occasional Paper, *May They All Be One*, Church House Publishing (GS MISC 459), 1997.

21. *Catholic News Service*, 9 July 1996—reporting an interview with the Polish Catholic Weekly *Tygodnik Powszechny*.

22. *Avvenire*, Mercoledì, 30 settembre 1998, 25.

23. *Catholic News Service*, 9 July 1996.

24. *Ecumenical News International*, a news and information publication of the WCC, 95–0122.

25. James L. Franklin, *Boston Globe*, 31 May 1995.

26. Unpublished text.

27. *IS*, No. 112 (2003/1), 10–11.

28. *L'Osservatore Romano* (hereafter *OR*), English Edition, No. 17, 28 April 2004, 11.

29. *IS*, No. 115 (2004/I–II), 47–48.

30. *SEIA* Newsletter on the Eastern churches and Ecumenism, Washington DC, No. 104, 31 May 2004, 23–24.

31. *IS*, No. 88 (1995/I), 2–3.

32. These can be found in *Information Service* No. 108 (2001/IV), 149.

33. Ibid., 148.

34. *The Mystery of the Church and of the Eucharist in the Light of the Mystery of the Holy Trinity* (Munich, 1982), *IS*, No. 49 (1982/II–III), 107–112; *Faith, Sacraments and the Unity of the Church* (Bari, 1987), *IS*, No. 64 (1987/II), 82–87; *The Sacrament of Order in the Sacramental Structure of the Church, with Particular Reference to the Importance of the Apostolic Succession for the Sanctification and Unity of the People of God* (26 June 1988), *IS*, No. 68 (1988/III–IV), 173–78.

35. *IS*, No. 78 (1991/III–IV), 204.

36. *IS*, No. 10 (1996/I–II), 91.

37. *Zenit News Agency: The World Seen from Rome*, "Quest for Christian Unity: Where It Stands," 29 January 2004, 1.

38. *SEIA*, No. 100, 31 January 2004, 19.

39. *IS*, No. 85 (1994/I), 54.

40. *The Ecumenical Society of the Blessed Virgin Mary* (Wallington, Surrey), Newsletter Third Series, No. 23, May 2003, 2–3.

41. *IS*, No. 111 (2002/IV), 230.

42. Ibid.

43. Joint letter dated February 6, 2004. See www.lutheranworld.org/Special_Events/LWF-Special_Events-Justification.html or www.vatican.va (go to Roman Curia—Councils—Council for Christian Unity).

44. *IS*, No. 109 (2002/1–11), 61.

45. *Catholic News*, 17 March 2004; see http://www.cathnews.com/news/403/93.php.

46. Cf. *IS*, No. 110 (2002/III), 178. This document can be read in *IS*, No. 111 (2002/IV) 241–51, together with a comment by Cardinal Avery Dulles (252–55).

47. Cf. *OR*, English edition, No.4, 28 January 2004, 4.

48. Brief reports on these meetings are found for 1998 in *IS*, No. 99 (1998/IV), 218; for 1999 in *IS*, No. 102 (1999/IV), 249; for 2000 in *IS*, No. 105 (2000/IV), 194.

49. Report to the 2003 plenary of the PCPCU in *IS*, No. 115 (2004/I–II), 66.

50. Report to the 2003 plenary of the PCPCU in *IS*, No. 115, 67.

51. *OR*, English edition, No. 12, 24 March 2004, 10.

52. *IS*, No.115 (2004/I–II), 61–62.

53. *IS*, No. 35 (1977/III), 6.

54. *IS*, No. 56 (1984/IV), 112.

55. *IS*, No. 60 (1986/I–II), 71–97. The report is accompanied by a review and appreciation of this document by Archbishop Kevin McNamara of Dublin, 97–102.

56. Report to the 2003 plenary of the PCPCU in *IS*, No. 115, 73.

57. A brief report is given in *IS*, No. 110, 177.

58. Report to 2003 plenary of the PCPCU in *IS*, No. 115, 73.

59. *IS*, No. 112 (2003/1), 1; audience of January 18, 2003.

60. *IS*, No. 99 (1998/IV), 192.

61. *Dictionary of the Ecumenical Movement*, sec. ed. (Geneva: WCC Publications, 2002), 461–63.

62. Ibid., 462.

63. The full text of this response is to be found in *IS*, No. 65 (1987/III–IV), 121–39.

64. *IS*, No. 65, 139.

65. At the time of writing, this paper has not been published, but remains an internal document of the WCC.

66. No. 118 of the unpublished text.

67. Cf. *IS*, No. 110, 173–76.

68. *Dictionary of the Ecumenical Movement*, 463.

69. *Vatican Information Service* (hereafter *VIS*), No. 189, 6 November 2003, 2.

70. *VIS*, No. 13, 22 January 2004, 1.

71. *Dictionary of the Ecumenical Movement*, 1203.

72. Full details of this service and of the participating delegations are given in *IS*, No. 103 (2000/I–II), 38ff.

73. Cf. *IS*, No. 62 (1986 /IV), 155–81, and No. 110 (2002/III), 115–46.

74. *IS*, No. 83 (1993/II), 61–77.

75. *IS*, No. 80 (1992/II), 17–28.

76. *IS*, No. 111, 215–17.

77. Ibid., 218–19.

78. Cf. *IS*, No. 110, 159–63.

79. *IS*, No. 102, 219–29.

80. *IS*, No. 111, 199–208.

81. *IS*, No. 110, 153–58.

82. *IS*, No. 107 (2001/II–III), 62–66.

83. *IS*, No. 109 (2002/I–II), 6–9.

84. *IS*, No. 112 (2003/I), 14–16.

85. *IS*, No. 110, 167–68.

86. *IS*, No. 111, 220.

87. Ibid., 221–25.

88. *IS*, No. 112, 27–34.

89. *IS*, No. 110, 169–72. The letter of congratulations from Pope John Paul II to Dr. Rowan Williams is also found under this report.

90. *IS*, No.112, 20–22.

91. *AustARC* (Australian Anglican–Roman Catholic Dialogue Commission), *Church as Communion:* A Discussion Resource for Anglicans and Catholics (Brisbane, Australia: Faith Education Services, 2004).

92. *IS*, No. 65 (1987), 140–45. Cf. *IS*, No. 110, 159–63.

93. PCPCU *Directory for the Application of Principles and Norms on Ecumenism (ED)*, No. 167.

94. *VIS*, 11 May 2004, 2.

95. *SEIA*, 31 October 2003, 1–2. This text and all those agreed on by the commission are available on the Web site of the U.S. Catholic Bishops' Conference at http//www.usccb.org/seia/dialogues.htm.

96. Published by Bayard, Fleurus-Mame and le Cerf. A report on this publication is given in *Service Orthodoxe de Presse* 288 (May 2004) and in *SEIA* Newsletter on the Eastern Churches and Ecumenism, Washington, DC, No. 104, 31 May 2004, 22–23.

97. *OR* English, No. 4, 28 January 2004, 4.

98. *The Tablet*, 8 November 2003, 27.

99. *OR*, English edition, No. 4, 28 January 2004, 4.

100. Reports on this historic event appeared in the local Australian press, for example, in *The Sydney Morning Herald*, 26 July 2004; in *The Catholic Weekly*, 1 August 2004; and in *Sharing*, the newsletter of the NSW Ecumenical Council, No. 68, July 2004, 3. The churches signing the covenant comprise the Catholic, Anglican, Uniting, Lutheran, and Congregationalist Churches, the Churches of Christ, Quakers, Salvation Army, and seven Orthodox Churches.

101. *Sharing*, No. 68, July 2004, 3.

102. *WARC Update*, Volume 14, No. 1, May 2004, 5–6.

103. Cardinal Walter Kasper, "A Vision of Christian Unity for the Next Generation," an address given during a 2003 visit to Australia and published by *Bread of Life Catholic Fellowship* (St. Marys, NSW), July 2003.

104. *OR*, English edition, No. 5, 4 February 2004, 5.

105. This letter conveyed the papal greeting to participants in a symposium on the theme "The Relationship between Spirituality and Christian Dogma in the East and the West" that took place in Ionnina, Epirus, Greece, from September 3 to 7, 2003, as part of a series of inter-Christian symposiums organized since 1992 by the Franciscan Institute of Spirituality at the Antonianum Pontifical Athenaeum in Rome and the Theology Faculty of the Aristotle University of Thessalonica of the Greek Orthodox Church. *VIS*, 4 September 2003, 2.

106. *OR*, English edition, No. 6, 11 February 2004, 9.

107. *SEIA*, No. 99, 31 December 2003, 9.

108. *SEIA*, No. 97, 31 October 2003, 14.

109. *Europaica*, 24 February 2004, 6 and 16–17.

110. *SEIA*, No. 102, 31 March 2001, 4.

111. *Europaica*, 18 May 2004, 8.

112. *Europaica*, 2 September 2004, 1–5.

113. *OR*, English edition, No. 27, 7 July 2004, 9.

114. Ibid., 1 and 9.

115. Congregation for the Doctrine of the Faith, *Dominus Jesus—Declaration on the Unicity and Salvific Universality of Jesus Christ and the Church* (Vatican City: Libreria Editrice Vaticana, 2000).

116. Pope Paul VI, in a homily in St. Peter's Basilica on March 8, 1964, on the occasion of the fourth centenary of the Council of Trent reported in *Attività della Santa Sede*, 1964, 124–25.

THE DECREE ON INTERRELIGIOUS RELATIONS: *NOSTRA AETATE*

1. Robert A. Graham, "Introduction to the Declaration on Non-Christians," in *The Documents of Vatican II*, 657.

2. Ibid.

3. When earlier councils, such as Lateran IV, spoke of Muslims and Jews, it was to disparage them, rather than seek to approach them in a positive way.

4. *Attività della Santa Sede* (an annual volume, hereafter *Attività*) 1966, 1201–2.

5. Ibid.

6. www.vatican.va/holyfather/paulvi/encyclicals/documents.

7. *The Pontifical Council for Interreligious Dialogue*, www.vatican.va/roman_curia/pontifical_councils/interelg.

8. *Attività* 1967, 1401.

9. Usually under the heading of sects or new religious movements, one finds groups whose approach to faith and whose doctrines and practices are alien to the Christian biblical tradition, and in some cases are directed against it. Among such movements are those who believe in a new revelation, such as the Latter-Day Saints (Mormons). See Hans-Diether Reimer's entry on "Sects" in the *Dictionary of the Ecumenical Movement*, WCC Publications, Geneva, 2002, p. 1030–31.

10. *Attività* 1976, 561.

11. *Information Service* (hereafter *IS*), No. 60 (1986/I–II), 6.

12. *IS*, No. 62 (1986/IV), 156.

13. Ibid., 174–75.

14. Ibid., 177–81.

15. *IS*, No. 83 (1993/II), 61–77.

16. Pope John Paul II, apostolic letter *Tertio Millennio Adveniente*, Vatican City, 10 November 1994.

17. *Attività* 2000, 1036.

18. *IS*, No. 110 (2002/III), 115.

19. *IS*, No. 110, 115–46.

20. PCID, Peace: *A Single Goal and a Shared Intention* (Vatican City: Libreria Editrice Vaticana, 2002).

21. *L'Osservatore Romano* (English edition, No. 41, 8 October 2003, 6–7; hereafter *OR*) contains a report on this meeting from which the information given here has been taken.

22. *OR*, English edition, No. 41, 6.

23. Ibid., 7.

24. www.vatican.va/roman_curia/pontifical_councils/interelg/documents.

25. Michael L. Fitzgerald, *Dialogue and Proclamation: Milestones in Interreligious Dialogue*, Rome/Lagos: Ceedee Publications, 2002, 210.

26. www.vatican.va/roman_curia/pontifical_councils/interelg/documents.

27. *Insegnament della Santa Sede* 1986, IX/2, 1262.

28. The French original is published in *La Documentation Catholique*, No. 1919 (1 June 1986), 547–554 and an English version in *Origins*, Vol. 16, No. 1 (22 May 1986), 1–10.

29. By means of the apostolic constitution *Pastor Bonus*, dated 28 June 1988, Pope John Paul II reformed the Roman curia, creating pontifical councils in the place of the secretariats set up after the Second Vatican Council, and defining clearly the competence of each of the Vatican dicasteries.

30. This document of the Pontifical Council for Culture and the Pontifical Council for Interreligious Dialogue was published by the Libreria Editrice Vaticana in 2002. An Australian edition has been made available by St. Paul's Publications, March 2003, www.stpauls.com.au.

31. Presentation of the Holy See's Document on "New Age" by Archbishop Michael L. Fitzgerald, his comment on chapter 5, at www.vatican.va/roman_curia/pontifical_councils/interelg/documents.

32. Ibid., comment on chapter 6.

33. *Vatican Information Service (VIS)*, 22 June 2004, 5.

34. PCID, *Journeying Together* (Vatican City: Libreria Editrice Vaticana, 1999).

35. PCID, *Spiritual Resources of the Religions for Peace* (Vatican City: Libreria Editrice Vaticana, 2003). Also available at www.vatican.va/ roman_curia/pontifical_councils/interelg/index.htm.

36. Chidi Denis Isizoh, ed., *Milestones in Interreligious Dialogue:* Essays in honour of Francis Cardinal Arinze (Rome/Lagos: Ceedee Publications, 2002).

37. Congregation for the Doctrine of the Faith, *Dominus Jesus—Declaration on the Unicity and Salvific Universality of Jesus Christ and the Church,* Vatican City, 6 August 2000.

38. PCID, *Meeting in Friendship*, Vatican City, 2003. The message for the end of Ramadan 2003 ('Id al-Fitr 1424 A.H) was entitled "Constructing Peace Today."

39. Several of these messages can be found on the Vatican Web site, www.vatican.va, under the Roman Curia–Pontifical Council for Interreligious Dialogue. The 2004 message to Buddhists for their annual festival of *Vesakh* had as its theme "Christians and Buddhists: We Both Regard Children as the Future of Humanity."

40. *Attività* 1988, 1487–92.

41. *IS*, No. 3 (1967/III), 24–25.

42. Pope Paul VI, apostolic constitution *Regimini Ecclesiae*, 15 August 1967, No. 94.

43. *IS*, No. 3, 25.

44. *IS*, No.17 (1972/II), 11–12.

45. *IS*, No. 25 (1974/III), 22.

46. The text is published in *IS*, No. 26 (1975/1), 1–7, and can also be found in the ILC publication *Fifteen Years of Catholic-Jewish Dialogue, 1970–1975*, edited by Pier Francesco Fumagalli (Vatican City: Libreria Editrice Vaticana, 1988), 293–98.

47. *IS*, No. 27 (1975/II), 32–35.

48. *IS*, No. 57 (1985/I), 16–21. This text is also found in *Fifteen Years*, 306–14.

49. *IS*, No. 49, 38.

50. *IS*, No. 45 (1981/1), 9.

51. *IS*, No. 49 (1982/II–III), 38.

52. *IS*, No. 14 (1971/II), 11.

53. *IS*, No. 17, 19–20.

54. Antwerp, 4–6 December 1973—*IS*, No. 23 (1974/I), 21–22; Rome, 7–10 January 1974—*IS*, No. 27, 34–37; Jerusalem, 1–3 March 1976—*IS*, No. 31 (1976/II), 17–18; Venice, 28–30 March 1977—*IS*, No. 34 (1977/II), 6–7: Madrid, 5–7 April 1978—*IS*, No. 37 (1978/II), 11–12; Regensberg, 22–25 October 1979 (*IS*, No. 41 (1979/IV), 11; London, 31 March–2 April 1981—*IS*, No. 45, 29–30: Milan, 6–8 September 1982—*IS*, No. 51 (1983/I–II), 36: Amsterdam, 27–29 March 1984—*IS*, No. 54 (1984/I), 21–22; Rome, 28–30 October 1985—*IS*, No. 59 (1985/III–IV), 37–39.

55. *IS*, No. 25, 22.

56. *IS*, No. 27, 34.

57. Ibid.

58. *IS*, No. 34, 6–7.

59. *IS*, No. 41, 11.

60. *IS*, No. 45, 29–30.

61. *IS*, No. 51, 36.

62. *IS*, No. 59, 33–39, where the Holy Father's address and that of Cardinal Willebrands are reported in full and there is a press release on the meeting.

63. *IS*, No. 63 (1987/I), 15–18.

64. *Fifteen Years of Catholic-Jewish Dialogue—1970–1985* is part of a series entitled "Teologia e Filosofia," sponsored by the Lateran University, Rome.

65. *IS*, No. 68 (1988/III–IV), 165–70.

66. *IS*, No. 6 (1969/I), 22.

67. *IS*, No. 27, 36–37; *Fifteen Years*, Appendix, 299–300.

68. *IS*, No. 40 (1979/III), 16–17.

69. *Fifteen Years*, 301–3.

70. *IS*, No. 60, 29–30.

71. Ibid., 26–28; *OR*, English edition, 21 April 1986, 6.

72. *IS*, No. 64 (1987/II); the full text of the two letters is found there on pages 76–78.

73. Earlier in the year, on March 11–14, a small committee had decided in Rome that the thirteenth plenary session of ILC would have as its theme "The *Shoah*: Significance and Implications in the Historical and Religious Perspectives"—*IS*, No. 67 (1988/II), 88–89.

74. *IS*, No. 64, 79–81 and *IS*, No. 67, 89.

75. *IS*, No. 65 (1987/III–IV), 116–20, where the full text of both speeches can be read.

76. *IS*, No. 70 (1989/II), 77.

77. Ibid., 78.

78. Ibid., 78–79.

79. Ibid., 77–78.

80. *IS*, No.101 (1999/III), 191–92. This article also explains more fully the background to the Vatican decision to attach Jewish-Christian relations to the Secretariat for Christian Unity, rather than to the Secretariat for Non-Christians.

81. *IS*, No. 73 (1990/II), 38.

82. *IS*, No. 75 (1990/IV), 173–78.

83. *IS*, No. 77 (1991/II), 72–77.

84. Ibid., 78–83.

85. Ibid., 83–84.

86. Ibid., 84–86.

87. *IS*, No. 81 (1992/III–IV), 135–36.

88. *IS*, No. 82 (1993/I), 32–38; and No. 84 (1993/III–IV), 132.

89. *IS*, No. 84 (1993/III–IV), 157.

90. *IS*, No. 88 (1995/I), 38–41.

91. *IS*, No. 87 (1994/IV), 231–36.

92. *IS*, No. 98 (1998/III), 152–54.

93. Address of Cardinal Edward Cassidy to the American Jewish Committee on receiving the Isaiah Interreligious Award at the organization's 95th annual meeting in Washington, DC, on May 2, 2001.

94. The *Drancy Statement* of the French Bishops, issued on October 2, 1997, for example, received almost universal praise from Jewish circles. It refers in particular to the period of the Vichy government, following the defeat of France by the German forces in 1940. While passing no judgment on the consciences of the people of that era, nor accepting guilt for what took place at that time, the French bishops acknowledge that "too many of the Church's pastors committed an offence, by their silence, against the Church herself and her mission" in face of the multifarious laws enacted by the government of that time. The bishops find themselves "obliged to admit the role, indirect if not direct, in the process which led to the *Shoah* which was played by commonly held anti-Jewish prejudices, which Christians were guilty of maintaining." At the same time they state: "This is not to say that a direct cause and effect link can be drawn between these commonly held anti-Jewish feelings and the *Shoah*, because the Nazi plan to

annihilate the Jewish people has its sources elsewhere." All the documents can be found on the Web site of Boston College's Center for Jewish-Christian Learning: http://www.bc.edu/research/cjl/.

95. *IS*, No. 75, 176: final statement of the Prague 1990 meeting of the ILC.

96. Letter of Pope John Paul II to Cardinal Cassidy on the occasion of the publication of *We Remember: A Reflection on the Shoah* in *IS*, No. 97 (1998/I–II), 18.

97. The full text is given in *IS*, No. 97, 18–22. It was also published as a separate small booklet by the Libreria Editrice Vaticana for distribution by the CRRJ at the time of its presentation.

98. Pope John Paul II, apostolic letter *Tertio Millennio Adveniente*, 10 November 1994, 33: *Acta Apostolicae Sedis*, No. 87 (1995), 25.

99. Quoted in an editorial of *The Philadelphia Inquirer*, 18 March 1998.

100. *The Jewish Advocate*, 3–9 April 1998.

101. *The Philadelphia Inquirer*, 18 March 1998.

102. *OR*, 1 November 1997, 6.

103. No. 8 of the Second Vatican Council's dogmatic constitution *Lumen Gentium* distinguishes "the society furnished with hierarchical agencies and the Mystical Body of Christ" and states that they are not to be considered as two realities. "Rather they form one interlocked reality which is comprised of a divine and a human element." This reality is compared by the council to the mystery of the Incarnate Word.

104. *IS*, No. 98, 165–73. The text of the *Common Declaration on Ecology* is found on pages 168–69.

105. *IS*, No. 98, 165.

106. *We Remember*, IV.

107. Idris Edward Cassidy, "Catholic-Jewish Relations—The Unfinished Agenda," a paper presented during an evening on Catholic-Jewish relations organized by the archdiocese of Baltimore on 18 February 1999 (private papers of Cardinal Cassidy).

108. *IS*, No. 108 (2001/IV), 178.

109. *IS*, No. 83, 93.

110. *IS*, No. 88, 37: 29 September 1994, representatives of the B'nai B'rith Anti-Defamation League; 6 February 1995, the American Jewish Committee.

111. *IS*, No. 87, 229–30.

112. Ibid., 229.

113. Ibid., 230.

114. *IS*, No. 93 (1996/IV), 165–66.

115. *IS*, No. 93, 165.

116. The Pontifical Biblical Commission was instituted by Pope Leo XIII on October 30, 1902, and given the task of promoting progress in biblical studies, and making sure that they were free of error. In 1971, Paul VI, in a general restructuring of the commission, associated it closely with the Congregation for the Doctrine of the Faith. The prefect of this congregation is *ex officio* and also president of the commission. (cf. *Annuario Pontificio* 2004, 1739).

117. *IS*, No. 95 (1997/II–III), 110–11.

118. *IS*, No. 96 (1997/IV), 141–42.

119. *IS*, No. 102 (1999/IV), 254–55.

120. *IS*, No. 103 (2000/I–II), 53–58.

121. Ibid., 77.

122. *IS*, No. 104 (2000/III), 107–11.

123. Ibid., 108–9.

124. Ibid., 107–8.

125. *IS*, No. 108. A full report on this meeting is given on pages 168–77, and unless otherwise indicated, all quotations in this commentary on the meeting will be found there.

126. *IS*, No. 108, 171.

127. Congregation for the Doctrine of the Faith, *Dominus Jesus—Declaration on the Unicity and Salvific Universality of Jesus Christ and the Church*, Vatican City, 6 August 2000.

128. *IS*, No. 108, 178.

129. *IS*, No. 17, 11.

130. *IS*, No. 98, 152.

131. Ibid., 165.

132. *IS*, No. 108, 171: *Recommendation on Education in Catholic and Jewish Seminaries and Schools of Theology.*

133. *IS*, No. 98, 167.

134. *The Bible, the Jews and the Death of Jesus: A Collection of Catholic Documents*, No. 5-618, USCCB publications.

135. *IS*, No. 98, 179.

136. Information given by Rabbi James Rudin, AJC's senior interreligious advisor, in his weekly religious news service commentary for 17 November 2003.

137. *IS*, No. 63, 17.

138. Information supplied by the secretary of the CRRJ to the 2003 plenary of the PCPCU.

139. *VIS*, 6 December 2003, 3.

140. This organization publishes a monthly ICCI update. Contact at iccijeru@icci.co.il.

141. The textbook for Australian students is *Jewish-Christian Relations*, edited by Maurice Ryan (Ringwood Vic.: David Lovell Publishing, 2004).

142. *IS*, No. 6, 20–22.

143. *IS*, No. 63, 17.

144. *IS*, No. 44 (1980/III–IV), 88.

145. *IS*, No. 77, 72–77.

146. *Attività* 1988, 1488.

147. *Attività* 1994, 1343–4.

148. *VIS*, 27 January 2004; *Pro Dialogo*, No. 115 (2004/1), 37–38.

149. www.vatican.va/roman_curia/pontifical_councils/interelg/index.htm; *OR*, English edition, No. 32/33, 11–18 August 2004, 2.

150. *Attività* 1990, 1306.

151. *Attività* 1991, 1435.

152. *OR*, English edition, No. 11, 17 March 2004, 2.

153. Cardinal Tauran had been for many years Secretary for Relations with the States within the Vatican Secretariat of State.

154. *VIS*, 28 May 2004, 2–3.

155. *VIS*, 29 May 2004, 2–3.

156. *VIS*, 2 June 2004, 2–3.

157. *IS*, No. 115, 83–84.

158. *Attività* 1985, 703–10.

159. Ibid., 1314–17.

160. *Attività* 1986, 1292.

161. *Attività* 1989, 1306.

162. *Attività* 1995, 970–74.

163. The acts of the proceedings are published in *Pro Dialogo*, No. 113 (2003/2).

164. www.vatican.va.

165. *Attività* 1995, 970–74.

166. *Attività* 2001, 974–79. For the Hindu philosopher, religion is strictly connected to birth, in the sense that each one is called to follow the religion into which he or she is born. There are various ways of reaching the summit of the mountain, as it were, and each is good, but only for those who are born into that religion. Conversion and mission are therefore rejected.

167. *Attività* 1988, 1487.

168. *Attività* 1992, 1279–83.

169. *Attività* 1996, 945–50.

170. *Attività* 1997, 1060–64.

171. *Attività* 1998.

172. *Attività* 1994, 1343.

173. Bari 1989; Malta 1990; Brussels 1992; Milan 1993; Assisi 1994; Florence 1995; Rome 1996; Padova and Venice 1997; Bucharest 1998; Lisbon 2000; Palermo 2002; Aachen 2003.

174. See the official Web site of the Sant'Egidio Community for further information on these various meetings: www.santegidio.org.

175. Franca Zambonini and Margaret Coen, *Chiara Lubich: A Life of Unity* (London: New City Press, 1992), 22–23.

176. Chiara Lubich, *La Dottrina Spirituale*, edited by Michel Vandeleene (Milan: Mondatori, 2001), 379–80.

177. *Attività* 1995, 970–74.

178. www.vatican.va/roman_curia/pontifical councils/interelg/documents.

179. *Attività* 1985, 1314.

180. www.vatican.va/roman_curia/pontifical councils/interelg/documents.

181. *OR*, English edition, 26 May 2004, 5.

182. *Attività* 1967, 1401.

183. *IS*, No. 63, 16.

184. *IS*, No. 70, 78.

185. The Eighteenth International Catholic-Jewish Liaison Committee Meeting, Buenos Aires, July 5–8, 2004, *Joint Declaration*, www.vatican.va/roman_curia/pontifical_councils.

186. The Jewish Klein Lecture on Judaic Affairs, Assumption College, 23 March 2000.

187. Institute for Jewish and Christian Studies, National Jewish Scholars Project, *Dabru Emet*, 13 September 2000, www.icjs.org/what/njps/dabruemet.htm.

188. Text sent to the author by Rev. John Pawlikowski on July 4, 2001.

189. At the 2001 ILC meeting Dr. David Berger pointed out that Jews were worried by the assertion in the document *Dominus Jesus* that followers of religions other than Christianity are in a gravely deficient situation in respect of salvation and that interreligious dialogue is part of the Church's mission to the nations.

190. *CNS Documentary Service*, 30–35 (February 15, 2000), 565–66. Quotations are to be found there.

191. *IS*, No. 112 (2003/I), 35–36.

192. *IS*, No. 114 (2003/IV), 200.

193. *Reflections on Covenant and Mission*, Office of Communications United States Conference of Catholic Bishops, Washington, 12 August 2002.

194. *The Tablet*, 12 July 2003, 13.

195. *OR*, English edition, 19 February 2003, 6.

196. *VIS*, 25 May 2004.

197. *IS*, No. 112, 36–37.

198. *Catholic News Service*—www.cathnews.com/news/401/90.php—20 January 2004.

199. *VIS*, 9 June 2004, 3. The two volumes consist of an inventory and documents, 1472 pages in all. In addition there are eight DVDs that contain the images of the original files in the archive and the names of 2,100,000 prisoners about whom information has been requested.

200. *The Tablet*, 31 January 2004, 29.

201. Ibid., 32.

202. *The Tablet*, 7 July 2001, *A Jewish-Christian revolution: 2—The Mission we can share*, 974–75.

203. *IS*, No. 17, 11.

204. A report on this meeting is to be found in *IS*, No. 87, 231, but these words of Dr. Wigoder are from the unpublished working papers of the meeting.

205. *Asia News*, 11 March 2004: www.asia news.it.

206. *Reflections on Covenant and Mission*, the conclusion.

207. *IS*, No. 109 (2002/I–II), 92.

208. *IS*, No. 111 (2002/IV), 232–38.

209. Cardinal Kasper refers here very positively to the document already mentioned of the Biblical Pontifical Commission entitled "The Jewish People and Their Sacred Scriptures in the Christian Bible." He states that this document "shows for me very convincingly that in a mere historical perspective and interpreted with mere historical methods both readings and both interpretations, the Jewish Rabbinical and the Christian one, are possible and legitimate. What reading we choose depends on what faith we have chosen."

210. *IS*, No. 111, 239.

PART V
FURTHER READING

GENERAL

Dizionario Comparato delle Religioni Monotheistiche, Ebaismo, Cristianesimo, Islam. Casale Monferrato, Italy: Edizioni Piemme, 1991.

Ehrenkranz, Joseph H. and David L. *Religion and Violence, Religion and Peace.* Fairfield, CT: Sacred Heart University Press, 2000.

ECUMENISM

Best, Thomas F., and Theodore J. Nottingham, eds. *The Vision of Christian Unity: Essays in Honor of Paul A. Crow, Jr.* Indianapolis: Oikoumene Publications, 1997.

Borelli, John, and John H. Erickson, eds. *The Quest for Unity: Orthodox and Catholics in Dialogue.* Crestwood, NY: St. Vladimir's Seminary Press and the United States Catholic Conference, 1996.

Braaten, Carl E., and Robert W. Jenson. *Union with Christ: The New Finnish Interpretation of Luther.* Grand Rapids, MI/Cambridge, UK: William B. Eerdmans Publishing Co., 1998.

Brancy, Alain, and Maurice Jourjon. *Mary in the Plan of God and in the Communion of Saints: Toward a Common Christian Understanding.* New York: Paulist Press, 2002.

Burgess, Stanley M., and Gary B. McGee eds.; Patrick H. Alexander, assoc. ed. *Dictionary of Pentecostal and Charismatic Movements.* Grand Rapids, MI: Zondervan Publishing House, 1988.

Colson, Charles, and Richard John Neuhaus, eds. *Evangelicals and Catholics Together: Toward a Common Mission.* Dallas: Word Publishing, 1995.

Confessing the One Faith, a Faith and Order Study Document. Geneva: WCC Publications, 1991.

Cunningham, Lawrence S., ed. *Ecumenism: Present Realities and Future Prospects.* Notre Dame, IN: University of Notre Dame Press, 1998.

Dictionary of the Ecumenical Movement, sec. ed. Geneva: WCC Publications, 2002.

Gassman, Günther, ed. *Documentary History of Faith and Order 1963–1993.* Geneva: WCC Publications, 1993.

Goventa, Beverly Roberts. *Mary: Glimpses of the Mother of Jesus.* Columbia, SC: University of South Carolina Press, 1995.

Hill, Christopher, and Edward Yarnold, eds. *Anglicans and Roman Catholics: The Search for Unity.* London: SPCK Publishing, 1994.

Hurley, Michael. *Christian Unity: An Ecumenical Second Spring?* Dublin: Veritas Publications, 1998.

International Theological Commission. *Memory and Reconciliation: The Church and the Faults of the Past.* Boston: Pauline Books and Media, 2000.

Kinnamon, Michael, and Brian E. Cope, eds. *The Ecumenical Movement: An Anthology of Key Texts and Voices.* Geneva: WCC Publications, 1997.

McDonald, Kevin. *Communion and Friendship: A Framework for Ecumenical Dialogue in Ethics.* PhD dissertation, University of St. Thomas, Rome, 1989.

McLoughlin, William, and Jill Pinnock, eds. *Essays on Mary and Ecumenism.* Leominster, Herefordshire: Gracewing, 2002.

McPartlan, Paul. *One in 2000? Towards Catholic-Orthodox Unity.* Middlegreen, UK: St. Paul's, 1993.

Paolo VI e l'Ecumenismo—Colloquio Internazionale di Studio, Brescia 1998. Brescia, Italy: Istituto Paolo VI, 2001.

Puglisi, James E., ed. *Petrine Ministry and the Unity of the Church.* Collegeville, MN: Liturgical Press, 1999.

Purdy, William. *The Search for Unity: Relations between the Anglican and Roman Catholic Churches from the 1950s to the 1970s.* London: Geoffrey Chapman, 1996.

Raiser, Konrad. *Ecumenism in Transition: A Paradigm Shift in the Ecumenical Movement?* Geneva: WCC Publications, 1991.

Rausch, Thomas P., ed. *Catholic and Evangelicals: Do They Share a Common Future?* Mahwah, NJ: Paulist Press, 2000.

Rusch, William G., ed. *Justification and the Future of the Ecumenical Movement: The Joint Declaration on the Doctrine of Justification.* Collegeville, MN: Liturgical Press, 2003.

Rusch, William G., and Jeffrey Gros, eds. *Deepening Communion: International Ecumenical Documents with Roman Catholic Participation.* Washington, DC: U.S. Catholic Conference, 1998.

Salachas, Dimitri. *Il Dialogo Teologico Ufficiale tra la Chiesa Cattolica-Romano e la Chiesa Ortodossa—iter e documentazione.* Bari, Italy: Quaderni di O Odigos, 1994.

Schmidt, Stjepan. *Augustin Bea: The Cardinal of Unity.* New York: New City Press, 1992.

Shea, Mark P. *By What Authority: An Evangelical Discovers Catholic Tradition.* Huntington, IN: Our Sunday Visitor, 1996.

Tillard, J.-M. R. *Church of Churches: The Ecclesiology of Communion.* Collegeville, MN: Liturgical Press, 1992.

Thurian, Max, ed. *Churches Respond to BEM: Official Responses to the Baptism, Eucharist and Ministry Text.* Geneva: WCC, 1986.

Van Elderen, Marlin. *Introducing the World Council of Churches.* Geneva: WCC Publications, 1990.

Wainwright, Geoffrey. *Worship with One Accord.* New York/Oxford: Oxford University Press, 1997.

Women in the Anglican Episcopate, The Eames Commission and the Monitoring Group Reports. Toronto: Anglican Book Centre, 1998.

INTERRELIGIOUS DIALOGUE

Ariarajah, S. Wesley. *Not Without My Neighbour: Issues in Interfaith Relations.* Vol. 85, Risk Book Series. Geneva: WCC Publications, 1999.

Arinze, Francis. *Inter-Religious Dialogue Today.* North Turramurra, NSW: Columban Mission Institute, 1997.

———. *Meeting Other Believers: The Risks and Rewards of Interreligious Dialogue.* Huntingdon, IN: Our Sunday Visitor, 1997.

———. *Religions for Peace: A Call for Solidarity to the Religions of the World.* New York: Doubleday, 2002.

Basset, Jean-Claude. *Le Dialogue Interreligieux, Histoire et Avenir.* Paris: Editions du Cerf, 1996.

Braaten, Carl E. *No Other Gospel! Christianity among the World's Religions.* Minneapolis: Fortress Press, 1992.

Burrows, William R., ed. *Redemption and Dialogue: Reading* Redemptoris Missio *and* Dialogue and Proclamation. Maryknoll, NY: Orbis, 1993.

Carmody, John Tully, and Denise Lardner Carmody. *Catholic Spirituality and the History of Religions.* Vol. 2, *Catholic Spirituality in Global Perspective.* Mahwah, NJ: Paulist Press, 1991.

D'Costa, Gavin. *The Meeting of Religions and the Trinity.* Maryknoll, NY: Orbis, 2000.

Dinoia, J. *The Diversity of Religions.* Washington: CUA Press, 1992.

Dupuis, Jacques. *Christianity and the Religions: From Confrontation to Dialogue.* Maryknoll, NY: Orbis Books, 2002.

———. *Toward a Christian Theology of Religious Pluralism*. Maryknoll, NY: Orbis, 2001.

Fredericks, James L. *Faith among Faiths: Christian Theology and Non-Christian Religions*. Mahwah, NJ: Paulist Press, 1999.

Gioia, Francesco, ed. *Interreligious Dialogue: The Official Teaching of the Catholic Church (1963–1995)*. Boston: Pauline Books and Media, 1997.

Isizoh, Chidi Denis, ed. *Milestones in Interreligious Dialogue: Essays in Honour of Francis Cardinal Arinze*. Rome/Lagos: Ceedee Publications, 2002.

May, John D'Arcy, ed. *Pluralism and the Religions: The Theological and Political Dimensions*. London: Cassell, 1998.

Panikkar, R. *The Cosmostheandric Experience: Emerging Religious Consciousness*. Maryknoll, NY: Orbis, 1993.

Pontifical Council for Interreligious Dialogue. *Journeying Together: The Catholic Church in Dialogue with the Religious Traditions of the World*. Vatican City: Libreria Editrice Vaticana, 1999.

———. *Recognise the Spiritual Bonds Which Unite Us: 16 Years of Christian-Muslim Dialogue*. Vatican City: PCID, 1994.

———. *Sangha in Buddhism and Church in Christianity:* Acts of the Third Buddhist-Christian Colloquium, Tokyo, Japan. *Pro Dialogo*, Bulletin 113, 2003/2.

———. *Spiritual Resources of the Religions for Peace*. Vatican City: PCID, 2003.

Ruokanen, Mikkha. *The Catholic Doctrine of Non-Christian Religions According to the Second Vatican Council*. Edited by Marc A. Spindler. Vol. 7, Studies in Christian Mission. Leiden, Netherlands: E. J. Brill, 1992.

Secretariat for Non-Christians. *The Attitude of the Church Towards the Followers of Other Religions: Reflections and Orientations on Dialogue and Mission*. Vatican City and Bombay: St. Paul's Publications, 1984.

———. *Fundamental Themes for a Dialogistic Understanding*. Roma-Milano: Editrice Ancona, 1970.

Vroom, Henrik. *No Other Gods: Christian Belief in Dialogue with Buddhism, Hinduism, and Islam*. Grand Rapids, MI/Cambridge, UK: William B. Eerdmans Publishing Company, 1996.

Wingate, Andrew. *Encounter in the Spirit: Muslim-Christian Meetings in Birmingham*. Geneva: World Council of Churches, 1977.

World Council of Churches. *Christians Meeting Muslims: WCC Papers on 10 Years of Christian-Muslim Dialogue*. Geneva: World Council of Churches, 1977.

———. "Ecumenical Considerations for Dialogue and Relations with People of Other Religions: Taking Stock of 30 Years of Dialogue and Revisiting the 1979 Guidelines." www.wcc-coe.org/wcc/what/interreligious/glines-e.html.

———. "Guidelines on Dialogue with People of Living Faiths and Ideologies." www.wcc-coe.org/wcc/what/interreligious.

CATHOLIC-JEWISH RELATIONS

Banki, Judith H., and John T. Pawlikowski. *Ethics in the Shadow of the Holocaust: Christian and Jewish Perspectives.* Franklin, WI: Sheed and Ward, 2001.

Bishops' Committee for Ecumenical and Interreligious Affairs. *The Bible, the Jews and the Death of Jesus.* Washington, DC: U.S. Conference of Catholic Bishops, 2004.

Boys, Mary. *Has God Only One Blessing? Judaism as a Source of Christian Self-Understanding.* Mahwah, NJ: Paulist Press, 2000.

Cunningham, Philip. *Education for Shalom: Religious Textbooks and the Enhancement of the Catholic and Jewish Relationship.* Collegeville, MN: Liturgical Press, 1995.

Dulles, Avery, SJ, and Rabbi Leon Klenicki. *The Holocaust, Never to Be Forgotten: Reflections on the Holy See's Document* We Remember. A Stimulus Book. Mahwah, NJ: Paulist Press, 2001.

Fisher, Eugene J. *Faith Without Prejudice: Rebuilding Christian Attitudes Toward Judaism.* New York: Crossroad Publishing Co., 1993.

Fisher, Eugene, and Leon Klenicki, eds. *In Our Time: The Flowering of Jewish-Catholic Dialogue.* New York: Paulist Press, 1990.

Flannery, Edward. *The Anguish of the Jews: Twenty-three Centuries of Anti-semitism.* Mahwah, NJ: Paulist Press, 1985.

Isaac, Jules. *Has Anti-Semitism Roots in Christianity?* New York: National Conference of Christians and Jews, 1961.

John Paul II. *Texts on Jews and Judaism 1979–1995.* Compiled by the Anti-Defamation League and edited by Eugene J. Fisher and Leon Klenicki. New York: a Crossroad Herder Book, 1995.

Kasimow, Harold, and Byron L. Sherwin, eds. *No Religion Is an Island: Abraham Joshua Heschel and Interreligious Dialogue.* Maryknoll, NY: Orbis Books 1991.

Klenicki, Leon, and Geoffrey Wigoder, eds. *A Dictionary of the Jewish-Christian Dialogue.* New York: Paulist Press, 1995.

Marchione, Margherita. *Yours Is a Precious Witness.* Mahwah, NJ: Paulist Press, 1997.

Moran, Gabriel. *Uniqueness: Problem or Paradox in Jewish and Christian Traditions.* Maryknoll, NY: Orbis Books, 1992.

Novak, David. *Jewish-Christian Dialogue: A Jewish Justification.* New York/Oxford: Oxford University Press, 1989.

Oesterreicher, John M. *The New Encounter Between Christians and Jews.* New York: Philosophical Library, 1986.

O'Hare, Padraic. *The Enduring Covenant: The Education of Christians and the End of Antisemitism.* Valley Forge, PA: Trinity Press International, 1997.

Pawlikowski, John. *Jesus and the Theology of Israel.* Wilmington, DE: Michael Glazier Books, 1989.

Pawlikowski, John T., and Hayim Goren Perelmuter, eds. *Reinterpreting Revelation and Tradition: Jews and Christians in Conversation.* Franklin, WI: Sheed and Ward, 2000.

Perelmuter, Hayim Goren. *Harvest of a Dialogue: Reflections of a Rabbi Scholar on a Catholic Faculty.* Edited by John Pawlikowski and Dianne Bergant. Jersey City, NJ: KTAV Publishing House, 1997.

Radici dell'Antigiudaismo in Ambiente Cristiano—Atti del Simposio Teologico-Storico, Città del Vaticano 1997. Vatican City: Libreria Editrice Vaticana.

Willebrands, Johannes. *Church and the Jewish People: New Considerations.* Mahwah, NJ: Paulist Press, 1992.

INDEX

Abraham's Heritage—A Christmas Gift, 248–50
Ad Petri Cathedram, 4
Al Albait Foundation Amman, 228
Al-Azhar University Cairo, 226, 228
Al-Qaradawi Youssef, 229
Alexy II, 112, 115, 116, 117
Alfeyev, Hilarion, 18
Amato, Angelo, 158
American Jewish Committee, 118, 172, 201
Anglican Communion, 44, 56–61, 62, 90, 108, 111
  Anglican–Roman Catholic International Commission (ARCIC), 38, 56, 59, 60, 111, 112
  The Church as Communion (1990), 57
  Episcopal Church USA, 237
  The Gift of Authority (1999), 57–58, 64
  International Anglican–Roman Catholic Commission for Unity and Mission (IARCCUM), 59–61, 111, 112
  Lambeth Conferences, 93
  Life in Christ: Morals, Communion and the Church (1993), 57
  Mary, Grace and Hope in Christ (2004), 58–59
  Mississauga Consultation (2000), 59

Anti-Catholicism, 244
Anti-Judaism, 246, 249
Anti-Semitism, 194, 195, 197, 199, 244, 248, 257, 258, 259
  Roots of Anti-Semitism in the Christian Milieu, Symposium, 213
Apple, Raymond, 205
Aram I, 47,80
Archives, Vatican, 209, 218–19, 257
  Actes et Documents du Saint-Siège rélatifs à la Seconde Guerre Mondiale, 209, 210
Arinze, Cardinal Francis, 158, 159, 226, 231, 233, 234, 235, 236, 238, 239
Armenian Apostolic Church, 47
Arns, Cardinal Paulo Evaristo, 195
Assisi Day of Prayer for Peace, 1986, 1993, and 2002, 92–94, 140–42, 143, 144, 145–46,151, 154, 231, 233, 234, 236, 240
Assyrian Church of the East, 46, 49
  Anaphora of Addai and Mari, 50–51
  Common Christological Declaration (1994), 49
  A Common Statement on Sacramental Life, 49–50
  Guidelines for Admission to the Eucharist between the Chaldean Church and the Assyrian Church of the East, 50

Joint Committee for Theological Discussion between the Catholic Church and the Assyrian Church of the East, 49–51

Athanagoras I, 8, 9, 90, 94, 117

Athanasios, Metropolitan, 91

Australia/Israel and Jewish Affairs Council (AIJAC), 222–23

Australian Lutheran–Roman Catholic Dialogue, 101

Baha'i, 237

Baptist World Alliance, 68–69
　Summons to Witness in Christ in Today's World (1990), 68

Bartholomew I, 54, 90, 91, 94, 95, 117, 146, 231

Baum, Gregory, 10

Bea, Cardinal Augustin, 5, 11, 20, 125, 126, 131, 132, 191

Bemporad, Jack, 193, 207

Berenbaum, Michael, 205

Beuchlein, Daniel, 67

Bidawid, Mar Raphael, 50

Bishops' Committee for Ecumenical and Interreligious Affairs, USA (BCEIA), 220, 252

B'nai B'rith Anti-Defamation League, 177, 179, 180, 221, 223

Bremer, Kristen Kyrre, 94

Brisbane College of Theology, 99

British Council of Christians and Jews (BCCJ), 222, 231, 258

Buddhism, 126,130, 137, 141, 144, 145, 158, 159, 161, 232, 233, 235, 237
　Budddhist-Christian Colloquium, 233
　Mount Hiei Day of Prayer, 233
　Rissho Kosei-Kai, 145, 232

Carey, George, 60, 91, 96, 146

Carmelite Convent Auschwitz, 190, 191, 192, 198, 207, 208

Casaroli, Cardinal Agostino, 188

Catholic Association of St. Willibrord, 4

Catholic Biblical Foundation, 99

Catholic Church–Oriental Orthodox Churches International Joint Commission for Dialogue, 47–48

Catholic Committee for Cultural Cooperation with the Orthodox Churches and the Oriental Orthodox Churches, 77, 99

Catholic Conference for Ecumenical Questions, 3, 78

Catholic-Jewish Relations at the National and Local Levels, 219–24

Catholics and Jews in Partnership, Millennium Conference, London, 2002, 222

CELAM (Episcopal Conferences of Latin America), 223

Center for Catholic-Jewish Studies, Florida, 221

Center for Muslim-Christian Understanding, Georgetown, USA, 236

Center for Jewish-Christian Relations, Cambridge, Great Britain, 236, 259

Centro *Pro Unione*, Rome, 179

Chalcedon, Council of, 46

Chaplin, Vsevolod, 116

Charriére, Bishop, 3

Chief Rabbinate in Israel, 244, 245, 250–52

Chooi, Teresa Ee, 144

Christian-Jewish Relations, 132

Christian World Communions, 68, 73, 75, 87

Christians, Jews and Muslims, 231
　Concert for Reconciliation of Christians, Jews and Muslims, Vatican, 231, 257

Christodoulos, Archbishop, 95
Christological Declarations, 46
Church of England, 38
Churches in union, 102
Clement, Oliver, 40
Coggan, Donald, 96
Columban Center for Christian-
    Muslim Relations, Sydney,
    Australia, 236
Commission for Religious Relations
    with the Jews (CRRJ), 163,
    166, 173, 179, 180, 188, 190,
    191, 192, 196, 197, 199, 200,
    201, 202, 205, 208, 209, 216,
    218, 219, 222, 224, 242, 243,
    250, 251, 257
    *Guidelines and Suggestions for
    Implementing the Conciliar Dec-
    laration Nostra Aetate N° 4,*
    (Guidelines) (1974), 164–66,
    183, 219
    *Notes on the Correct Way to Present
    Jews and Judaism in Preaching
    and Catechesis in the Roman
    Catholic Church* (Notes)
    (1985), 166–72, 219
Condemnations, 8–9, 115
Conference of European Churches
    (CEC), 100
Confucianism, 145, 233, 235
Congar, Yves, 4
Congregation of the Doctrine of the
    Faith (CDF), 49, 50, 64, 84,
    150
Congregation for the Evangelization
    of Peoples, 150, 261
Coptic Orthodox Church, 45, 46,
    47
Council of Centers on Jewish-
    Catholic Relations, 221
Council of Episcopal Conferences of
    Europe (CCEE), 100
Council for Public Affairs of the
    Church, 173

Councils of Churches, National and
    Regional, 99–100
Couturier, Paul, 89
Covenant and Mission, 252–56, 260
Covenants between Churches, 102–3
Crow, Paul, 41, 67
Cullman, Oscar, 10, 11

Dabru Emet, 245–48, 250
Dalai Lama, 137, 233
Damaskinos, Metropolitan, 39
Deicide, Teaching of Contempt, 127,
    244
Di Segni, Riccardo, 256
Dignitatis Humanae, 171
Dimitrios I, 52, 90, 94
Dinka IV, Mar, 49, 50
Disciples of Christ (Christian
    Church), 44, 66–68, 90
    Disciples of Christ–Roman
    Catholic Dialogue:
    First Phase: *Apostolicity and
    Catholicity in the Visible Unity
    of the Church* (1977–81), 66
    Second Phase: *The Church as Com-
    munion in Christ* (1983–92), 67
    Third Phase: *Receiving and Hand-
    ing on the Faith: The Mission
    and Responsibility of the Church*
    (1995–2002), 67
    Fourth Phase: *The Presence of Christ
    in the World with Special Refer-
    ence to the Eucharist* (2003–), 68
*Dominus Jesus—Declaration on the
    Unicity and Salvific Universality
    of Jesus Christ and the Church*
    (CDF), 64, 119, 120, 158,
    217, 248, 249
Dulles, SJ, Cardinal Avery, 67

Ecclesiam Suam, 134, 239
*Ecumenical Collaboration on Regional,
    National and Local Levels,*
    SPCU (1975), 29

Ecumenical Directories, 20–30, 97, 98, 106
El-Hage, Dr., 230
Eritrean Orthodox Church, 47
Etchegaray, Cardinal Roger, 172
Ethiopian Orthodox Church, 46, 47
Evangelii Nuntiandi, 152

Faith and Order Commission, 38, 79, 82–87, 88, 92, 106
  Major Studies:
  The Apostolic Faith Study, 83
  Baptism, Eucharist and Ministry (BEM), 84
  Churches Respond to BEM: Official Responses to the Baptism, Eucharist and Ministry Text (1986–88), 84; Catholic Response to BEM, 84
  Toward a Common Expression of the Apostolic Faith Today, 84–85
  The Unity of the Church and the Renewal of Humankind, 83
Farrell, Brian, 55
Federation of Asian Bishops' Conferences (FABC), 235
  BIRA meetings, 235
Federici, Tommaso, 253
Feiner, Johannes, 10
Feldman, Leon, 193
Fifteen Years of Catholic-Jewish Dialogue, 1970–1985, 180–82
Fisher, Eugene, 220
Fitzgerald, Michael, 160, 228, 229, 230, 234, 236
Focolare Movement, 98, 232, 234, 237–38
Fogarty, Gerard, 218
Frizzell, Lawrence, 217
FUCI, International Federation of Catholic Universities, 158
Fumagalli, Francesco, 180, 193
Fundamental Agreement between the Holy See and the State of Israel, 198, 207, 259

Gadecki, Stanislaw, 223
Gassman, Günter, 86
Gordis, David, 206
Guidelines for Interconfessional Cooperation in Translating the Bible, 99
Gulf States Center, University of Qatar, 229

Hackel, Sergis, 115
Hamid Bin Ahmad Al-Rifaie, 228, 229
Hamid Bin Khalifa Al-Thani, 229
Hassan II ben Mohammed, 232
Henrix, Hans Herman, 199
Hertzberg, Arthur, 172
Hinduism, 126, 130, 141, 145, 158, 159, 161, 226, 234, 237
  Christian-Hindu Meetings
    Varanasi 1992, Madurai 1995, Mumbai 2001, 234
  Swadhyaia Family, 234
Hockhuth, Rolf, *The Deputy*, 209
Humanae Salutis, 5, 9

International Catholic-Jewish Liaison Committee (ILC), 172–80, 182, 190, 191, 193–95, 198, 199, 200, 207, 210, 216, 218, 220, 242, 243, 259
  Protecting Religious Freedom and Holy Sites (2001), 216
  Recommendation on Education in Catholic and Jewish Seminaries and Schools of Theology (2001), 216
International Council of Christians and Jews (ICCJ), 222
International Jewish Committee for Interreligious Consultations (IJCIC), 172, 177, 188, 191, 192, 196, 197, 209, 210, 216, 242, 243
Interreligious Assembly, Vatican, 1999, 143–45

Interreligious Coordinating Council in Israel (ICCI), 222
Islam, 126, 130, 141, 142, 143, 144, 145, 158, 159, 190, 226, 233, 236, 237, 241
    Christian-Muslim Dialogue, 226, 241
    Islamic-Catholic Liaison Committee, 227
    Islamic Forum for Dialogue, Jeddah, 228
    Islamic International Council for Da'wah and Humanitarian Aid, 226
    Islamic-Muslim League, 226
    Islamic World Conference, 226
    Islamic World Congress, 226
    Organization of the Islamic Conference, 226
    Qatar Conference on Muslim-Christian Dialogue, 2004, 229–30
    Visit of Pope John Paul II to Morocco, 232
    World Islamic Society, 226
    World Muslim League, 226
Israeli Delegation for Relations with the Catholic Church, 222
Israel Jewish Council for Interreligious Dialogue, 177
Israeli Jewish Council for Interreligious Relations (IJCIR), 222

Jadot, Jean, 137, 138
Jainism, 141, 145, 158, 235
John XXIII, 4–7, 9, 35, 125, 126,129, 131, 184, 185, 243
John Paul I, 167
John Paul II, 13, 15, 30, 31, 32, 35, 36, 37, 40, 42, 44, 46, 47, 49, 52, 55, 60, 77, 80, 88, 90, 91, 92, 93, 94, 95, 96, 100, 101, 104, 107, 109, 110, 112, 116, 117, 120, 128, 132, 140, 141–46, 147, 151, 167, 168, 169, 171, 172, 177, 178, 179, 180, 182–86, 187, 188, 189, 190, 191, 192, 193, 196, 198, 200, 202, 204, 206, 208, 210–16, 223, 224, 228, 231, 232, 233, 235, 236, 240, 242, 243, 250, 256, 257, 260
    Crossing the Threshold of Hope, 233
Jubilee Year 2000, 81, 90–91, 118, 145
Jubilee Year and the Jewish People, 213, 214–16
Judaism, 141, 142, 145, 158, 161, 164, 175, 177, 183, 185, 196, 233

Karekin I, 46
Kasper, Cardinal Walter, 55, 63, 69, 86, 95, 96, 107, 108, 110, 111, 115, 116, 117, 216, 217, 219, 224, 250, 253, 256, 260, 261, 262, 263
Kazan, Icon of Our Lady of, 116–17
Keonig, Cardinal Franz, 196
Kessler, Edward, 259
Kirill, Metropolitan, 115
Klein, Laurentius, 174
Klenicki, Leon, 205, 217
Kolbe, Maximilian, 190
Kondrusiewicz, Tadeus, 114
Kopnick, Rabbi, 206

L'Arche community, 98
Leisner, Karl, 212
Lichtenberg, Bernhard, 212
Loughran, James, 217
Lubachisky, Cardinal, 54
Lustiger, Cardinal Jean-Marie, 224, 258
Lutheran World Federation, 44, 61–63, 75, 90, 93, 96, 98, 108, 237
    Apostolicity of the Church, Ministry and Church Teaching, 63

International Lutheran/Roman
   Catholic Commission for
   Unity, 61, 63
*Joint Declaration on the Doctrine of
   Justification* (JD) (1999), 61,
   69, 77, 98, 100
Plenary Assembly 2003, 63

Macharski, Cardinal Franciszek, 191
Malankara Orthodox Churches, 45,
   46, 47, 48
   Joint International Commission
      for Theological Dialogue
      between the Catholic Church
      and the Malankara Orthodox
      Syrian Church, 47, 48
   Joint International Commission
      for Theological Dialogue
      between the Catholic Church
      and the Malankara Syrian
      Orthodox Church, 48
Marella, Cardinal Paolo, 133, 136
Marrus, Michael 218
Martin, Dr. J. M., 7
Martini, Cardinal Carlo Maria, 42
Mejia, Cardinal Jorge, 192, 251
Mennonite World Conference,
   69–72, 93
   Called Together to be Peacemakers
      (2003), 70,71
   Mennonite World Assembly
      2003, 71
Middle East Council of Churches
   (MECC), 49
Millennium World Peace Summit
   2000, United Nations Orga-
   nization, 235
Musial, Stanislaw, 192
Muszynski, Henryk, 191, 223
Myochikai, 145

National Council of Synagogues
   USA, 252
Nazarbayev, Nursultan, 147
Neuhaus, John, 37

Nikkyo Niwano, 232
Nikodim, Metropolitan, 115
Noko, Ismael, 63, 146
Nordic Lutheran Churches, 93, 94,
   101–2
North American Orthodox-Catholic
   Theological Consultation,
   100–101
Novak, David, 217

Observers at the Second Vatican
   Council, 9–12
Oesterreicher, John A., 221
Opochensky, Milan, 40
Oriental Orthodox Churches, 44,
   45–51, 90
Orthodox Churches, 51–56, 90, 108,
   237
   Balamand Document, 53
   French Joint Committee for
      Catholic Orthodox Theologi-
      cal Dialogue, 101
   Joint International Commission
      for Theological Dialogue
      between the Catholic Church
      and the Orthodox Church,
      52–54, 117
   Official visits Rome and Constan-
      tinople, 94, 117–18

Pandurangshastri Athavale, 234
Pastor Bonus, 154
Paul VI, 8, 11, 36, 77, 90, 94, 96,
   117, 120, 132, 133, 134, 136,
   160, 161, 163, 167, 174, 182,
   183, 223, 232, 241
Pawlikowski, John T., 221, 248
Pentecostal Churches, 72–73, 90
   Documents:
   First Phase Final Report (1976),
      72
   Second Phase Final Report
      (1982), 72
   Third Phase: *Perspectives on
      Koinonia* (1989), 72

Fourth Phase: *Evangelization, Proselytism and Common Witness* (1997), 72
Pignedoli, Cardinal Sergio, 139
Pius IX, 217
Pius XI, 2, 257
Pius XII, 209, 217, 257, 258
Poland, Church of, 190, 198, 201, 223
Pontifical Biblical Commission, 212
Pontifical Council for Culture, 154, 158
Pontifical Council for the Family, 235
Pontifical Council for Interreligious Dialogue (PCID), 82, 132, 136, 143, 145, 154, 157, 158, 159, 225, 226, 227, 232, 233, 234, 235, 236, 238, 239, 240, 241
    Commission for Religious Relations with Muslims, 229, 241
    Interreligious Assembly, Rome, 1999, 240
    Publications:
    Christianity in Dialogue with African Traditional Religion and Culture, 235
    Dialogue and Mission (*DM*), 148–49
    Dialogue and Proclamation (*DP*), 150–54, 238, 239
    Interreligious Dialogue Directory (2001), 236
    Jesus Christ, The Bearer of the Water of Life, 154–58
    Journeying Together, 158
    Meeting in Friendship, 159
    Milestones in Interreligious Dialogue, 158
    On the Eve of the Third Millennium 1999, Collaboration between Different Religions, 144
    Peace: A Single Goal and a Shared Intention, 145

Spiritual Resources of the Religions for Peace: Exploring the Sacred Texts in Promotion of Peace, 158
Spirituality in Dialogue, Dialogue of Spirituality, 238
Pontifical Council for Non-Believers, 154, 158
Pontifical Council for Promoting Christian Unity (PCPCU), 22, 50, 55, 56, 61, 63, 64, 65, 68, 69, 71, 72, 73, 74, 76, 79, 80, 83, 84, 88, 93, 97, 154, 158, 192, 200, 219, 238
Pontifical Gregorian University, 256
    Cardinal Bea Institute for Jewish Studies, 257
Pontifical Lateran University, 180, 196
Pontifical University of St. Thomas Aquinas, 179
Pro Oriente Foundation, 47
Putney, Michael, 65

Raiser, Konrad, 40
Ramsey, Michael, 96
Ratzinger, Cardinal Joseph, 248–50, 253
Redemptoris Missio, 135, 150
Regimini Ecclesiae, 161
Reich, Seymour, 192, 207, 216
Reigner, Gerhart, 172, 177, 181, 192, 193, 208
Rossano, Pietro, 181
Ruini, Cardinal Camillo, 256
Runcie, Robert, 96
Russian Orthodox Church, 113, 114, 115, 116

Sachs, Dr. Jonathan, 258
Sant'Egidio Community, 98, 236–37
    Christian-Muslim Summit 2001, 236
    Meetings *Religion and Peace*, 236
Schmemann, Alexander, 11,12
Schmidt, Helmut, 176

Secretariat for Christian Unity
(SPCU), 4, 9, 10, 20, 29, 78,
89, 121, 161, 162
Secretariat for Non-Christians, 132,
135, 136, 140, 145, 148, 150,
239, 241
Christian-Islam Congress,
Tripoli, 1976, 138–40
Publications:
*The Attitude of the Church toward
the Followers of Other Religions,*
(1984), 239
*Orientations pour un Dialogue entre
crétiens et musulmans* (1969),
136
A la recontre des Religions Africanes
(1969), 136
Toward a meeting with Buddhism
(1970), 136
Toward a Culture of Dialogue, 145
Vers la recontre des Religions (1967),
136
Sects (New Religious Movements),
137, 154, 157
Seventh Day Adventists, 75
Shar Yishur Cohen, 250
Shenouda III, 47, 229
Shintoism, 141, 145
Shoah (Holocaust), 126, 128, 188-91,
193, 194, 196, 197, 198, 200-
205, 207, 249, 258
Concert to Remember the *Shoah,*
Vatican, 211
European Episcopal Conferences,
202, 215
SIDIC (Service International de
Documentation Judeo-
Chrétienne), 177, 179
Siegman, Henry, 172, 174, 175
Signer, Michael, 217
Sikhism, 141, 145, 158, 233, 235,
237
Singer, Israel, 146, 193, 207
Sobel, Henry I, 195, 223

Sodano, Cardinal Angelo, 235
Stein, Edith, 186, 217
Stransky, Thomas, 10
Synagogue Council of America, 172
Synod of Bishops
Special Assembly for Europe, 197
Synod for Lebanon, 230

Taizé Community, 98
Tanenbaum, Marc, 172, 193
Tantawi, Sheik Al-Azhar
Mohammed, 146, 226, 229
Taoists, 235, 237
Tappouni, Cardinal, 127
Tauran, Cardinal Jean-Louis, 229
Tendai, 145
Tenrikyo, 145, 235
Tertio Millennio Adveniente, 91, 143,
202
Teshuva, 194, 204
Theoctist, Patriarch, 95
Theresienstadt, 193
Thijssen, Franz, 4
Thurian, Max, 34, 84
Toaff, Elio, 184, 211, 212, 256
Tomko, Cardinal Josef, 147
Traditional Religions, 235, 237
African Religions, 141, 145, 235
Amerindian Religions, 141

Ukrainian Greek Catholic Church,
112, 113, 114, 115
Uniatism, 52, 53, 54, 101, 108, 112
Union of Religious Superiors, 157
Union of Utrecht, 76, 87
United Nations Organization, 140
Ut Unum Sint (UUS), 30–43, 54, 80,
88, 91, 92, 93, 104, 107, 108,
109, 120

Virgin Mary and Ecumenism, 108
Ecumenical Society of the Blessed
Virgin Mary, 59
Vischer, Lucas, 40

Wagle, Finn, 94
Waldheim, Kurt, 186, 187, 188
Wainwright, Geoffrey, 65
Wattson, Paul, 89
Waxman, Mordecai, 177, 187, 189, 193
We Remember: A Reflection on the Shoah, 200–205, 248
    Reactions to the Document, 205–7
Week of Prayer for Christian Unity, 4, 5, 86, 88, 89, 90, 98, 108, 111, 140
Wigoder, Geoffrey, 259
Willebrands, Johannes, 4, 20, 162, 165, 166, 178, 179, 181, 187, 188, 191, 192, 219, 242, 259
Willams, Rowan, 96, 111, 112
World Alliance of Reformed Churches (WARC), 44, 62, 65–66, 75, 93, 106, 118
    Church as Community of Common Witness to the Kingdom of God (1988–), 66
    Presence of Christ in the Church and in the World (1970–77), 66
    Roman Catholic–World Alliance of Reformed Churches Dialogue, 66
    Toward a Christian Understanding of the Church (1984–90), 66
World Council of Churches, 4, 9, 75–82, 83, 90, 97, 106, 107, 135, 157, 159–160, 161

Commission on World Mission and Evangelism (CWME), 79
Joint Working Group, 79–80, 160
World Conference of Religions for Peace, 233
World Evangelical Alliance (WEA), 73–75
    Reports of Conversations with the PCPCU:
    The Evangelical–Roman Catholic Dialogue on Mission (1977–84), 73
    Church Evangelization and the Bonds of Koinonia (1993–2001), 74–75
World Evangelical Fellowship, 73
World Methodist Council, 44, 62, 63–65, 90, 237
    The Apostolic Tradition (1991), 63–64
    International Methodist-Catholic Dialogue Commission, 63–65
    Speaking the Truth in Love (2001), 64
    The Word of Life—A Statement on Revelation and Faith (1996), 64
World Religions Congress, Astana 2003, 147–48
World Jewish Congress, 177, 209, 258

Yoffe, Eric H., 245

Zakka I Iwas, Mar, 47
Zoroastrian Religion, 141, 145, 158, 237